READINGS IN

CLASSICAL CHINESE

POETRY AND PROSE

GLOSSARIES

ANALYSES

袁乃瑛　　　唐海濤　　　蓋杰民
Naiying Yuan　　Haitao Tang　　James Geiss

PRINCETON UNIVERSITY PRESS

PRINCETON, NEW JERSEY

Published by Princeton University Press, 41 William Street,
Princeton, New Jersey 08540
In the United Kingdom: Princeton University Press, 3 Market Place,
Woodstock, Oxfordshire OX20 1SY

Library of Congress Control Number: 2005931446

ISBN-13: 978-0-691-11832-1
ISBN-10: 0-691-11832-9

British Library Cataloging-in-Publication Data is available

This publication has been made possible by generous grants from
The Mercer Trust and The Consortium for Language Teaching and Learning

The publisher would like to acknowledge the authors of this volume for
providing the camera-ready copy from which this book was printed

Printed on acid-free paper

pup.princeton.edu

Printed in the United States of America

10 9 8 7 6 5 4 3 2 1

Foreword

Selected Readings in Classical Chinese Poetry and Prose is the literary supplement to *Classical Chinese -- A Basic Reader*. It applies the same rigorous standard set forth in the *Basic Reader* and reinforces its linguistic lessons with carefully chosen exemplary works in literature to expand the scope of linguistic contact to a new realm.

Literature is a linguistic art. It uses language as the medium to create pieces of writing that have lasting value because of their excellence of form, great emotional effects, remarkable imagination, etc. Chinese writers in ancient times were all influenced by the Confucian humanism and the Taoist naturalism. As a result, traditional Chinese literature demonstrated the linguistic characteristics of the Chinese language in its form, and to various degrees, either coverttly or overtly, embodied the essentials of the Confucian and the Taoist teachings.

1. The Contents:

    This volume comprises three sections: Poetry, Lyrics, and Prose. Section one contains thirty-two poems chosen from *the Book of Odes*, Hàn dynasty anonymous poems, Wèi and Jìn pentasyllabic poems, six dynasties folk songs and poems by known authors, and down to Táng dynasty ancient poems and regulated verses in pentasyllabic and heptasyllabic meters, with the last poem drawn from the Sòng dynasty. Section two contains nine lyrics chosen from Táng, Five Dynasties, and Sòng times, plus the last selection which is a Yuán dynasty song-poem. Section three contains 15 short pieces of prose from Warring States period down to the Qīng dynasty, including one from the *Chǔ Cí* at the beginning, and a parallel prose at the end. These selections represent a great variety of themes and styles, showing the richness and colorfulness of Chinese literary works. They are arranged in chronological order with an exception of the parrallel prose, placing Chinese literature in a historical perspective to reveal its continuity and change over a long course of development. In addition, two brief introductions, to regulated verse and to parallel prose, are provided so as to enable users of this book to get a better sense of the linguistic and artistic characteristics of these two highly sophisticated literary forms.

2. The Formats:

    As poetry and lyrics are intimately related to music, and prose writings also needs to be chanted or read aloud, so each selection is here romanized in Hànyǔpīnyīn, with special attention called upon to redupicative, alliterative, and rhyming compounds as these are frequently used devices for versification. The end rhymes of poems and lyrics are listed at the end of each selection, and their reconstructed sound values (of C. 600-1000 A.D.) are also given, so that users can get a feeling of the auditory effects they created. Regulated verses, lyrics, and song-poems are highly developed forms of Chinese literature. In order to highlight their respective structural characteristics we have provided specific rules for four regulated verses, two lyrics and one song-poem to show the cadence and tonal design in each form.

A brief biographical sketch is given to each of the known author as a study aid.

The glosses are explained in both modern Chinese and in English, as brief and to the point as possible. The grammatical categories and parts of speech of the glosses are determined by their functions in their immediate contexts. When a gloss has two readings, both readings are given.

Noteworthy grammatical points and sentence patterns are explained or analyzed immediately under the glosses where they appear.

Some key words in the explanation of glosses are further explained, with a ◆ sign preceding them.

Set phrases derived from the text are marked with a ✳ sign.

Additional vocabulary that can help clarify or elucidate the meaning of the text are given with a ◎ sign preceding them.

3. Understanding and Appreciation of Literature:

As a linguistic art, literature is very difficult to understand fully. One needs to go beyond the basic linguistic meaning--lexical, syntactic, and onerall structural--to grasp its descriptive, lyrical, narrative, or expository mode of expression; to perceive its visual, auditory and psycological appeal; to apprehend its theme and philosophical implication. Whether a work of literature is serene, lively, dashing, grand, cheerful, sorrowful, contemplative, or soul-stirring, it can be understood and appreciated through carefully analyzing its special linguistic effects--diction, imagery, alliteration, assonance, etc., and its literary techniques--allegory, contrast, allusion, personification, inversion, hyperbole, antithesis, etc. For each of the fifty-seven selections we have provided an introductory note to point out what we regard as some remarkable features of the work, in the hope that students can explore the work further along these lines. If students, after such exploration, can come up with their own understanding and critical assessments, it will be a very good substitute for routine linguistic exercises.

4. The Goals:

    Like philosophy and history, literature is a major component of culture. Poetry and prose hold the leading position in Chinese literarure. They touch upon the exploration of men and universe, the glorification of Nature, the adherence to life's ideals, the pursuit of love and beauty, and the lament for *anitya* or the impermanence of life and the eventual transcendence of that sorrow. They amply reveal the depth and breadth of Chinese culture.

    Through reading these selections students will further improve their knowledge in classical Chinese: such as the monosyllabic, tonal nature of Chinese morphemes and the grammatical versaltility of Chinese words; will strengthen their command of major grammatical rules; at the same time, through carefully analyzing the forms and contents of these texts, will better comprehend and appreciate the artistic conceptions created in these literary works, and gain a better and deeper understanding of the thoughts, ideals, and aspirations of their authors, wherein lies the inner secret of Chinese culture. If in this process students develop a keen interest in the study of Chinese literature, we would regard that as an added gain.

                                                                                    The Authors

Acknowledgments

First and foremost, we want to express our heartfelt gratitude to Professor Frederick Wade Mote, the founder of the East Asian Studies Department at Princeton University, and to the late Professor Ta-Tuan Ch'en, Director of the Chinese Language Program in the EAS Department. This textbook project would not have been undertaken, much less completed, had it not been for their insight in recognizing that classical Chinese is a critical link in the teaching of Chinese culture. It was thanks to their strong support that we were encouraged to improve teaching materials and methods.

L.L.D. David Finkelstein, President of Pro Re Nata, inc. Margaret Hsü, and Professor Andrew Plaks, three friends known since the 1960s, helped to proofread and comment on the English portion of this text. We thank them all heartily.

An earlier version of this book was sponsored and funded by the Consortium for Language Teaching and Learning. The publication of the current book was generously subsidized by the Mercer Trust Fund. To both institutions we are immensely grateful.

Our Introductions to Regulated Verse and Parallel Prose were to a great extent based on works done by the late Professor Wáng Lì of Běijīng University, to whom the credit goes; we are solely responsible for any misrepresentation of his main ideas in these introductions.

The Authors

詩選目錄

End T'ang poetry

詞曲選目錄

—Prose—

文選目録

第一首

關雎

詩經　周南

關關雎鳩，在河之洲。窈窕淑女，君子好逑。
參差荇菜，左右流之。窈窕淑女，寤寐求之。
求之不得，寤寐思服。悠哉悠哉，輾轉反側。
參差荇菜，左右采之。窈窕淑女，琴瑟友之。
參差荇菜，左右芼之。窈窕淑女，鐘鼓樂之。

Zhùyīn:

Guān guān jū jiū, zài hé zhī zhóu. Yǎo tiǎo shú nǔ, jūn zǐ hǎo qiú.

Cēn cī xìng cài, zuǒ yòu liú zhī. Yǎo tiǎo shú nǔ, wù mèi qiú zhī.

Qiú zhī bù dé, wù mèi sī fú. Yōu zāi yōu zāi, zhǎn zhuàn fǎn cè.

Cēn cī xìng cài, zuǒ yòu cǎi zhī. Yǎo tiǎo shú nǔ, qín sè yǒu zhī.

Cēn cī xìng cài, zuǒ yòu mào zhī. Yǎo tiǎo shú nǔ, zhōng gù yào zhī.

篇旨

關雎是一首情歌，描寫一個男子愛慕一個美麗的
淑女，極力追求她，希望能跟她結為夫婦，過幸
福、美滿的婚姻生活。詩中描述追求之急切，心
情之憂慮，憧憬求得後之快樂，情意真摯，委曲
周至，可稱千古情詩之祖。

This is a love song, describing a man admiring a beautiful and virtuous young woman, trying every means to win the heart of her, hoping that she would marry him and lead a blissful and happy life together. The poem gives a detailed account of the eagerness of courting, the anxiety over the unknown prospect, and the vivid imagination of a happy ending. It is sincere and earnest, suave and meandering, can be called the progenitor of love poems through all ages.

注解

1. **關雎**
   Guānjū
   【名詞】篇名。古時詩先於題，詩經每篇都用第一句的兩個或幾個字作為篇名
   title of an ode. In ancient times, poems existed first and titles were later added to them. In the *Book of Odes*, it usually adopts the first two (sometimes more than two) characters in an ode as its title.

2. **南** Nán
   【名詞】南方之國 the states in the south

   周南
   Zhōu Nán
   【名詞】周王朝所直轄的南方之國，在今河南省黃河以南偏西之地
   The southern states directly under the jurisdiction of the Zhōu court, in present-day Hénán province, south of the Yellow River and slightly toward the west

3. **關關**
   guān guān
   【象聲詞】雎鳩鳥的和鳴聲
   the harmonious sounds of osprey

   ◆ **象聲詞**
   xiàngshēngcí
   an onomatopoeia

4. **雎鳩**
   jū jiū
   【名詞】魚鷹 osprey
   據說這種鳥很凶猛，雌雄有固定的配偶，古人稱之為貞鳥
   It was said that ospreys are fierce but theadily stay with a fixed mate, so ancients called them "chaste birds"

   ◆ **雌** *cí*   female
   ◆ **雄** *xióng*   male

5. **河** hé
   【名詞】黃河 the Yellow River

6. **洲** zhōu
   【名詞】水中沙洲 an islet in a river
   詩人以在沙洲上叫的雎鳩引出下文的兩句話，這種表達的方法叫"興"(xìng)。"興"是用一種事物引出自己要說的事物，兩種事物之間有一定的聯繫，但在解釋時不能牽強附會。

Here the sound of the osprey on the islet is used to introduce the next two lines; such a device is called 'xìng' or incitement/ association. The initial thing and the thing it leads into must have some kind of connection, but in reading such poems one should not force an interpretation with far-fetched ideas.

◆ 引出 *yǐnchū*　　　　to draw forth; to lead to

◆ 聯繫 *liánxì*　　　　connection; relationship

◆ 牽強附會　　　　　to give a forced interpretation; to
　qiānqiǎngfùhuì　　strain the sense

7. 窈 yǎo　　【形容詞】內心文靜　quiet; demure

8. 窕 tiǎo　　【形容詞】容貌美麗　beautiful; pretty

　　窈窕　　【形容詞】疊韻聯綿詞 a rhyming compound
　　yǎo tiǎo　　　　嫻靜美麗　demure and pretty

　　　　　　◆ 疊韻 *diéyùn*　　　rhyming
　　　　　　◆ 聯綿詞　　　　a compound

9. 淑 shu/shū　【形容詞】賢淑；品德好　virtuous

　　窈窕淑女【名詞語】文靜美麗的賢淑女子
　　yǎo tiǎo shú nǚ　　　demure, pretty, and virtuous young lady

10. 君子　　【名詞】才德出眾的人
　　jūn zǐ　　　　a person with extraordinary talent and virtue
　　　　　　詩經中的君子多指有官爵者而言
　　　　　　In *Book of Odes* it often refers to a member of the ruling class

11. 逑 qiú　　【名詞】配偶 (pèiǒu) a spouse

　　好逑　　【名詞語】好配偶 a good spouse
　　hǎo qiú

12. 參差　　【形容詞】雙聲聯綿詞　an allitarative compound
　　cēn cī　　　　長短不齊；高矮不一樣
　　　　　　　　of varied sizes; some tall, some short

　　　　　　◆ 雙聲 *shuāngshēng*　alliterative

3

◆ **聯綿詞**　　　　　　　a compind
　　liánmiàncí

13. 荇菜　【名詞】荇，一種水草，可以吃，故稱荇菜
　　xìng cài　　　nymphoides, a kind of edible water plants;
　　　　　　　　　water mallows

14. 左　zuǒ　【方向詞】左邊 to the left

15. 右　yòu　【方向詞】右邊 to the right

16. 流　liú　【動詞】擇取；尋求；物色 to choose; to look for

17. 求　qiú　【動詞】追求 to pursue [something]; to court [a woman]

18. 寤　wù　【形容詞】醒著 awake

19. 寐　mèi　【形容詞】睡著；睡夢中 in sleep; in one's dream

20. 思　sī　【助詞】句中語氣詞，無義 a particle that does not have a
　　　　　　　　　lexical meaning but conveys only a tone or mood

21. 服　fú　【動詞】思念 to think about [a person];
　　　　　　　　　to miss [something or someone]

22. 悠　yōu　【動詞】思念 to miss; to think of; to remember with longing

23. 哉　zāi　【助詞】表感嘆；可譯成"啊" a modal particle

　　悠哉悠哉【動詞語】思念啊！思念啊！不停地思念 oh! I think
　　yōu zài yōu zài　　　of ...continuously and incessantly

24. 輾　zhǎn　【動詞】轉一半儿 to turn half over

25. 轉　zhuǎn　【動詞】轉動 to turn round

　　輾轉　【動詞】雙聲疊韻聯綿詞 an alliterative and rhyming compound
　　zhǎn zhuǎn　　　來回轉動 to toss and turn

26. 反　fǎn　【動詞】反身 to flip ... over

27. 側 cè 【動詞】 側身 to roll ... on side

反側
fǎn cè 【動詞】 翻來覆去 to toss this way or that

※ 輾轉反側 【成語】 翻來覆去，形容心有所思，睡不安穩
zhǎn zhuǎn fǎn cè to turn around in bed and can not get a sound sleep, as one has something bothering in mind

28. 采 cǎi 【動詞】 採 to pick

29. 琴 qín 【名詞】 一種樂器，有七弦(xián)或五弦
a five or seven stringed Chinese lute or guitar

30. 瑟 sè 【名詞】 一種樂器，形狀似琴，長八尺多，古有
五十弦，後改為二十五弦，弦各有柱
(zhù)，可上下移動。
A large horizontal musical instrument about nine feet long with movable bridges for tuning; originally it had 50 strings which was later reduced to 25.

31. 友 yǒu 【動詞】 親近；友愛 to be intimate with; to love

琴瑟友之 【動詞語】 彈琴鼓瑟來表達愛她的心意
qín sè yǒu zhī to express love through playing stringed music

◆ 彈 tán   to play a stringed musical instrument
◆ 鼓 gǔ   to beat or play a certain musical instrument

32. 芼 mào 【動詞】 拔 to pull out

33. 鐘 zhōng 【名詞】 樂器，銅製中空，敲擊可發聲 a bell;
a hollow metal object made to sound a musical note when struck by a clapper

◆ 敲擊 qiāojī   to beat [a bell]; to toll [a bell]

34. 鼓 gǔ 【名詞】 一種把皮蒙(méng)在木桶上的樂器，以鼓槌
或手打擊可發聲 a drum; a musical instrument made of a hollow round frame with skin stretched tightly across one or both end, it can be played with sticks or with hands

5

35. 樂 yào 　　【動詞】使…快樂 to make happy; to please

鐘鼓樂之【動詞語】敲鐘打鼓(用鐘鼓奏樂)來使她快樂
zhōng gǔ yào zhī 　　　　to please her with tolling the bells and playing the drums

◆ 奏樂 zòuyuè 　　　to play music

※ 　韻 yùn 　　　rhyme
押韻 yāyùn 　　to rhyme
節奏 jiézòu 　　rhythm

韻部

鳩、洲、逑	əu	幽部
流、求	-əu	幽部
得、服、側	-ək	職部
采、友	-ə	之部
芼	- au	宵部
樂	- auk	藥部

第二首

桃夭

詩經　周南

桃之夭夭，灼灼其華。之子于歸，宜其室家。
桃之夭夭，有蕡其實。之子于歸，宜其家室。
桃之夭夭，其葉蓁蓁。之子于歸，宜其家人。

Zhùyīn:

Táo zhī yāo yāo, zhuó zhuó qí huá. Zhī zǐ yú guī, yí qí shì jiā.

Táo zhī yāo yāo, yǒu fén qí shí. Zhī zǐ yú guī, yí qí jiā shì.

Táo zhī yāo yāo, qí yè zhēn zhēn. Zhī zǐ yú guī, yí qí jiā rén.

篇旨

這是一首祝賀女子出嫁的的短詩。詩人以紅艷的桃花比喻新娘，讚美她的美麗，並熱情地祝她婚後生活美滿幸福。風格輕快活潑，充滿歡樂的氣氛。

This is a short poem congratulating a marrying bride. The poet likens the bride to the bright and brilliant peach blossom, praising her unusual beauty, and ardently wishes her a nuptial life with much bliss. Lively and sprightly, it is full of joyful atmosphere

注解

1. 桃 táo 【名詞】桃樹 a peach tree

2. 夭夭 yāo yāo 【形容詞】疊字 reduplication; a reduplicative compound
   〔樹木〕少壯美好
   [said of trees] young and pretty

   ◆ 疊字 diézì a reduplicative compound

3. 灼灼 zhuó zhuó 【形容詞】疊字 a reduplicative compound
   紅色鮮明；亮麗
   [of colour] bright and brilliant

4. 華 huā 【名詞】古 "花" 字 flowers; blossoms

   灼灼其華 zhuó zhuó qí huā 【描寫句】其華灼灼；桃樹的花很鮮明
   桃樹的花像火一般地鮮明亮麗
   The peach blossoms are as bright and brilliant as fire

7

5. 之子
zhī zǐ   【名詞語】是子，這位少女   this young lady

6. 于 yú   【助詞】在詩中用來配合句子的音節，字本身沒
有甚麼意義   a prefix of a verb to fill in the needed syllable, and itself does not carry any lexical meaning

7. 歸 guī   【動詞】婦人謂嫁曰歸   [said of a girl] to get married

    于歸
yú guī   【動詞】出嫁   [said of a girl] to enter into matrimony

8. 宜 yí   【形容詞】和諧   harmonious; peaceful

9. 室 shì   【名詞】夫婦居住的屋子 the bed room of the couple

10. 家 jiā   【名詞】一門之內；整個家庭 the entire family

    宜其室家 【動詞語】使其室家宜
yí qí shì jiā   使她的家庭和諧
to make her [new] home harmonious and orderly

11. 有 yǒu   【助詞】在詩中用來配合句子的音節，字本身沒
有甚麼意義   a prefix of an adjective to fill in the needed syllable but without lexical meaning in itself

12. 蕡 fén   【形容詞】又大又多 plumpy and plentiful

13. 實 shí   【名詞】果實，指桃子 the fruit, meaning peaches

    有蕡其實 【描寫句】它的果實又大又多
yǒu fén qí shí   its fruits are plumpy and plentiful

14. 家室
jiā shì   【名詞】室家；家庭 family

15. 葉 yè   【名詞】葉子；樹葉 the leaves

16. 蓁蓁
zhēn zhēn   【形容詞】疊字   a reduplicative compound
茂盛 luxuriant

其葉蓁蓁 【描寫句】它的葉茂盛；它的葉子非常茂盛
qí yè zhēn zhēn　　　　　　its leaves are luxuriant

17.家人　　　【名詞語】一家的人；全家的人　family members
jiā rén

※ 宜室宜家 【成語】使家庭和諧
yí shì yí jiā　　　　　　to make a harmonious and orderly home [used as a congratulatory message on wedding]

韻部

華、家	-a	魚部
實、室	-et	質部
蓁、人	-en	真部

第三首

上山採蘼蕪

漢　樂府

上山採蘼蕪，下山逢故夫。長跪問故夫，新人復何如？
新人雖言好，未若故人姝。顏色類相似，手爪不相如。
新人從門入，故人從閣去。新人工織縑，故人工織素。
織縑日一匹，織素五丈餘。將縑來比素，新人不如故。

Zhùyīn:

Shàng shān cǎi mí wú, xià shān féng gù fū.　Cháng guì wèn gù fū, xīn rén fù hé rú?
Xīn rén suī yán hao, wèi ruò gù rén shū.　Yán sè lèi xiāng sì, shǒu zhǎo bù xiāng rú.
Xīn rén cóng mén rù, gù rén cóng gé qù.　Xīn rén gōng zhī jiān, gù rén gōng zhī sù.
Zhī jiān rì yì pǐ, zhī sù wǔ zhàng yú.　Jiāng jiān lái bǐ sù, xīn rén bù rú gù.

9

作者　本篇是民間歌謠，作者不詳。

This is a folk song and its author is unknown

篇旨

敍述棄婦遇見故夫時兩人之問答，談話淳樸坦率，而微妙的神情，細膩的心理，婉曲傳出。

This poem records the dialogue between a deserted wife and her former husband; the conversation was very simple, direct, and sincere, yet all the subtle expression and the minute detail of mentality were delicately and tactfully displayed.

注解

1. 上山
shàng shān
【動詞語】登上山去 to ascend a mountain

2. 採 cǎi
【動詞】採摘；採取 to pick; to gather

3. 蘼蕪
mí wú
【名詞】草名，開白色小花，有清香
Gracilaria confervoides, a kind of fragrant herb

4. 下山
xià shān
【動詞語】走下山來；從山上下來 to descend a mountain; to come down from a mountain

5. 逢 féng
【動詞】遇 to meet; to come across

6. 故夫
gù fū
【名詞語】從前的丈夫；前夫 former husband

7. 跪 guì
【動詞】跪下；兩膝(xī)彎曲著(zhuó)地 to kneel

長跪
cháng guì
【動詞語】伸直腰地跪〔表示尊敬〕
to kneel upright [in a solemn and respectful way]

8. 新人
xīn rén
【名詞語】新娶的妻子 a new wife

9. 復 fù
【副詞】又 again; then

10. 何如　hé rú　【準繫詞語】像什麼？怎麼樣？ to be like what? How does she look? How do you think of her?

11. 言　yán　【動詞】說 to say; to be said

12. 好　hǎo　【形容詞】美好 good; fair

13. 未若　wèi ruò　【準繫詞語】不像；不如 not as ... as ...; not equal to...; inferior to ...

14. 姝　shū　【形容詞】美麗 pretty

15. 顏色　yán sè　【名詞】容貌 looks; appearance

16. 類　lèi　【副詞】大致 roughly

17. 相　xiāng　【副詞】此處指你 here: it stands for the patient--you

相字原表示彼此對待的關係，但若只有一方發出的動作行為涉及於另一方時，相字起指代接受動作一方的作用，可以是第一身、第二身、或第三身。

The adverb "xiāng" means "mutually" or to "each other," indicating a reciprocal relationship. But when only one party acts upon the other party, the word "xiāng" then assumes the function of a pronoun which stands for the patient/receiver of action, and it can be either in the first person, the second person, or the third person.

18. 似　sì　【準繫詞】像 to be similar; to be alike

類相似　lèi xiāng sì　【動詞語】大致像你 roughly similar to you

19. 手爪　shǒu zhǎo　【名詞】手指；此處指紡紗、織布、縫紉等技能 fingers; dexiterity; here referring to skills in spinning, weaving and other needleworks

不相如　bù xiāng rú　【準繫詞語】不如你；比不上你 to be not as good as you; inferior to you

20. 閣　gé　【名詞】女子的閨房 a woman's chamber

21. 去　qù　【動詞】離去 to leave; to depart

11

22. 工 gōng 【形容詞】工〔於〕；善〔於〕；很會 be good at

23. 織 zhī 【動詞】織布 to weave

24. 縑 jiān 【名詞】淺黃色細絹 a fine, yellowish silk

25. 素 sù 【名詞】白色的生絹 pure white silk

26. 一匹 yì pī 【數量詞】長四丈 a length slightly over 13 meters

◆ 丈 zhàng a unit of length (=3.33 metres)

27. 餘 yú 【形容詞】多 more than

28. 將 jiāng 【動詞】拿；把 to take

押韻

蕪、夫	-u	上平聲七虞
如	-io	上平聲六魚
姝	-u	上平聲七虞
如	-io	上平聲六魚
去	-io	去聲六御
素	-u	去聲七遇
餘	-io	上平聲六魚
素、故	-u	去聲七遇

在古詩中平仄聲可以通押（混合在一起押韻）

In ancient style poems, words of different tones can rhyme with each other, so long as the sound values are similar.

第四首

行行重行行

漢　　古詩十九首

行行重行行，與君生別離。相去萬餘里，各在天一涯。
道路阻且長，會面安可知。胡馬依北風，越鳥巢南枝。
相去日已遠，衣帶日已緩。浮雲蔽白日，遊子不顧返。
思君令人老，歲月忽已晚。棄捐勿復道，努力加餐飯。

Zhùyīn:

Xíng xíng chóng xíng xíng, yǔ jū shēng bié lí. Xiāng qù wàn yú lǐ, gè zài tiān yì yí.

Dào lù zǔ qiě cháng, huì miàn ān kě zhī? Hú mǎ yī běi fēng, yuè niǎo cháo nán zhī.

Xiāng qù rì yǐ yuǎn, yī dài rì yǐ huǎn. Fú yún bì bái rì, yóu zǐ bú gù fǎn.

Sī jūn lìng rén lǎo, suì yuè hū yǐ wǎn. Qì juān wù fù dào, nǔ lì jiā cān fàn.

篇旨

描述思婦想念遠遊在外的丈夫，由於他久留不歸，內心產生種種疑慮。情意真摯，哀怨中不失溫婉。

This poem describes a pensive wife's thinking of her husband on a long journey. Since he has stayed away for a long time with no intention to return, she becomes suspicious and worrisome. The sentiment is sincere and cordial; though unavoidably plaintive, yet the tone can be regarded as mild.

注解

1. 行 xíng　　【動詞】走 to walk

2. 重 chóng　　【副詞】又 again

行行重行行【動詞語】走啊又走，走個不停
xíng.x chóng xíng.x　　　　　to walk (travel) on and on

3. 君 jūn　　　【名詞】您 you [used in addressing a male in formal speech]

4. 生別離　　【動詞語】活著別離 to part in life
　　shēng bié lí

楚辭《九歌・少司命》："悲莫悲兮生別離"。

Chǔ Cí, Nine Songs, The Lesser Master of Fate : "No sorrow is greater than the parting of the living"; translated by David Hawkes.

5. 去 qù　　　【動詞】距離 be apart from

6. 萬 wàn　　【數詞】一萬 ten thousand

7. 里 lǐ　　　【名詞】長度單位，三分之一公里
　　　　　　　　　　　a unit of linear measure; 1/3 of a kilometer

萬餘里　　【名詞語】一萬多里 more than ten thousand lǐ
wàn yú lǐ

8. 各 gè　　　【代詞】各自 each

9. 涯 yí/yá　　【名詞】邊際 margin; limit; boundary

天一涯　　【名詞語】天的一邊 the end of the world
tiān yì yí

10. 道路　　　【名詞】道路 the road
　　dào lù

11. 阻 zǔ　　　【形容詞】險阻 dangerous and difficult

12. 長 cháng　　【形容詞】遙遠 distant; remote; faraway

13. 會面　　　【動詞語】見面 to meet face to face
　　huì miàn

14. 安 ān　　　【副詞】何；怎麼 how

14

15. 可 kě　　　【助動詞】能　can

16. 知 zhī　　　【動詞】知道　to know; to be known

17. 胡馬　　　【名詞語】北方胡地所產的馬　horses bred in the North
    hú mǎ

18. 依 yī　　　【動詞】依戀　to feel persistent attachment [for a thing or a
    person]; to lean toward

19. 風 fēng　　　【名詞】風　wind

    北風　　　【名詞語】從北方吹來的風
    běi fēng　　　　　　　wind blowing from the North

20. 越鳥　　　【名詞語】南方越地的鳥　birds inhabiting in the South
    yuè niǎo

21. 巢 cháo　　　【動詞】作巢；搭窩　to build a nest

22. 枝 zhī　　　【名詞】樹枝　branches; boughs

    南枝　　　【名詞語】對著南方的樹枝　twigs facing the south;
    nán zhī　　　　　　　southern boughs

23. 相去　　　【動詞語】互相分開　to be apart from each other
    xiāng qù

24. 日 rì　　　【名詞】天　day

    　　　　　　【用作副詞】一天天地　day by day; daily

25. 已 yǐ　　　【副詞】已經　already

26. 遠 yuǎn　　　【形容詞】遙遠　distant; far away in distance

27. 帶 dài　　　【名詞】腰帶子　sash

28. 緩 huǎn　　　【形容詞】寬鬆　loose

15

衣帶緩
yī dài huǎn
【描寫句】委婉地說自己由於思念，一天天消瘦，腰圍縮小了
to say tactfully that because she thinks of her husband she is becoming more emaciated each day, and her waist size has shrunk

29. 浮 fú 【形容詞】浮動的 floating

30. 雲 yún 【名詞】雲 clouds

浮雲
fú yún
【名詞語】浮動的雲 the floating clouds

31. 蔽 bì 【動詞】遮蔽；擋住 to cover; to obscure

32. 白日
bái rì
【名詞語】明亮的太陽，比喻遠遊未歸的丈夫
the bright sun, standing for her wandering husband

33. 遊子
yóu zǐ
【名詞語】遠遊在外的人 a wanderer
此處指丈夫 here: her husband

34. 顧 gù 【動詞】念；想 to think of; to care for

35. 反 fǎn 【動詞】同“返”，回來 to come back; to return

36. 思君
sī jūn
【動詞語】想念您 to think of you; to miss you

37. 令人老
lìng rén lǎo
【動詞語】使人變老；使我變老 to cause one to become old; to cause me to become old

38. 歲月
suì yuè
【名詞語】年月；時間 years and months; time

39. 忽 hū 【副詞】很快地 quickly

40. 晚 wǎn 【形容詞】晚 late

歲月忽已晚
suì yuè hū yǐ wǎn
【敘述句】一生的時間很快地到了晚期
one's life time quickly comes to its late period

41. 棄捐
qì juān
【動詞】拋 (pāo)棄 to abandon; to desert

42. 道 dào 　　【動詞】說 to speak of; to mention

　　勿復道 　　【動詞語】不要再說 not to mention again
　　wù fù dào

43. 努力 　　【動詞語】勉力 to make great efforts to
　　nǔ lì

44. 加 jiā 　　【動詞】增加 to increase

45. 餐飯 　　【名詞】食物 food; meal
　　cān fàn

　　努力加餐飯【祈使句】努力多進飲食，保重身體。意思是
　　nǔ lì jiā cān fàn 　　說，儘管你不顧念我，可是我還是
　　希望你注意飲食，健康快樂。
　　《禮記・經解》："溫柔敦厚，詩教
　　也。" 從本詩可以得到一個證明。
　　This line "strive to eat more" meant that even
　　though you betrayed me, I still wish that you will
　　take good care of yourself and be healthy and
　　happy.　In the JīngJiě chapter of the *Book of
　　Rites,* it says: "Tenderness and sincerity, these
　　are the teaching of the Odes."　This poem can
　　testify to such a pronouncement.

　　◆ 祈使句 　　　　an imperative sentence
　　　 qíshǐjù
　　◆ 溫柔 wēnróu 　　warm and tender
　　◆ 敦厚 dūnhòu 　　honest and sincere

押韻

離、涯、知、枝　　-i 　　　　　　　　上平聲四支

遠 -iuɐn 　　晚　　-uɐn 　　返、飯 　　-ɐn 　　上聲十三阮

緩 　　　　　　-uɑn 　　　　　　　　上聲十四旱

古詩可以轉韻：從一個韻換到另一個韻

In ancient style poems, rhymes are allowed to change--to switch from one
rhyme to another.

第五首

迢迢牽牛星

漢　　古詩十九首

迢迢牽牛星，皎皎河漢女。纖纖擢素手，札札弄機杼。
終日不成章，泣涕零如雨。河漢清且淺，相去復幾許？
盈盈一水間，脈脈不得語。

Zhùyīn:

Tiáo tiáo Qiānniú xīng, jiǎo jiǎo Héhàn nǚ. Xiānxiān zhuó sù shǒu, zházhá nòng jī zhù.
Zhōng rì bù chéng zhāng, qì tì líng rú yǔ. Hé Hàn qīng qiě qiǎn, xiāng qù fù jǐ xǔ?
Yíngyíng yì shuǐ jiàn, mòmò bù dé yǔ.

篇旨

借牽牛星織女星的神話，表達男女相愛，遭受到
不合理的壓迫，不能自由相聚的痛苦。作者連用
迢迢、皎皎等六個疊字來突顯織女的美麗形象與
綿綿情意，是本詩的藝術特色。

Using the myth of the Herd Boy and the Weaving Maid to express the agony experienced by lovers unreasonably kept apart. Using six reduplicative compounds in a sequence to illustrate the beauty of the Weaving Maid and her tender love toward the Herd Boy is the artistic characteristics of this poem.

注解

1. 迢迢　　　【形容詞】疊字 a reduplicative compound
   tiáo tiáo　　　　遙遠的　remote

2. 牽牛星 　【名詞】又名河鼓，在天河南，與天河北的織
　qiān niú xīng 　　　　女星相對
　　　　　　　　the constellation of the Herd Boy, some stars in
　　　　　　　　Aquila; the star Altair

3. 皎皎 　【形容詞】疊字 a reduplicative compound
　jiǎo jiǎo 　　　　潔白明亮的　white and bright

4. 河漢 　【名詞】天河；銀河；星河 the Milky Way
　hé hàn

　河漢女 　【名詞】指天河北的織女星　the Weaving Maid
　hé hàn nǔ

　　　　　◆織女星 　　　　the Spinning Damsel -- the Star Vega in
　　　　　　zhīnǔxīng 　　　the constellation Lyra

5. 纖纖 　【形容詞】疊字 a reduplicative compound
　xiān xiān 　　　　柔細的，多用來描寫女子的手
　　　　　　　　delicate [hands of a woman]

6. 擢 zhuó 　【動詞】引；伸；[從袖中]伸出來　to stretch out
　　　　　　　　[from the sleeves]

7. 素手 　【名詞語】白皙的手；潔白的手 white hands
　sù shǒu

8. 札札 　【象聲詞】織布時織布機所發出來的聲音；
　zhá zhá 　　　　卡拉卡拉地 sound of weaving on a loom

　　　　　◆象聲詞 　　　　an onomatopoeia
　　　　　　xiàngshēngcí

9. 弄 nòng 　【動詞】用／拿…做… to work with; to use a particular
　　　　　　　material to produce something

10. 機 jī 　【名詞】織布機 a loom

11. 杼 zhù 　【名詞】織布用的梭 (suō) 子 a shuttle

　弄機杼 　【動詞語】拿杼在織布機前織布
　nòng jī zhù 　　　　to weave with a shuttle on a loom

19

12. 章 zhāng 　　【名詞】花紋　a pattern

　　不成章 　【動詞語】不能織成花紋；織不成花紋，即織不
　　bù chéng zhāng 　　　　　　成一段布　unable to weave into a piece of cloth

13. 泣 qì 　　【名詞】眼淚　tears

14. 涕 tì 　　【名詞】眼淚　tears

　　泣涕 　　【名詞】眼淚　tears
　　qì tì

15. 零 líng 　　【動詞】落　to fall

　　零如雨 　【動詞語】落得像下雨一樣
　　líng rú yǔ 　　　　　　to fall as if raining

16. 清且淺 　【形容詞】又清又淺；又清澈又不深
　　qīng qiě qiǎn 　　　　　　clear and shallow

17. 去 qù 　　【動詞】距；隔　to be apart

　　相去 　　【動詞語】相距；互相距離　be apart from each other
　　xiāng qù

18. 復 fù 　　【副詞】又　again

19. 幾許 　　【副詞】多少　how much; how many
　　jǐ xǔ 　　　　　　這裡的意思是 "多麼遠" here: how far

20. 盈盈 　　【形容詞】疊字　a reduplicative compound
　　yíng yíng 　　　　　　清清澈澈的　clear and limpid

21. 一水 　　【名詞語】一條河；一道銀河
　　yì shuǐ 　　　　　　a river; the Milky Way

22. 間 jiàn 　　【動詞】間隔；分隔　to separate; to set apart

23. 脈脈 　　【副詞】疊字　a reduplicative compound
　　mò mò 　　　　　　同 "眽眽"，深情地注視
　　　　　　to gaze affectionately

20

黙黙不語地用眼神表達愛戀的情意
quietly sending the message of love

24. 得 dé 　　【助動詞】能 can; be able to

不得語 　　【動詞語】不能說話 can not talk; be unable to talk
bù dé yǔ

最後兩句詩的大意是端莊美麗的織女隔著一條又清又淺的銀河
深情地注視牛郎，可是不能跟他談話

The general sense of the last two lines is that the dignified and pretty Weaving Maid, affectionately gazes at her lover, the Herd Boy, across the Milky Way, but she is unable to talk with him.

◆ 端莊 duāngzhuāng　sober; dignified

神話說牽牛織女原是夫婦，但因過受懲終年分離，
僅一年一度在七月七日之夕，由喜鵲在銀河上搭橋
，容許夫妻一會。第七首曹丕之《燕歌行》及宋秦
觀之《鵲橋仙》詞，皆歌詠此一神話

According to a Chinese myth, the Herd Boy and the Weaving Maid were originally a couple; they committed a minor offense and were separated as a punishment. They were allowed to unite once a year on the seventh night of the seventh lunar month, when magpies build a bridge over the Milky Way for them to get together. Both Poem no. 7 and Lyric no.7 dwell on this legend as well.

押韻

| 女、杼、許、語 | -io | 上聲六語 |
| 雨 | -iu | 上聲七麌 |

古詩上聲六語跟上聲七麌可通押
In ancient style poems these two rhymes are interchangeable.

第六首

贈從弟三首之二

漢　劉楨

亭亭山上松，瑟瑟谷中風。風聲一何盛，松枝一何勁！
冰霜正慘淒，終歲常端正。豈不罹凝寒，松柏有本性。

Zhù yīn:

Tíngtíng shān shàng sōng, sèsè gǔ zhōng fēng. Fēngshēng yī hé shèng, sōngzhī yī hé jìng!
Bīngshuāng zhèng cǎnqī, zhōngsuì cháng duānzhèng. Qǐbù lí nínghán, sōngbó yǒu běnxìng.

作者　劉楨 (d. 217)，字公幹，東平（今山東平陰縣）人
。"建安七子"之一。詩的風格剛勁有力。曹丕
稱讚他的五言詩"妙絕時人"，鍾嶸《詩品》列
爲"上品"。有《劉公幹集》。

Liú Zhēn (d. 217 A.D.), courtesy name Gōnggàn, was a native of Dōngpíng,
present-day Píngyīn district in Shāndōng province. He was one of the
"Seven Literary Masters of the Jiàn'ān Period." His poetic style was famous
for being vigorous and forceful. Cáo Pī praised his poems as superior to
those of his contemporaries, and the Liáng dynasty critic Zhōng Hóng ranked
him in the 'upper category' in his *Classification of Poets*. His work is entitled
Collected Works of Liú Gōnggàn.

篇旨

《贈從弟》共三首，這是其中第二首。作者勉勵
他的堂弟要有松柏一樣的堅貞品質，不要因環境
的艱苦而改變操守。風格極剛健雄勁。所謂魏晉
風骨，從此詩可領略一二。

This is the second poem in a series of three. In the poem the poet exhorts his
cousin to uphold a strong integrity, like the pines and cypresses that withstand

the most adverse circumstances. The style is extremely vigorous and powerful. The strength of character and vigor of style, said to be characteristics of the Wèi-Jìn period, can be sensed in this poem.

注解

1. 贈 zèng 【動詞】送給 to give to

2. 從弟 cóng dì 【名詞語】堂弟；叔伯兄弟 a cousin

3. 亭亭 tíng tíng 【形容詞】疊字 a reduplicative compound 聳立；高聳挺直地立著 tall and erect

4. 松 sōng 【名詞】松樹，一種常綠喬木 pine trees; a kind of evergreen tree

5. 瑟瑟 sè sè 【象聲詞】摹擬 (mónǐ)大風的聲音；蕭颯 (xiāosà) 的 simulating the rustling sound of the wind

   ◆ 象聲詞 xiàngshēngcí an onomatopoeia

6. 谷 gǔ 【名詞】山谷 a gorge; a deep valley

7. 風 fēng 【名詞】風 wind

8. 風聲 fēng shēng 【名詞語】風的聲音 the rustling sound of the wind

9. 一何 yī hé 【副詞】多麼 how

10. 盛 shèng 【形容詞】盛大；強烈；響 powerful; strong; loud

11. 松枝 sōng zhī 【名詞語】松樹的枝條 the branches of pine trees

12. 勁 jìng 【形容詞】強勁；堅強有力 strong; sturdy

13. 冰 bīng 【名詞】冰；水在寒冷時凝結成的固體 ice; water that has frozen and become solid

23

14. 霜 shuāng　【名詞】霜；附著在地面上的水氣因寒冷而凝結成的白色結晶體　frost; a white frozen dew coating the ground at night

15. 正 zhèng　【副詞】正在　in the course of; in the state of ...

16. 慘淒 cǎn qī　【形容詞】肅殺寒冷；嚴酷寒冷　severe and cold; harsh and cold

17. 終歲 zhōng suì　【副語】一年到頭　throughout the year; year round; the whole year

18. 常 cháng　【副詞】總是　always; constantly

19. 端正 duān zhèng　【形容詞】挺直的　upright

20. 豈不 qǐ bù　【副詞】難道不…；用於反問句表肯定　Isn't it...? Doesn't it...? Would it not...? Could it not...? Here: a rhetorical negative question is used to emphasize an affirmative meaning.

21. 罹 lí　【動詞】遭遇　to encounter

22. 凝寒 níng hán　【名詞語】嚴酷的寒冷　severe cold

23. 柏 bó　【名詞】柏樹；一種常綠喬木　cypress; a tall, straight, evergreen tree

24. 本性 běn xìng　【名詞語】固有的性質；耐寒的天性　intrinsic nature; a cold resistant nature

韻部

松、風			-ung	上平聲一東
盛、正	- ng	勁、性	-i ng	去聲二十四敬

第七首

燕歌行

魏　曹丕

秋風蕭瑟天氣涼，草木搖落露為霜。
群燕辭歸雁南翔，念君客游思斷腸。
慊慊思歸戀故鄉，君何淹留寄他方？
賤妾煢煢守空房，憂來思君不敢忘。
不覺淚下霑衣裳。
援琴鳴絃發清商，短歌微吟不能長。
明月皎皎照我床，星漢西流夜未央。
牽牛織女遙相望，爾獨何辜限河梁？

Zhùyīn:

Qiūfēng xiāosè tiānqì liáng, cǎomù yáoluò lù wéi shuāng.
Qún yàn cí guī yàn nán xiáng, niàn jūn kè yóu sī duàn cháng.
Qiànqiàn sī guī liàn gùxiāng, jūn hé yānliú jì tuōfāng?
Jiànqiè qióngqióng shǒu kōngfáng, yōu lái sī jūn bù gǎn wàng.
Bù jué lèi xià zhān yīshāng.
Yuán qín míng xián fā qīngshāng, duǎn gē wēi yín bùnéng cháng.
Míngyuè jiǎojiǎo zhào wǒ chuáng, xīng hàn xī liú yè wèi yāng.
Qiānniú Zhīnǚ yáo xiàng wàng, ěr dú hégū xiàn hé liáng?

作者　曹丕 (187-226 A.D.)，字子桓，篡漢自立，史稱魏文帝
　　　。他著作的"典論論文"，是中國最早的文學批
　　　評論著，他的"燕歌行"，也被認爲現存最早的
　　　七言詩，在中國文學史上佔重要地位。他也是歷

史上有文學成就的皇帝之一。

Cáo Pī (187-226 A.D.), courtesy name Zǐhuán, was known as Emperor Wén of Wèi, after he usurped the collapsing Hàn regime and founded the new dynasty. He wrote an "Essay on Literature," which is regarded as the earliest important work of Chinese literary criticism. His "Song of Yān" is also regarded as the earliest extant poem written in the septasyllabic form. He held an important position in the history of Chinese literature, and was one of a few rulers who had achieved literary excellence.

篇旨

描寫思婦在寒涼的秋夜想念遠遊他方的丈夫，憂傷難寐的淒清情境，委婉細膩，動人心弦。篇末以爲牛郎織女無辜被銀河阻隔鳴不平，來抒發自己對夫妻久離的哀怨。餘韻悠悠，耐人尋味。本篇是最早的七言詩，有如在楚辭與唐詩間搭了一座橋。在中國詩的發展史上有重要的地位。

This poem depicts the scene of a pensive woman thinking of her far away husband in a lonesome, chilly, and sleepless autumnal night; is a pensive but tactful and exquisite playing upon one's heartstrings. At the end of the poem, through crying out against an injustice imposed on the Weaving Maid and the Herd Boy, the heroine lamented over her own distress, leaving a lingering aftertaste for one to savor. This is probably the earliest poem with septasyllabic lines, with rhymes falling on the end of each line. It built a bridge between Chǔcí and Táng verses, and played an important role in the development of Chinese poetry.

注解

1. 燕歌行　　【名詞語】屬《樂府・相和歌・平調曲》，燕為
   Yān gē xíng　　地名。樂府詩以地名為題的，是表示
   曲調的地方特點，後世曲調失傳，於
   是就只用來歌詠當地的風土人情

   This is a tune of the Music Bureau Ballads and it belongs to the Even Melody choral songs. Yān is the name of an ancient place. When a ballad uses a place name in its title, it indicates the characteristics of the local music in that specific area. Later the music of the tune is lost, and the ballad depicts only the local conditions and customs of the said region.

2. 蕭瑟
   xiāo sè
   【象聲詞】形容風吹樹木的聲音
   the rustling sound of the autumn wind

   ◆ 象聲詞
   xiàngshēngcí
   an onomatopoeia

3. 搖落
   yáo luò
   【動詞】凋殘，零落
   to wither and fall

4. 露 lù 【名詞】露水 dew

5. 霜 shuāng 【名詞】霜 frost

6. 燕 yàn 【名詞】燕子 swallows

7. 辭 cí 【動詞】告辭 to bid farewell; to take leave

8. 歸 guī 【動詞】回家 to return; to go home

9. 雁 yàn 【名詞】鴻雁 wild geese

10. 南翔
    nán xiáng
    【動詞語】南飛；向南方飛
    to fly southward

11. 念 niàn 【動詞】想念 to think of; to miss

12. 客游
    kè yóu
    【動詞語】在外地客居或遊歷 to travel in a distant place

13. 思 sī 【動詞】思念 to think of; to miss

14. 斷腸
    duàn cháng
    【動詞語】心碎 to break the heart; to be heart-broken

15. 慊慊
    qiàn qiàn
    【形容詞】疊字 a reduplicative compound
    含恨；不滿 resentful and discontent

16. 戀 liàn 【動詞】戀念 to feel a persistent attachment to

27

戀故鄉
liàn gùxiāng
【動詞語】戀念故鄉；思念故鄉
to feel attached to and miss one's native place

17. 淹留
yān liú
【動詞語】久留 to stay for a long period of time

18. 寄 jì
【動詞】寄居 to sojourn

19. 他方
tuō fāng
【名詞語】別處；他鄉；外地
other places; a land away from home

寄他方
jì tuō fāng
【動詞語】寄居在外地
to sojourn in a remote place

20. 賤妾
jiàn qiè
【名詞語】古代婦人謙稱自己為賤妾 your concubine;
I; a self-reference among women of ancient time

21. 煢煢
qióng qióng
【形容詞】疊字 a reduplicative compound
孤孤單單的 lonely

21. 守 shǒu
【動詞】堅持呆在 to keep staying/living in

22. 空房
kōng fáng
【名詞語】空空的屋子 an empty room; a deserted room

23. 援琴
yuán qín
【動詞語】拿過琴來 to pick up a lute

24. 鳴弦
míng xián
【動詞語】使弦鳴；彈起琴弦來
to sound the strings; to play on the strings

25. 清商
qīng shāng
【名詞語】樂調名；清商之調，節奏短促，聲音
細微悲涼 a tune in the Qīngshāng mode, with
short, abrut rhythm and tenuous sound

26. 短歌
duǎn gē
【動詞語】短促地歌唱 to sing a song briefly

27. 微吟
wēi yín
【動詞語】低微地吟詠 to chant in a low pitch

28. 皎皎　　　【形容詞】疊字 a reduplicative compound
    jiǎo jiǎo　　　　　　潔白明亮 white and bright

29. 星漢　　　【名詞語】眾星及銀河
    xīng hàn　　　　　　the stars and the Milky Way

30. 西流　　　【動詞語】向西方流動
    xī liú　　　　　　　to move/shift westward

31. 央　yāng　【動詞】盡；完 to finish; to end

    未央　　　【動詞語】未盡 not yet ended; not yet finished
    wèi yāng

32. 牽牛　　　【名詞語】牽牛星；又名河鼓，在銀河南
    Qiān niú　　　　　　the star Herd Boy, to the south of the Milky Way

33. 織女　　　【名詞語】織女星，在銀河北
    Zhī nǚ　　　　　　　the star Weaving Maid, to the north of the Milky
    　　　　　　　　　　Way

34. 遙相望　【動詞語】遠遠地互相望著
    yáo xiāng wàng　　　 to gaze at each other from afar

35. 爾　ěr　【代名詞】你；你們 you (here referring to both the stars and
    　　　　　　　　　　the husband)

36. 獨　dú　【形容詞】單獨 alone

37. 辜　gū　【名詞】罪；過失 sin; crime; offense

    何辜　　　【名詞語】何罪；有何罪過；犯了什麼罪
    hé gū　　　　　　　what reason? what offense?

38. 限　xiàn　【動詞】限制；隔離（此處為被動意）
    　　　　　　　　　　to confine; to be confined [by]

39. 河梁　　　【名詞語】橋樑；此處指銀河
    hé liáng　　　　　　 the bridge; here referring to the Milky Way

平日銀河上無橋梁相通，故牛、女為銀河所限，不

29

舩聚首。 Usually, there was no bridge over the Milky Way, and thus the couple, Herd Boy and Weaving Maid, was unable to unite.

韻部

涼、翔、鄉、央、梁	-iang;
腸、方、房、裳、商、長	-ang
霜、忘、床、望、	-uang　　　　下平聲七陽

第八首

雜詩六首之四

魏　曹植

南國有佳人，容華若桃李。朝遊江北岸，夕宿瀟湘沚。
時俗薄朱顏，誰為發皓齒？俛仰歲將暮，榮耀難久恃。

Zhùyīn:

Nán guó yǒu jiā rén, róng huá ruò táo lí. Zhāo yóu jiāng běi àn, xī sù Xiāo Xiāng zhǐ. Shí sú bó zhū yán, shéi wèi fā hào chǐ? Fǔ yǎng suì jiāng mù, róng yào nán jiǔ shì.

作者　　曹植(192-232 A.D.)，字子建，是建安時代成就最高的
　　　　詩人。他才思敏捷，志向遠大，早期詩風俊爽，
　　　　充滿昂揚奮發的精神；後因在政治上飽受壓抑，
　　　　內心憤懑，風格轉為沈鬱，寫了很多慷慨不平的
　　　　詩篇，最後終於郁郁而死。詩評家鍾嶸在《詩品
　　　　》中把他列為上品，盛讚他的詩"骨氣奇高，詞采
　　　　華茂，情兼雅怨，體備文質。"

Cáo Zhí (192-232 A.D.), courtesy name Zǐjiàn, was a man of great talent and aspiration. He is considered the most accomplished poet of the Jiàn'ān period. His early poems are sprightly and dashing, full of ambition and high spirit, but his later works are gloomy and indignant, reflecting his frustration and depression after suffering repeated political suppression. He eventually died a disheartened man. The Liáng dynasty critic Zhōng Hóng ranked Cáo Zhí in the 'top category' in his renowned *Classification of Poets*, and extolled his poems as: "extremely lofty in spirit, luxuriant and ornate in diction, plaintive yet elegant in poetic mode, and combining cultivated grace with naturalness."

篇旨

本篇以佳人容華絕世不受時人賞識作比喻，來發抒賢士懷才而不受重用的悲哀。前人認爲是曹植自傷之詞。

In this poem the poet uses an extraordinary beauty's not being admired as a metaphor to express the sadness of a talented man who was not given a chance to serve. Traditionally this poem has been regarded as a lament for the author himself.

注解

1. **雜詩** zá shī 　【名詞語】興致不一，不拘流俗，遇物即言之詩 poems with various moods, not confined by convention, written to spontaneous occasions; miscellaneous poems

2. **南國** nán guó 　【名詞語】江南 the southern states; south of the Yángzǐ River

3. **佳人** jiā rén 　【名詞語】美人 a beauty

4. **容** róng 　【名詞】容貌 appearance; looks

5. **華** huá 　【形容詞】美麗 pretty; gorgeous

6. **若** ruò 　【準繫詞】像 to be like; to resemble

7. **桃李** táo lǐ 　【名詞語】桃花、李花 blossoms of peaches and plums

8. 朝 zhāo 【時間詞】早晨；早上 morning; in the morning

9. 江北岸
Jiāng běi àn 【名詞語】長江的北岸 the northern bank of the Yángzǐ River

10. 暮 mù 【時間詞】薄暮；傍晚 dusk; at dusk

11. 宿 sù 【動詞】住；過夜 to dwell; to stay over night

12. 瀟湘
Xiāo Xiāng 【名詞】瀟水，湘水，在湖南省 the Xiāo River and the Xiāng River, both in Húnán province

13. 沚 zhǐ 【名詞】水中小洲 a sandy islet in a stream

14. 時俗
shí sú 【名詞語】當時的風尚 the current fad

15. 薄 bó 【動詞】鄙薄；不看重 to slight; to belittle; to look down upon

16. 朱顔
zhū yán 【名詞語】美麗的容貌；此處比喻過人的才華 beautiful looks; here it stands for outstanding talent

17. 誰為
shéi wèi 【介詞語】為誰？ for whom

疑問代詞用作賓語時，提在介詞之前 When an interrogative pronoun functions as the object in a prepositional phrase, it musg be transposed in front of the preposition.

18. 發 fā 【動詞】開；展露 to open; to reveal

19. 皓齒
hào chǐ 【名詞語】潔白的牙齒 sparkling teeth

發皓齒
fā hào chǐ 【動詞語】展露潔白的牙齒，指言笑或歌唱；喻展露才華 to grin; to speak, smile, or sing; meaning: to show one's talent

20. 俛仰
fǔ yǎng 【動詞】俯首仰首；低頭抬頭 to lower and to raise one's head

【副詞】俯仰之間；在很短的時間之內

32

in a short while; in an instant

21. 歲 suì 　　【名 詞】一年 a year
　　　　　　　　　比喻人生 a life

22. 云 yún 　　【助 詞】無義 a particle that has no lexical meaning

23. 暮 mù 　　【形 容 詞】晚 late

　　歲暮 　　【時 間 詞】一年將盡 approaching the end of the year
　　suì mù 　　　　　　　比喻一生將盡 approaching the end of the life

24. 榮耀 　　【形 容 詞】〔花木〕茂盛鮮豔 luxuriant and resplendent
　　róng yào

25. 難 nán 　　【形 容 詞】不容易 difficult; not easy to

26. 久 jiǔ 　　【時 間 詞】長久地 for long; longlasting

27. 恃 shì 　　【動 詞】仗恃；依賴；憑藉 to rely on

韻 部

李、沚、齒、恃　　　　-i　　　　上聲四紙

第九首

歸園田居

晉　　陶潛

33

少無適俗韻，性本愛丘山。誤落塵網中，一去三十年。
羈鳥戀舊林，池魚思故淵。開荒南野際，守拙歸園田。
方宅十餘畝，草屋八九間。榆柳蔭後簷，桃李羅堂前。
曖曖遠人村，依依墟里煙。狗吠深巷中，雞鳴桑樹顛。
戶庭無塵雜，虛室有餘閒。久在樊籠裡，復得返自然。

Zhùyīn:

Shào wú shì sú yùn, xìng běn ài qiū shān. Wù luò chén wǎng zhōng, yí qù sān shí nián.
Jī niǎo liàn jiù lín, chí yú sī gù yuān. Kāi huāng nán yě jì, shǒu zhuó guī yuán tián.
Fāng zhái shí yú mǔ, cǎo wū bā jiǔ jiān. Yú liǔ yìn hòu yán, táo lǐ luó táng qián.
Ai ài yuǎn rén cūn, yī yī xū lǐ yān. Gǒu fèi shēn xiàng zhōng, jī míng sāng shù diān.
Hù tíng wú chén zá, xū shì yǒu yú xián. Jiǔ zài fán lóng lǐ, fù dé fǎn zì rán.

作者

陶潛 (365-427 A.D.) 字淵明，東晉潯陽柴桑 (今江西九江) 人。曾為江州祭酒及彭澤令，厭惡官場的巧詐腐敗，辭官歸田。擅長描寫隱居田園的生活，是中國田園詩人之祖。

Táo Qián (365-427 A.D.), courtesy name Yuānmíng, was a native of Cháisāng in Xúnyáng prefecture, present-day Jiǔjiāng in Jiāngxī province. At one time he served as the libator (chancellor) of the Provincial School of Jiāngzhōu, and the magistrate of Péngzé district, but he became disillusioned with the cynicism and corruption of officialdom and resigned to lead a carefree rural life. He excelled in writing about nature and country life, and is held to be the originator of the form of Chinese pastoral verse known as 'field and garden poetry'.

◆ 江州 *Jiāngzhōu* — the name of a prefecture
◆ 祭酒 *jìjiǔ* — Libator; head-master of a school
◆ 彭澤 *Péngzé* — the name of a county
◆ 令 *lìng* — County Magistrate (offical title in former time)

篇旨

描寫厭惡官場的巧詐，辭官歸田，重獲精神自由的歡欣，與鄉居生活的樂趣。

This poem depicts the poet's loathing of the cunning officialdom, and his resigning from his official post to return to farm land. It also depicts his elation in regaining his mental freedom and the pleasure he finds in his rural life.

注解

1. 少 shào　　　【形容詞】少年；年輕 young
   此處指"年少時" while [I was] young

2. 適 shì　　　　【動詞】適合 to suit; to adapt to

3. 俗 sú　　　　【形容詞】世俗 secular; worldly; conventional

4. 韻 yùn　　　　【名詞】氣質；性情 temperament; disposition

   適俗韻　　　　【名詞語】適合世俗的性情 a temperament that suits the
   shì sú yùn　　　　　　　social convention

5. 性 xìng　　　　【名詞】本性；天性 natural temperament; intrinsic nature

6. 丘 qiū　　　　【名詞】小山 hills

7. 誤 wù　　　　【副詞】錯誤地 mistakenly; unwittingly

8. 落 luò　　　　【動詞】落入；掉進 to fall into

9. 塵 chén　　　　【名詞】塵世；現實的社會 the mundane world

10. 網 wǎng　　　【名詞】用線、繩等結成的捕魚捉鳥的用具 a net;
    a web; a type of material made of string or rope, woven
    or tied together with small space in between that is used
    for catching fish or birds

   塵網　　　　　【名詞語】塵世的網；人在世間受到種種束縛，
   chén wǎng　　　　　　如魚在網，故稱"塵網"。此處指仕途
   　　　　　　　　　　；誤落塵網是指誤入仕途 the web of the

35

world's dust; one's life in the world is restricted by all kinds of social conventions, just as a fish living in a net, so the world is likened to a web; here, it refers to a career in officialdom

11. 三十年
sānshí nián

【名詞語】有人認為應當寫作十三年。因陶淵明從出仕到辭官是十二年，此詩作於歸田後的第二年，前後剛好是十三年。

Some thought that thirty was an error and it should be thirteen, bacause Táo served in official career for a total of twelve years. This poem was written one year after his resignation, exactly thirteen years from his first assuming official duty.

12. 羈 jī
【動詞】束縛 (fù)；限制 to bind; to confine; to restrain

羈鳥
jī niǎo
【名詞語】籠鳥；被關在籠子裡的鳥
birds confined in a cage

13. 戀 liàn
【動詞】戀念；思念 to think of ...with affection

14. 舊 jiù
【形容詞】故舊的；從前的 old; former

15. 林 lín
【名詞】樹林 forest; woods

16. 池 chí
【名詞】池子 a pond

池魚
chí yú
【名詞語】池子裡的魚 fish in a pond

17. 故 gù
【形容詞】故舊的；從前的 old; former

18. 淵 yuān
【名詞】深水 deep water; an abyss

19. 開荒
kāi huāng
【動詞語】開墾 (kěn)荒地 to open up wasteland

20. 野 yě
【名詞】荒野 wilderness; open country

21. 際 jì
【名詞】邊 edge; side

22. 守 shǒu
【動詞】守著；不改變 to keep to; to maintain

23. 拙 zhuō 【形容詞】笨拙 stupid; awkward; slow and clumsy
不善於巧詐；不會逢迎
not good at crafty schemes; unable to ingretiate

守拙
shǒu zhuō
【動詞語】守著愚拙〔不學巧偽，不爭名利〕；
指歸耕田園 to hold on to one's clumsiness;
meaning "to return to farmland to lead a rural life"

24. 方宅 fāng zhái 【名詞語】方形的宅院 a rectangular homestead

25. 畝 mǔ 【名詞】土地的量詞；一畝約等於 0.16 英畝 one sixth of an acre

26. 榆 yú 【名詞】榆樹 the elm trees

27. 柳 liǔ 【名詞】柳樹 the willow trees

28. 蔭 yìn 【動詞】蔭蔽；遮蔽 to shelter

29. 簷 yán 【名詞】屋簷 the eaves

30. 桃 táo 【名詞】桃樹 the peach trees

31. 李 lǐ 【名詞】李樹 the plum trees

32. 羅 luó 【動詞】羅列；排列 to line up; to stand in lines

33. 堂 táng 【名詞】廳堂 the hall; the living room

34. 曖曖 ài ài 【形容詞】疊字 a reduplicative compound
昏昧模糊；模模糊糊 dim; vague; indistinct

35. 村 cūn 【名詞】村莊 a village

36. 依依 yī yī 【形容詞】疊字 a reduplicative compound
輕柔的 soft and gentle
裊裊 (niǎo) 上升的 spiralling up

37

37. 墟里
xū lǐ
【名詞】村落；村莊　village; hamlet

38. 煙　yān
【名詞】炊(chuī)煙　smoke from kitchen chimneys

39. 狗　gǒu
【名詞】狗　dogs

40. 吠　fèi
【動詞】〔狗〕叫　to bark

41. 巷　xiàng
【名詞】胡同　a lane; an alley

深巷
shēn xiàng
【名詞語】離大街很遠的長巷；偏僻的長胡同
a deep, secluded lane or alley

42. 雞　jī
【名詞】雞　chickens; cocks

43. 鳴　míng
【動詞】叫　to crow

44. 桑　sāng
【名詞】桑樹　the mulberry trees

45. 顛　diān
【名詞】頂　the top

46. 戶　hù
【名詞】門　door; gate

47. 庭　tíng
【名詞】庭院；院子　the courtyard

48. 塵雜
chén zá
【名詞語】人世間的煩雜瑣事　worldly affairs that are
complicated and difficult to handle

49. 虛室
xū shì
【名詞語】空室；空空的屋子
empty rooms
比喻澄靜無雜念的心靈
here it stands for a mind that is pure and serene

50. 餘閒
yú xián
【名詞語】剩餘下來的閒暇；很多的閒暇
excessive leisure; spare time

51. 樊籠
fán lóng
【名詞語】關鳥獸的籠子　a cage

詩人用樊籠來比喻限制和束縛；人住在塵俗的社會
中好像鳥獸被關在籠中一樣失掉自由

The poet likens restrictive human living condition to a bird cage; one lives in a conventional mundane society is like a bird locked in a cage, with no freedom at all.

52. 復 fu4 　　【副詞】又 once again

53. 得 dé 　　【助動詞】能 can; be able to

54. 返 fǎn 　　【動詞】回到 to return to

55. 自然 　　【名詞】自然界 the great nature; natural environment
　　zì rán 　　　　　　指淳樸的農村生活 the simple rural life

押韻

山 　　-an;　　　　間、閒 　　-ian　　　　上平聲十五刪

年、田、簷、前、煙、顛、然 　　-iɛn;

淵 　　iuɛn　　　　　　　　　　　　　下平聲一先

下平一先、上平十五刪，二韻古詩可以通押

In ancient style poems these two rhymes were interchangeable.

第十首

結廬在人境

晉　　陶潛

結廬在人境，而無車馬喧。問君何能爾？心遠地自偏。
採菊東籬下，悠然見南山。山氣日夕佳，飛鳥相與還。
此中有真意，欲辯已忘言。

Zhùyīn:

Jié lú zài rén jìng, ér wú chē mǎ xuān, Wèn jūn hé néng ěr? Xīn yuǎn dì zì piān.

Cǎi jú dōng lí xià, yōu rán jiàn nán shān. Shān qì rì xī jiā, fēi niǎo xiāng yǔ huán.

Cǐ zhōng yǒu zhēn yì, yù biàn yǐ wàng yán.

作者   見詩選《歸園田居》p.34

篇旨

作者描述自己遠離塵俗，從觀賞自然美景的和諧
靜謐中領悟到心神怡適難以言傳的人生真實意味
。

In this poem the author depicts himself as one keeps far away from the maddening world, and comprehends the true meaning of life while observing the harmony and serenity of Nature and feeling pleasant and content in his heart, a feeling that is beyond verbal expression.

注解

1. 廬 lú   【名詞】茅廬；茅舍；簡陋的草頂房子 a hut;
            a simple and crude dwelling; a thached cottage

   結廬   【動詞語】蓋簡陋的草頂的房子 to build a thatched hut
   jié lú

2. 人境   【名詞語】人所居止的地方 human habitations
   rén jìng

3. 喧 xuān   【動詞】喧鬧；嘈(cáo)雜 to clamor; to make noise

4. 爾 ěr   【準繫詞語】如此；像這樣 to be thus; to be like this

5. 偏 piān   【形容詞】偏僻(pì) secluded

6. 採 cǎi   【動詞】摘取 to pick; to pluck

7. 菊 jú   【名詞】菊花 chrysanthemums

8. 籬 lí　　【名詞】籬笆(bā)；用竹子作的矮牆　fences; a structure made of bamboo supported with posts that is put between two areas of land as a boundary

9. 悠然 yōu rán　　【副詞】閒適地；恬淡地　leisurely and tranquilly

10. 南山 nán shān　　【名詞】南面的山　mountain in the south

11. 氣 qì　　【名詞】很淡的煙霧 (yānwù)　mist; vapor

　　山氣 shān qì　　【名詞語】山上淡淡的煙霧　mountain vapor; mist

12. 日夕 rì xī　　【時間詞】黃昏；日落的時候　dusk

13. 佳 jiā　　【形容詞】美好　good; fine; beautiful

14. 飛鳥 fēi niǎo　　【名詞語】飛翔著的鳥　flying birds

15. 相與 xiāng yǔ　　【動詞語】互相在一塊兒　together; in flocks

16. 還 huán　　【動詞】返回；飛回　to return; to fly home

17. 辯 biàn　　【動詞】辯說；清楚地說明　to explain
　　"此中有真意，欲辯已忘言"這兩句詩的大意是從大自然的景色中領悟到一種人生的真實的意味，本想很清楚地說明一下這真意是甚麼，可是又忘了要說的話。其實這真意是只能用心靈去感受而無法用語言表達出來的

The general sense of the two last lines is that in the idyllic beauty of Nature, one can comprehend a certain truth about life, but as soon as one tries to explain it, one gets lost in the words. In fact, such truth can only be perceived mentally; it is beyond verbal description.

◆ 領悟 lǐngwù　　to comprehend; to grasp
◆ 感受 gǎnshòu　　be affected by; to perceive

41

◆心靈 *xīnlíng*   heart; spirit; soul

◎和諧   【形容詞】 harmonious
hé xié

◎恬淡   【形容詞】 serene; indifferent to worldly gains
tián dàn

押韻

喧	-iuɐn	言	-iɐn		上平聲十三元
偏	-iɛn				下平聲一仙
山	-an	還	-uan		上平聲十五刪

此三韻音相近，古詩通押

These three rhymes sound similar, and they are interchangeable in ancient style poems.

第十一首

敕勒歌

民歌

敕勒川，陰山下。
天似穹廬，籠蓋四野。
天蒼蒼，野茫茫，風吹草低見牛羊。

Zhùyīn:

Chì lè chuān, Yīn shān xià.
Tiān sì qióng lú, lǒng gài sì yě.
Tiān cāng cāng, yě máng máng, fēng chuī cǎo dī xiàn niú yáng.

篇旨

本篇是敕勒的民歌，以簡短的歌詞，明快的節奏，歌唱出西北大草原的遼闊、牛羊的眾多，富有北方民族的粗曠豪邁的特色。

This is a folk song prevalent in the Chìlè area. With a short verse and in quick tempo, it ably presents the spaciousness of the steppe and the numerous cattle and sheep. Bold, unconstrained, carefree, and straightforward, it is full of the characteristics distinctive of northern ethnic tribesmen.

注解

1. 敕勒
   Chì-lè
   【名詞】民族名，是匈奴的後裔，北齊時 (550-577A.D.)居住在朔 (Shuò)州 (今山西省西北部一帶) Name of a tribe that descended from the Huns and lived in th northwestern part of Shānxī

   ◆ 後裔 hòuyì　　　descendants

2. 川 chuān
   【名詞】平原　a plain; a prairie

   敕勒川
   Chì-lè Chuān
   【名詞語】敕勒平原
   the plain/prairie of Chì-lè

3. 陰山
   Yīn Shān
   【名詞】山名，在今內蒙古南境 Mt. Yīn, situated in the southern parts of inner-Mogolia

4. 穹廬
   qióng lú
   【名詞語】圓頂氈帳 (zhān zhàng) felt tents with rounded tops; a yurt

5. 籠蓋
   lǒng gài
   【動詞】籠罩 (zhào)；蓋住 to cover; to shroud

6. 野 yě
   【名詞】原野；又平坦又廣大的郊野　wilderness

   四野
   sì yě
   【名詞語】四面的原野 wilderness on four sides

7. 蒼蒼
   cāng cāng
   【形容詞】疊字 a reduplicative compound
   青色的；藍色的 blue; azure

43

天蒼蒼　　【描寫句】天非常青；天非常藍
tiān cāng cāng　　The sky is azure.

8. 茫茫　　【形容詞】疊字 a reduplicative compound
máng máng　　廣大無邊 vast; boundless

野茫茫　　【描寫句】原野廣大無邊
tiān cāng cāng　　The wilderness is boundless.

9. 草 cǎo　　【名詞】草 grass

10. 低 dī　　【動詞】彎下去；倒下去 to bend

11. 見 xiàn　　【動詞】"現" 的古字 to reveal; to show; to make visible

12. 牛羊　　【名詞】牛和羊 cattle and sheep
niú yáng

押韻

| 下、野 | | -ia | 上聲二十一馬 |
| 蒼、茫 -ang | 羊 | -iang | 下平七陽 |

由上聲二十一馬換韻到下平聲七陽

The rhymes change from rising tone 21 to level tone B7

第十二首

木蘭詩

北方民歌

唧唧復唧唧，木蘭當戶織。不聞機杼聲，唯聞女嘆息。
問女何所思？問女何所憶？女亦無所思，女亦無所憶。
昨夜見軍帖，可汗大點兵。軍書十二卷，卷卷有爺名。
阿爺無大兒，木蘭無長兄。願為市鞍馬，從此替爺征。

Zhùyīn:

> Jī jī fù jī jī, Mù Lán dāng hù zhī. Bù wén jī zhù shēng, wéi wén nǚ tàn xí.
>
> Wèn nǚ hé suǒ sī? wèn nǚ hé suǒ yì? Nǚ yì wú suǒ sī, nǚ yì wú suǒ yì.
>
> Zuó yè jiàn jūn tiě, Kè Hán dà diǎn bīng. Jūn shū shí èr juàn, juàn juàn yǒu yé míng.
>
> Ā yé wú dà ér, Mù Lán wǔ zhǎng xiōng. Yuàn wèi shì ān mǎ, cóng cǐ tì yé zhēng.

篇旨

本篇屬於古樂府民歌，作者姓名不詳。敘述木蘭女扮男裝，代父從軍，英勇作戰，得勝歸來的故事。語言樸實，風格自然，充分表現民歌的特色。是中國少數敘事詩歌名篇之一。

This ballad is preserved in the Music Bureau collection; it tells the story of Mùlán's joining the army while dressed in a man's clothing on behalf of her aged father, fighting bravely, and returning in triumph. Composed in simple language and naturalistic style, it is one of a few epic poems in Chinese poetic tradition.

◆ 樂府 *yuèfǔ*		the Music Bureau; ballads
◆ 風格 *dēng gé*		style of a work of literature
◆ 敘事詩 *xùshìshī*		epics

注解

1. 唧唧　【象聲詞】嘆息的聲音 the sound of sighing; to sigh
   jī jī

   ◆ 象聲詞　an onomatopoeia
   xiàngshēngcí

2. 復 fù　【副詞】又 again

3. 木蘭　【名詞】人名，姓花，名木蘭，據唐人考證，木
Mù lán　蘭為河南商邱人，約生活在北魏時代
personal name; surnamed Huā and named Mùlán,
according to the study of a Táng dynasty scholar, she
was a native of Shāngqiū in Hénán province, and lived
during the Northern Wèi period(386-534 A.D.)

4. 當 dāng　【動詞】面對著 to face; facing

5. 戶 hù　【名詞】門 the door

當戶　【動詞語】對著門 facing the door
dāng hù

6. 織 zhī　【動詞】織布 to weave

7. 機 jī　【名詞】織布機 a weaving loom

8. 杼 zhù　【名詞】織布用的梭子 a shuttle

9. 嘆息　【動詞】嘆氣 to sigh
tàn xí

【名詞】嘆氣的聲音 the sighing sound

10. 思 sī　【動詞】思索 to ponder; to think

所思　【名詞語】所＋ V = N
suǒ sī　　　　　思索的事 things that you are pondering

"所"字用在及物動詞之前，組成一個名詞語（所＋
V＝N），表示"V的N"。"所"字的作用好像是代替名
詞充當動詞後的賓語，在這種情況下，這個"所"
字可以看作是代詞。

When the word "suǒ" occurs before a transitive verb, the combination
"suǒ + v" functions like a noun phrase (suǒ + v = n). This phrase is
equivalent in meaning to the construction 'n of v'. The word "suǒ"
serves both as a pronoun and as the object of the verb, much like the
word "what" does in English.

何所思　【倒裝句】所思〔為〕何；思索的事是什麼
hé suǒ sī　　　　思索什麼
What are you pondering?

11. 憶 yì 【動詞】回憶 to reminisce

所憶
suǒ sī
【名詞語】所＋V＝N
回憶的人、事
persons or things that you are reminiscing

何所憶
hé suǒ yì
【倒裝句】所憶〔為〕何；回憶的人、事是什麼
回憶什麼 What are you reminiscing?

12. 亦 yì 【動詞】也 also; either...neither

無所思
wú suǒ sī
【動詞語】無所思者 Nothing was I pondering of.
沒有思索的事
沒思索什麼事
I was not pondering of anything

無所憶
wú suǒ yì
【動詞語】無所回憶者 Nothing was I reminiscing.
沒有想念的人、事
沒想念什麼人、事
I was not reminiscing anyone or anything

13. 昨夜
zuó yè
【名詞語】昨天晚上 last night

14. 軍帖
jūn tiě
【名詞語】軍事的文告 a military proclamation

15. 可汗
Kè Hán
【名詞】大王 the Khan; the chieftain (a term mainly used in northern tribes)

16. 點兵
diǎn bīng
【動詞語】徵召 (zhēng zhào) 兵士 to call roll of the troops

17. 軍書
jūn shū
【名詞語】軍事文書 military documents

18. 卷 juàn 【名詞】冊；本 rolls; volumes

19. 爺 yé 【名詞】父親 father

20. 阿爺
ā yé
【名詞】父親 father

21. 大兒
dà ér
【名詞語】長大的兒子 a grown-up son

22. 長兄
zhǎng xiōng
【名詞語】大哥；排行最大的哥哥
one's eldest brother

23. 為 wèi
【介詞】為了；為〔此〕 for; for [this reason]

24. 市 shì
【動詞】買 to buy

25. 鞍 ān
【名詞】馬鞍 a saddle

26. 馬 mǎ
【名詞】戰馬 a horse

27. 從此
cóng cǐ
【介詞語】從現在〔開始〕 from now on

28. 替 tì
【動詞】代替 to substitute; to take the place of

29. 征 zhēng
【動詞】出征；作戰；打仗 to go fighting

東市買駿馬，西市買鞍韉，南市買轡頭，北市買長鞭。
旦辭爺娘去，暮宿黃河邊。
不聞爺娘喚女聲，但聞黃河流水鳴濺濺。
旦辭黃河去，暮至黑山頭。
不聞爺娘喚女聲，但聞燕山胡騎鳴啾啾。

Dōng shì mǎi jùn mǎ, xī shì mǎi ān jiàn. Nán shì mǎi pèi tóu, běi shì mǎi cháng biān.
Dàn cí yé niáng qù, mù sù Huáng Hé biān.
Bù wén yé niáng huàn nǔ shēng, dàn wén Huáng Hé liú shuǐ míng jiàn jiàn.
Dàn cí Huáng Hé qù, mù zhǐ Hēi Shān tóu.
Bù wén yé niáng huàn nǔ shēng, dàn wén Yān Shān Hú jì míng jiū jiū.

30. 東市
dōng shì
【名詞語】東邊的市場 the eastern market

31. 駿馬
jùn mǎ
【名詞語】良馬；好馬 a steed horse

32. 西市
xī shì
【名詞語】西邊的市場 the western market

33. 鞍韉
ān jiàn
【名詞】鞍下的墊子 the under-pad of a saddle

34. 南市
nán shì
【名詞語】南邊的市場 the southern market

35. 轡頭
pèi tóu
【名詞】馬籠頭 a bridle

36. 北市
běi shì
【名詞語】北邊的市場 the northern market

37. 長鞭
cháng biān
【名詞語】策馬的長鞭 a long horse whip

38. 旦 dàn
【時間詞】早上 in the morning

39. 辭 cí
【動詞】辭別 to bid farewell

40. 爺娘
yé niáng
【名詞】父母 father and mother

41. 暮 mù
【時間詞】傍晚 at dusk

42. 宿 sù
【動詞】住宿；過夜 to stay over night

43. 黃河
Huáng Hé
【名詞】黃河 the Yellow River

44. 邊 biān
【處所詞】旁邊；岸邊 side; bank

45. 喚 huàn
【動詞】呼喚 to call

46. 流水
    liú shuǐ
    【名詞語】流動的水 the running water; the current

47. 鳴 míng
    【動詞】發出⋯聲音來 to sound; to make a sound

48. 濺濺
    jiàn jiàn
    【象聲詞】嘩啦嘩啦水流得很急的聲音 gurgling

    鳴濺濺
    míng jiàn jiàn
    【動詞語】發出嘩啦嘩啦水流得很急的聲音
    to make a gurgling sound

49. 至 zhì
    【動詞】到 to arrive at

50. 黑山
    Hēi Shān
    【名詞】山名；今北京昌平天壽山 the Black Mountain;
    present-day Tiānshòu Mountain in Chāngpíng, under
    the juridiction of Běijīng

51. 頭 tóu
    【處所詞】最高的地方；頂端 head; top

52. 燕山
    Yān Shān
    【名詞】山名，在今河北省北部及北京一帶 the Yān
    Mountain, in the northern part of present-day Héběi
    province and near Běijīng.

53. 胡騎
    Hú jì
    【名詞語】胡馬；胡人的馬 barbarian horses

54. 啾啾
    jiū jiū
    【象聲詞】馬的嘶叫聲 the neighing sound of a horse

    鳴啾啾
    míng jiàn jiàn
    【動詞語】發出淒切尖細的嘶叫聲
    to make a long, high neighing sound

萬里赴戎機，關山度若飛。朔氣傳金柝，寒光照鐵衣。
將軍百戰死，壯士十年歸。

Wàn lǐ fù róng jī, guān shān dù ruò fēi. Shuò qì chuán jīn tuò, hán guāng zhào tiě yī.
Jiāng jūn bǎi zhàn sǐ, zhuàng shì shí nián guī.

55. 萬里
    wàn lǐ
    【名詞語】一萬里 ten thousand li

50

56. 赴 fù 【動詞】奔赴 to rush to; to hasten to

57. 戎機 róng jī 【名詞語】軍機；重要的軍事任務；戰爭 a military mission; a war

赴戎機 fù róng jī 【動詞語】參加軍事行動；參加戰爭 to take part in a military action/a war

58. 關山 guān shān 【名詞】關隘山嶺 strategic positions or passes on the border and mountains

59. 度 dù 【動詞】度過；越過 to cross; to pass by

60. 若飛 ruò fēi 【準繫詞語】像飛一樣 as if flying

度若飛 dù ruò fēi 【動詞語】像飛似的度過 to pass by as if flying

61. 朔 shuò 【形容詞】北方的 north; northern

朔氣 shuò qì 【名詞語】北方的寒氣 the northern cold air

62. 傳 chuán 【動詞】傳佈到…上 to pass on to; to spread on to

63. 金柝 jīn tuò 【名詞語】即刁斗；古代軍中用器，斗形有柄銅質；白天用作炊具，晚上擊以巡更 a pot made of copper in the shape of a dipper with a handle, used by the army in ancient time for cooking during the day, and as a night-watchman's bell while making rounds

64. 寒光 hán guāng 【名詞語】寒冷的星月之光 the chilly star-light and moonlight

65. 照 zhào 【動詞】照射 to shine upon

66. 鐵衣 tiě yī 【名詞語】鎧 (kǎi) 甲 armor

67. 將軍　　【名詞】高級將領　a military leader of high rank; a general
jiāng jūn

68. 百戰　　【動詞語】作戰百次　to conduct a hundred battles
bǎi zhàn

69. 壯士　　【名詞語】勇武的戰士　valiant warriors
zhuàng shì

70. 歸 guī　　【動詞】歸來　to return

歸來見天子，天子坐明堂。策勳十二轉，賞賜百千強。
可汗問所欲，木蘭不用尚書郎。願借明駝千里足，送兒
還故鄉。

Guī lái jiàn Tiānzǐ, Tiānzǐ zuò míngtáng. Cè xūn shíêr zhuǎn, shǎngcì bǎi qiān qiáng.
Kè Hán wèn suǒ yù, Mù Lán bú yòng Shàngshū Láng.
Yuàn jiè míng tuó qiān lǐ zú, sòng ér huán gù xiāng.

71. 天子　　【名詞】君主；指可汗　the emperor; here: the Khan
Tiān Zǐ

72. 明堂　　【名詞語】殿堂；古代帝王宣明政教的地方
Míng Táng　　　　　　a palace hall; an audience hall

73. 策 cè　　【動詞】登錄　to record

74. 勳 xūn　　【名詞】功勳：戰功　merits; contribution

75. 轉 zhuǎn　　【名詞】升遷一級為一轉　rounds; stages [of promotion]

76. 賞賜　　【動詞】上贈給下　to bestow
shǎng cì

77. 強 qiáng　　【名詞】通“繦”，穿錢的繩子，也指穿好的錢貫
，即一千錢
same as "qiǎng", a cord used to string coins together; it
also stands for the coins strung together, 1000 coins

52

百千強　【名詞語】百千貫錢；很多很多錢　a hundred million
bǎi qiān qiáng　　　　　　　　of coins; a lot of money

78. 所欲　【名詞語】想要的　what one desires
suǒ yù

79. 用 yòng　【動詞】需要　to need

80. 尚書郎　【名詞語】尚書省的郎官；高官 a high official;
Shàngshū Láng　　　　　Gentleman in the Imperial Secretariat

81. 借 jiè　【動詞】借　to borrow; to be allowed to ride

82. 明駝　【名詞語】能走遠路而且走得很快的駱駝
míng tuó　　　　　name of a special kind of camel that can run as fast
as a steed horse

83. 千里　【形容詞】日行千里的 to run a thousand li a day
qiān lǐ

84. 足 zú　【名詞】腳力　foot strength; speed

85. 還 huán　【動詞】返回　to go back to; to retrun

86. 故鄉　【名詞語】老家；家鄉　the homeland
gù xiāng

爺娘聞女來，出郭相扶將。阿姊聞妹來，當戶理紅妝。
小弟聞姊來，磨刀霍霍向豬羊。

　　Yé niáng wén nǚ lái, chūguō xiāng fújiāng.　Azǐ wén mèi lái, dānghù lǐ hóng zhuāng.
　　Xiǎo dì wén zǐ lái, mó dào huò huò xiàng zhū yáng.

87. 聞 wén　【動詞】聽見　to hear

88. 郭 guō　【名詞】外城　the outer city wall

　　出郭　【動詞語】出城　to go out of the city wall
chū guō

53

89. 相 xiāng 【名詞】 互相 mutually

90. 扶將 fú jiāng 【動詞】 攙 (chān) 扶 to support with one's hand

91. 阿姊 ā zǐ 【名詞】 姊姊 elder sister

92. 理 lǐ 【動詞】 整理 to arrange; to do; to apply

93. 妝 zhuāng 【名詞】 妝飾 makeup

紅妝 hóng zhuāng 【名詞語】 美麗的妝飾，因婦女妝飾多用紅色，故稱紅妝 pretty makeup, as women's makeup is generally in red, so comes the term red makeup.

94. 小弟 xiǎo dì 【名詞語】 小弟弟 little brother

95. 磨刀 mó dāo 【動詞語】 磨刀；把刀放在磨石上磨 to sharpen the knife on a stone

96. 霍霍 huò huò 【象聲詞】 磨刀聲 the sound of knife-sharpening

97. 向 xiàng 【動詞】 對著 to face; to look at

98. 豬羊 zhū yáng 【名詞】 豬和羊 pig and sheep

開我東閣門，坐我西閣床。脫我戰時袍，著我舊時裳。
當窗理雲鬢，對鏡帖花黃。出門看伙伴，伙伴皆驚忙。
同行十二年，不知木蘭是女郎。

Kāi wǒ dōng gé mén, zuò wǒ xī gé chuáng. Tuō wǒ zhàn shí páo, zhuó wǒ jiù shí shāng. Dāng chuāng lǐ yún bìn, duì jìng tiē huā huáng. Chū mén kàn huǒ bàn, huǒ bàn jiē jīng máng. Tóng xíng shí èr nián, bù zhī Mù Lán shì nǚ láng.

99. 開 kāi 【動詞】打開 to open

100. 東閣 dōng gé 【名詞語】東邊的閣樓 the eastern loft

101. 門 mén 【名詞】門 door

102. 西閣 xī gé 【名詞語】西邊的閣樓 the western loft

103. 床 chuáng 【名詞】床 bed

104. 脫 tuō 【動詞】脫掉；脫下 to take off; to remove

105. 戰時 zhàn shí 【名詞語】作戰時候 war time

106. 袍 páo 【名詞】〔戰〕袍 rope; garment

107. 著 zhuó 【動詞】穿上 to put on

108. 舊時 jiù shí 【名詞語】從前時候 in former times

109. 裳 shāng 【名詞】衣裳 outfit

110. 當窗 dāng chuāng 【動詞語】對〔著〕窗子 facing the window

111. 理 lǐ 【動詞】梳理：整理 to comb

112. 雲鬢 yún bìn 【名詞語】像雲般濃密的鬢髮 cloud-like hair

113. 對鏡 duī jìng 【動詞語】對〔著〕鏡子 facing a mirror

114. 貼 tiē 【動詞】貼 to paste on; to apply

115. 花黃　　【名詞語】黃色的花瓣；古代女子臉部的裝飾
　　　huā huáng　　　　　　　yellow flower petals used for facial makeup

　　　貼花黃　　【動詞語】以黃色花瓣貼額，來裝飾自己
　　　tiē huā huáng　　　　　to apply yellow flower petals on the forehead as makeup

116. 伙伴　　【名詞】〔軍中的〕同伴　companions; peers
　　　huǒ bàn

117. 驚忙　　【形容詞】驚訝怪異　surprised; astonished
　　　jīng máng

118. 同行　　【動詞語】一起行動　to march together
　　　tóng xíng

119. 女郎　　【名詞】年輕女子　a young woman; a girl
　　　nǚ láng

雄兔腳撲朔，雌兔眼迷離。雙兔傍地走，安能辨我是雄雌？

Xióng tù jiǎo pū shuò, cī tù yǎn mí lí. Shuāng tù bàng dì zǒu, ān néng biàn wǒ shì xióng cí?

120. 雄 xióng　　【形容詞】雄性的；公的　male

121. 兔 tù　　【名詞】兔子　hare; rabbit

122. 腳 jiǎo　　【名詞】腳　feet

123. 撲朔　　【形容詞】毛蓬鬆，一跳一跳的　fluffy and jumping
　　　pū shuò

124. 雌 cí　　【形容詞】雌性的；母的　female

125. 眼 yǎn　　【名詞】眼睛　eyes

126. 迷離　　【形容詞】模糊看不清　blurred; dim of vision
　　　mí lí

※ 撲朔迷離 【成語】 形容事情錯綜複雜，不易看清真相
　　pū shuò mí lí 　　　　　vague or ambiguous; complicated and confusing

127. 雙兔 　　【名詞語】 一雙兔子；兩隻兔子 two hares
　　shuāng tù

128. 傍地 　　【動詞語】 貼近地面 close on to ground
　　bàng dì

129. 走 zǒu 　　【動詞】 跑 to run

130. 安 ān 　　【疑問副詞】 何；怎麼 how

131. 辨 biàn 　　【動詞】 辨別；分清楚 to distinguish; to make out

押韻

唧			-it	入聲四質
織	-ǝk;	息	-iǝk	入聲十三職
思			-i;	上平聲四支
憶			-i;	去聲四實

以上為一組，四韻音近通押

兵、名	-iɐng	兄	-iuɐng	征	-ɐng	下平聲八庚
韉、鞭、邊、濺					-iɛn	下平聲一先
頭	-ǝu	啾	-iɐu			下平聲十一尤
機、飛、衣	-ɚi	歸	-uɐi			上平聲五微
堂、郎	-ang	強、鄉	-iang			下平聲七陽
將、羊	-iang	裳、忙、郎	-ang			
妝、床、黃					-uang	下平聲七陽
離、雌					-i	上平聲四支

北方話入聲韻尾消失較早，故能與平聲通押

In northern dialects the entering tone was lost and merged into other tones by this time.

第十三首

登幽州臺歌

唐　　陳子昂

前不見古人，	Qiān bú jiàn gǔ rén,
後不見來者。	Hòu bú jiàn lái zhě.
念天地之悠悠，	Niàn tiān dì zhī yōu yōu,
獨愴然而涕下。	Dú chuàng rán ér tì xià.

作者　陳子昂 (661 - 702 A.D.) 字伯玉，四川人，初唐著名詩人。

Chén Zǐáng (661-702 A.D.), courtesy name Bóyù, was a native of Sìchuān, and a famous poet in the early years of the Táng dynasty

篇旨

作者登高望遠，感慨在遼闊的蒼穹，茫茫的大地間，一代一代的人匆匆來去，自己是多麼的渺小孤獨。再深思到與永無窮盡的天地相較，人生又是何等短暫，不禁悲傷落淚。全詩充滿慷慨悲悵的情調。

While the poet gazed far and wide on top of a watch tower, his heart brimmed with the feeling that between the boundless heaven and earth, men passed by generation after generation so lonely and so insignificantly. He further brooded over the idea that in comparison with the vast and endless universe, human lives were extremely fleeting; and his tears rolled down uncontrollably. The entire poem is full of such sorrowful, disconsolate sentiment.

注解

1. 登 dēng 【動詞】登上 to ascend

2. 幽州 Yōu zhōu 【名詞】州名。漢代十三州之一，轄境相當今河北北部及遼寧等地，唐時一度改稱范陽郡，不久又改回原名 the Commandery of Yōu, one of the thirteen commanderies of Hàn, under its jurisdiction were the northern part of Héběi province and the entire Liáoníng region. It was once renamed as the Prefecture of Fànyáng during the Táng dynasty, but soon changed back to the original name.

3. 臺 tái 【名詞】居高臨下，可以瞭望四方的建築物 a terrace; a watch tower, from which one can watch for danger or incoming enemy

    ◆ 瞭望 liàowàng　to watch from a height or a distance; to look down from a higher place

   幽州臺 Yōu zhōu 【名詞】幽州台即薊(Jì)北樓，故址在北京市北 Tower of Yōuzhōu, also known as the Storeyed Building of Jīběi, situated to the north of Běijīng

4. 念 niàn 【動詞】思考；沈思 to brood upon; to contemplate

5. 悠悠 yōu yōu 【形容詞】久遠；悠久；無窮無盡 long-lasting; infinite; endless

6. 獨 dú 【副詞】獨自；自己一個人 alone

7. 愴然 chuàng rán 【形容詞】悲傷 broken-hearted; sad; sorrowful

8. 涕 tì 【名詞】眼淚 tears

9. 下 xià 【動詞】流下；落下 to roll dowm

押韻

者　　-a　　　　下　　-ia　　　　上聲二十一馬

第十四首

登鸛雀樓

唐　　王之渙

白日依山盡，	Bái rì yī shān jìn,
黃河入海流。	Huáng Hé rù hǎi liú.
欲窮千里目，	Yù qióng qiān lǐ mù,
更上一層樓。	Gèng shàng yì céng lóu.

作者　王之渙 (688 - 742 A.D.) 字季淩，唐晉陽 (今山西太原)

人，盛唐時著名詩人。

Wáng Zhīhuàn (668-742 A.D.), courtesy name Jìlíng, was a native of Jìnyáng, present-day Tàiyuán city in Shānxī province. He was a famous poet during the High Táng period.

篇旨

描寫登樓所見北方山河的壯闊景色，思考並形

象地說明欲望遠須更登高的人生哲理。

This poem presents a magnificent view of the landscape of north China from the top of a tower, and the poet ponders over and then figuratively expounds the truth of life that one must stand high to see things far away.

注解

1. 鸛雀　　【名詞】一種長喙、長頸、長腿、黑白色的水鳥
　 guàn què 　　　　，居住在水邊，但築巢在高大建築物的
　　　　　　　　　　　頂上
　　　　　　　　　a large black and white bird with a long beak and neck
　　　　　　　　　and long legs, that lives near water but often builds its
　　　　　　　　　nest on the top of a high building; a stork

2. 鸛雀樓　【名詞】故址在今山西省永濟縣西南，樓高三
　 guān què lóu 　　層，向前可看到中條山，向下可看到黃
　　　　　　　　　河。由於時有鸛雀棲止在上面，所以叫
　　　　　　　　　鸛雀樓　the old site of the Stork Tower was to the
　　　　　　　　　southwest of present-day Yǒngjì district, in Shānxī
　　　　　　　　　province. It was a three-storied tower facing the Zhōng-
　　　　　　　　　tiáo Mountain and overlooking the Yellow River. It
　　　　　　　　　was so named because there were often storks perching
　　　　　　　　　on it.

3. 白日　　【名詞語】明亮的太陽　the bright sun
　 bái rì

4. 依 yī　　【動詞】靠　to lean against

5. 盡 jìn　　【動詞】窮盡；完全没有了　exhausted; to come to an end
　　　　　　　　　此處：完全落下去了
　　　　　　　　　here:　　to go down below the horizon

6 黃河　　【名詞】黃河　the Yellow River
　 Huáng hé

7. 海 hǎi　　【名詞】海　a sea

8. 流 liú　　【動詞】流　to flow

　入海流　【動詞語】流進海裡去
　 rù hǎi liú 　　　　　to flow into the sea

9. 欲 yù　　【動詞】想要　to want to; to intend to

10. 窮 qióng　【動詞】窮盡。此處：用盡；用完　to exhaust

11. 千里目　【名詞語】能看到一千里遠的目力
　 qiān lǐ mù 　　　　the eye sight that can see things a thousand li away

61

12. 更 gèng 　　【副詞】再 again; once more

13. 上 shàng 　　【動詞】登上 to climb up; to ascend

14. 層 céng 　　【名詞】層 one floor [of a multistoried building]

15. 樓 lóu 　　【名詞】兩層及兩層以上的房屋
　　　　　　　　　　　　a building of two stories or more; a tower

一層樓 　　【名詞語】另一層樓
yì céng lóu 　　　　　　another floor of a tower

押韻

流　　-iəu　　　　樓　　-əu　　　　下平聲十一尤

第十五首

春曉

唐　孟浩然

春眠不覺曉，	Chūn mián bù jué xiǎo,
處處聞啼鳥。	Chù chù wén tí niáo.
夜來風雨聲，	Yè lái fēng yǔ shēng,
花落知多少。	Huā luò zhī duō shǎo.

作者　孟浩然 (689-740 A.D.)，湖北襄陽人，盛唐著名田園派
　　　詩人。

Mèng Hàorán (689-740 A.D.), was a native of Xiāngyáng in Húběi province,

62

and a famous pastoral poet during the High Táng period.

篇旨

作者以春曉啼鳥處處點出春光爛漫，又以風雨摧殘春花惋惜春光易逝。賞春愛春惜春之情，躍然紙上。

This poem depicts the glorious spring scene when the dawn chorus is heard everywhere, it also laments for flowers ruined by storm. The poet's appreciation and love of Spring, along with his mournful feeling over the fleeting glory of Spring, is ably presented in this short verse.

注解

1. 春 chūn 　【名詞】春天　spring season; spring time

2. 眠 mián 　【動詞】睡覺　to sleep

3. 覺 jué 　【動詞】覺得　to sense; to be conscious of

4. 曉 xiǎo 　【動詞】黎明；天亮　to dawn; to be daybreak

5. 處處 chù chù 　【副詞】到處　everywhere; all over

6. 聞 wén 　【動詞】聽見　to hear; to be heard

7. 啼 tí 　【動詞】叫　to chirp *chirping birds*

8. 鳥 niǎo 　【名詞】鳥　birds

9. 夜來 yè lái 　【時間副詞】昨夜以來　since last night

10. 風雨聲 fēng yù shēng 　【名詞語】颱風下雨的聲音　the sound of wind and rain

11. 花 huā 　【名詞】花；花朵　flowers; flower petals

63

12. 落 luò 　【動詞】掉落；掉下 to fall

13. 多少 　【數詞】多少 how many
　　duō shǎo

　　知多少 　【反問句】知道有多少嗎 Do you know how many?
　　zhī duō shǎo 　　　　不知道有多少 Don't know how many.
　　　　　　　　　　大概很多吧 probably very many.

押韻

曉、鳥、少　　　　-iɛu　　　　上聲十七篠

第十六首

渭城曲

（送元二使安西）（陽關曲）（陽關三疊）

唐　　王維

渭城朝雨浥輕塵，　　Wèi Chéng zhāo yǔ yì qīng chén,
客舍青青柳色新。　　Kè shè qīng qīng liǔ sè xīn.
勸君更盡一杯酒，　　Qùn jūn gèng jìn yì bēi jiǔ,
西出陽關無故人。　　Xī chū Yáng Guān wú gù rén.

作者　　王維(701-761 A.D.)，字摩詰，唐代著名的山水、田園
　　　　詩人，也善於畫山水畫儿。宋朝的蘇軾曾讚美他
　　　　"詩中有畫，畫中有詩"。

Wáng Wéi (701-761 A.D.), courtesy name Mójié, was a famous landscape and pastoral poet of Táng dynasty, and he was also a great painter. Sū Shì of the Sòng dynasty once praised him, "there is a painting in his poem and there is a poem in his painting."

篇旨

詩題本作"送元二使安西"，後入樂傳唱，改稱"渭城曲"，又稱"陽關曲"，"陽關三疊"。詩人藉滿目細柔的青青垂柳抒寫自己的依依離情，是唐代以來最著名的送別曲。

The original title of this poem was "Seeing Master Yuán Off on His Mission to Kucha", later when it was sung with music, the title was changed to " The Song of Wèichéng," or "The Song of Yángguān," or "The Song of Yángguān with a Thrice Repeated Refrain". In this poem the poet likens the wavering of the tender drooping willow to the sadness and reluctance of parting; it has become the most famous seeing-off poem since the Táng dynasty.

注解

1. **渭城** Wèichéng 【名詞】秦時的咸陽城，漢改稱渭城，在長安西北(在今陝西省西安市西北)渭水北岸，是王維給元二餞別的地方 Wèi Chéng, to the north-west of Xī-ān of Shǎnxī province, was where Wáng Wéi offered a farewell party to his friend Yuán, the second.

2. **曲** qǔ 【名詞】歌曲 a song

3. **元二** Yuán Èr 【名詞】姓元，排行第二 Mr. Yuán, the second among his siblings

4. **使** shì 【動詞】出使；奉君主命令到⋯去做大使 to serve as an envoy; to be sent by the emperor to...as an envoy

5. **安西** Aňxī 【名詞】唐代安西都護府的治所，在今新疆庫車附近 place name; the site of the office of Aňxī Garrison of Táng dynasty, it is located in present-day Xīnjiāng province, near Kùchē.

65

6. 朝雨　　　　【動詞語】早晨下雨　to rain in the morning
　　zhāo yǔ

7. 浥 yì　　　　【動詞】沾濕　to moisten

8. 輕塵　　　　【名詞語】地面上的浮土　light dust on the surface of
　　qīng chén　　　　　　　　　the ground

9. 客舍　　　　【名詞語】旅舍；旅館　a guest house; an inn
　　kè shè

10. 青青　　　　【形容詞】疊字　a reduplicative compound
　　 qīng qīng　　　　　　　綠綠的　green

11. 柳色　　　　【名詞語】柳樹的顏色　color of the willow
　　 liǔ sè

12. 新 xīn　　　　【形容詞】清新　fresh; refreshing

13. 勸 quàn　　　　【動詞】勸勉；鼓勵　to urge

14. 君 jūn　　　　【代詞】您　you

15. 更 gèng　　　　【副詞】再　again; once more

16. 盡 jìn　　　　【動詞】飲乾；喝完　to drink up; to finish off

17. 杯 bēi　　　　【名詞】酒杯　a wine cup

　　 一杯酒　　　　【名詞語】一杯酒　a cup of wine
　　 yì bēi jiǔ

18. 出 chū　　　　【動詞】走出　to go out; to go beyond

　　 西出　　　　【動詞語】向西走出　a go westward and out of ...
　　 xī chū

19. 陽關　　　　【名詞】古代關名，在今甘肅省敦煌縣西南，是
　　 Yángguān　　　　　唐代通往西域的要道。陽關在中原地區
　　　　　　　　　　　外，安西更在陽關外　the Yáng Pass, to the
　　　　　　　　　southwest of present-day Dūnhuáng district in Gānsù
　　　　　　　　　province. It was on the main road leading to the western

region. Yángguān was outside the central area of China, and Ānxī was beyond Yángguān.

20. 故人　　　【名詞】舊交；老朋友　long time acquaintance; old frieds
　　gù rén

Note　　折柳：灞(Bà)橋在長安東，跨水作橋，漢人送客至此，折柳作別。《詩・小雅・采薇》："昔我注矣，楊柳依依；今我來思，雨雪霏霏"。漢人折柳作贈，大概是借細柔的柳條來表達依依惜別之情。

The Bà Bridge (a bridge over the Bà river) was located to the east of Chángān. Since the Hàn dynasty it has become a custom that when one sends a friend off, one breaks a willow at the Bà bridge and gives it to the departing friend as a token. This practice perhaps begins with the lines in the Ode "Pluck the Bracken": "Long ago, when we started, the willows spread their shade. Now that we turn back, the snow flakes fly." The soft and tender willow is used to stand for the tender feeling and affection between the parting friends.

押韻

塵、新、人　　　　　-in　　　　上平聲十一真

第十七首

輞川閒居贈裴秀才迪

唐　王維

寒山轉蒼翠，　　　Hán shān zhuǎn cāng cuì,

秋水日潺湲。　　　qiū shuǐ rì chán yuán.

|　｜　－　－　｜

倚杖柴門外，　　　　Yǐ zhàng chái mén wài,

－　－　｜　｜　－

臨風聽暮蟬。　　　　lín fēng tīng mù chán.

－　－　｜　｜

渡頭餘落日，　　　　Dù tóu yú luò rì,

－　｜　｜　－　｜

墟里上孤煙。　　　　xū lǐ shàng gū yān.

｜　｜　－　－　｜

復值接輿醉，　　　　Fù zhí Jiē Yú zuì,

－　－　｜　｜　－

狂歌五柳前。　　　　kuáng gē wǔ liǔ qián.

－ indicates a level-tone word; ｜ indicates a deflected-tone word;
⊥ indicates a deflected-tone word appearing in a levl-tone position;
├ indicates a level-tone word appearing in a deflected-tone position.

作者　　見詩選《渭城曲》p.64

篇旨

作者藉欣賞日落時絢麗靜謐的田園風光表達自己
幽居山林、蕭然物外的生活情趣。篇末以楚狂接
輿比裴迪，以陶潛比自己，點出與志趣相同的好
友的相知相契。

Describing a gorgeous and tranquil pastoral scene at dusk, the poet sings the
praises of a reclusive life that is carefree and beyond social restrictions. At the
end, the poet likens his friend Péi Dí to Chǔ Kuáng and likens himself to Táo
Qián, to illustrate the understanding and agreement between friends of
congeniality.

注解

1. 輞川
   Wǎng chuān
   【名詞】河水名。此處指王維的輞川山莊，在陝西省藍田縣南，景致極美 the Wǎng River. Here it refers to his 'mountain villa at Wǎngchuan', to the south of Lántián district in Shǎnxī province, with great landscape and scenes.

2. 閒居
   xián jū
   【動詞語】安閒地住在家裡 to lead a quiet, retired life

3. 贈 zèng
   【動詞】贈送；送給 to present to

4. 裴迪
   Péi Dí
   【名詞】人名，是王維好友，常在王維的輞川山莊作客 name of a good friend of Wáng Wéi, who often visits Wáng Wéi and stays at Wǎngchuān

5. 秀才
   xiù cái
   【名詞】泛指才能秀出的人；凡應舉而尚未成進士者也稱秀才 a talented scholar; it also refers to those scholars who have taken parts in the civil service examinations but haven't succeeded.

6. 寒山
   hán shān
   【名詞語】寒冷季節的山；蕭寂的山；冷清寂靜的山 chilly mountains; desolate and tranquil mountains; lonely and quiet mountains

7. 轉 zhuǎn
   【動詞】轉變成 to change to; to turn into

8. 蒼翠
   cāng cuì
   【形容詞】雙聲聯綿詞 an alliterative compound 深綠色 dark green

   ◆ 雙聲 shuāng shēng   alliterative
   ◆ 聯綿詞 liánmiámcí   disyllabic words

9. 潺湲
   chán yuán
   【形容詞】疊韻聯綿詞 a rhyming compound 水流徐緩；〔水〕輕緩地流 water flowing slowly

   ◆ 疊韻 diéyùn   a rhyming compound

10. 倚杖
    yǐ zhàng
    【動詞語】靠著拐杖 leaning on a cane

69

11. 柴門　【名詞語】用樹枝編做的門
chái mén　a door of brushwood

12. 臨風　【動詞語】面對〔著〕風　facing the wind
lín fēng

13. 暮 mù　【時間詞】日落時；黃昏時　dusk

14. 蟬 chán　【名詞】知了　cicadas
蟬高居悲鳴飲露，詩文中多用牠來比喻品行高潔的人　cicadas live in high trees, shrill in sad sounds, and drink dews, and they are often likened to noble and pure persons in literature

15. 渡頭　【名詞】渡口；過河的地方　a ferry
dù tóu

16. 餘 yú　【動詞】剩餘；剩下　to leave behind

17. 墟里　【名詞】村落　a village
xū lǐ

18. 上 shàng　【動詞】上升；升起　to ascend

19. 孤煙　【名詞語】一縷(lǚ)炊煙　a wisp of kitchen smoke
gū yān
◆ 炊煙 chuīyān　smoke from a kitchen chimney

20. 值 zhí　【動詞】遇到；碰上　to meet; to happen

21. 接輿　【名詞】人名，姓陸，名通，字接輿，楚國的隱者，與孔子同時。為了避世，假裝瘋狂，世稱楚狂。作者借以比喻裴迪
Jiē yú　name of a hermit in the state of Chǔ, surnamed Lù, named Tōng, and courtesy name Jiēyú, who was contemporary with Confucius. In order to avoid the society, he pretended to be mad, so he was called the lunatic of Chǔ. Here the poet likened him to Péi Dí.

22. 狂歌　【動詞語】縱情地唱歌　to sing loudly and heartily
kuáng gē

23. 五柳　　【名詞語】五柳先生陶潛（淵明），作者借以比
　　wǔ liǔ　　　喻自己

Master Five Willows, i.e., the recluse Táo Qián, whom the poet Wáng Wéi used to liken himself

押韻

| 湲 | -iuɐn | 上平十三元 |
| 蟬 –iuɛn;　　煙、前 | -iɛn; | 下平一先 |

先、元兩韻通押

These two rhymes are interchangeable.

第十八首

獨坐敬亭山

唐　　李白

眾鳥高飛盡，	Zhòng niǎo gāo fēi jìn,
孤雲獨去閒。	Gū yún dú qù xián.
相看兩不厭，	Xiāng kàn liǎng bú yàn,
只有敬亭山。	Zhǐ yǒu Jìng Tíng Shān.

作者　　李白 (701-762) 字太白，號青蓮居士，盛唐時最著名的浪漫派詩人，世稱詩仙。

Lǐ Bái (701-762 A.D.), courtesy name Tàibái and style name 'Recluse Scholar of Qīnglián,' was the most celebrated romantic poet of the High Táng period. He is frequently referred to as a divine 'Immortal among Poets'.

◆ 浪漫派   school of Romanticism
    làngmàn pài

◆ 詩仙 *shīxiān*   the Poet Immortal; an immortal among poets

篇旨

描寫山中獨坐靜賞鳥飛雲浮之清興，及 "我看青
山多嫵媚，料青山看我亦如是" 之閒情逸致。

This poem depicts the poet's refined interest in sitting alone, watching the
birds' flying and the clouds floating, and reveals his peaceful and comfortable
mood that "I find the blue mountains very charming, and figure that the blue
mountains regard me likewise."

注解

1. 獨 dú   【副詞】獨自；自己一個人 alone

2. 敬亭山   【名詞】在今安徽 (huī) 宣城縣北 Mt. Jìngtíng, to the
   Jìngtíng shān   north of present-day Xuānchéng in Ānhuī province

3. 眾 zhòng   【形容詞】眾多；很多 many

4. 鳥 niǎo   【名詞】鳥 birds

5. 盡 jìn   【副詞】完；光 totally; exhaustedly

6. 孤 gū   【形容詞】孤獨；孤單 solitary; lone

7. 雲 yún   【名詞】雲 clouds

   孤雲   【名詞語】孤單的雲；一片雲 a lone cloud
   gū yún

8. 去 qù   【動詞】離去；浮走 to float away

9. 閒 xián   【副詞】悠閒地 leisurely

   獨去閒   【動詞語】獨自悠閒地浮走 to float away alone leisurely
   dú qù xián

10. 相看　　　【動詞語】互相地看　a look at each other
　　 xiāng kàn

11. 厭 yàn　　　【動詞】厭倦；厭煩；對某種活動失去興趣而不
　　　　　　　　　願意繼續

　　　　　　　　to be tired of; to feel having had enouph; to have lost
　　　　　　　　interest in an ongoing activity

押韻

　　　　閒、山　　　　　　　-an　　　　　　上平聲十五刪

第十九首

下江陵

唐　李白

朝辭白帝彩雲間，　　　Zhāo cí Bái Dì cǎi yún jiān,
千里江陵一日還。　　　Qiān lǐ Jiāng Líng yí rì huán.
兩岸猿聲啼不住，　　　Liǎng àn yuán shēng tí bú zhù,
輕舟已過萬重山。　　　Qīng zhōu yǐ guò wàn chóng shān.

作者　　見詩選《獨坐敬亭山》p.71

篇旨

　　　此詩又名"早發白帝城"，是李白被流放夜郎
　　　（今貴州桐梓），至白帝城遇赦東歸時所作。風
　　　格俊逸，節奏輕快，歡欣鼓舞之情充分流露。

73

This poem was composed when Lǐ Bái was pardoned at Báidì Chéng, half way on his exile to Yèláng (or present-day Tóngzǐ in Guìzhōu province). It was also called "Set Off from Báidìchéng in the Morning". The style was elegant, unrestained, and expressive; the rhythm was sprightly and lively, revealing an elation the poet was enjoying.

注解

1. 下 xià 【動詞】順著流水向下駛 to sail down with the current

2. 江陵 Jiānglíng 【名詞】地名，今湖北省江陵縣 name of a district in present-day Húběi province

3. 早 zǎo 【時間詞】早晨；早上 morning

4. 發 fā 【動詞】出發 to set out; to start off

5. 白帝城 Báidì chéng 【名詞】城名，故址在今四川奉節縣白帝山上。從山下仰望，如在雲中。 the City of Báidì, on the Báidì mountain of present-day Fèngjié district in Sìchuān province. Looked up from the foot of the Bai-dì mountain, the Báidì City seems to be in the clouds

6. 朝 zhāo 【時間詞】早晨；早上 morning

7. 辭 cí 【動詞】辭別；告辭 to take leave

8. 彩雲 cǎi yǔn 【名詞語】各種顏色的雲；絢 (xuàn) 麗的雲 colored clouds; gorgeous clouds

9. 間 jiān 【處所詞】中間 midst

10. 里 lǐ 【量詞】長度單位 a unit of linear measure about 1/3 of a mile

♦ 量詞 *liàngcí*   a measure word; a classifier

千里 qiān lǐ 【名詞語】一千里路 a journey of 1000 li

11. 一日 yí rì 【名詞語】一天 one day

12. 還 huán 【動詞】返回；回來 to return; to come back to

13. 岸 àn 【名詞】江邊的陸地 banks of a river

    兩岸 【名詞語】兩邊岸上 both banks; either bank
    liǎng àn

14. 猿 yuán 【名詞】長臂猿 a small ape with long arms; gibbons

    猿聲 【名詞語】猿〔叫〕的聲音 crying sound of gibbons
    yuán shēng

15 啼 tí 【動詞】叫 to cry

    啼不住 【動詞語】叫不停；叫個不停 to cry incessantly
    tí bú zhù 猿叫的聲音，此起彼落，連綿不絕
    the crying sound of gibbons rises and falls in turn
    continuously

16. 輕舟 【名詞語】輕快的小船 a light boat
    qīng zhōu

17. 已 yǐ 【副詞】已經 already

18. 過 guò 【動詞】駛過 to sail pass

19. 重 chóng 【量詞】層；座 layer; a measure word for mountains

    萬重山 【名詞語】數不清的連綿不斷的山
    wàn chóng shān countless unbroken mountains

押韻

間、山　　-an　　還　-uan　　　上平聲十五刪

第二十首

月下獨酌

唐　李白

花間一壺酒，獨酌無相親。
舉杯邀明月，對影成三人。
月既不解飲，影徒隨我身。
暫伴月將影，行樂須及春。
我歌月徘徊，我舞影凌亂。
醒時同交歡，醉後各分散。
永結無情遊，相期邀雲漢。

Zhùyīn:

Huā jiān yì hú jiǔ, dú zhuó wú xiāng qīn.
Jǔ bēi yāo míng yuè, duì yǐng chéng sān rén.
Yuè jì bù jiě yǐn, yǐng tú suí wǒ shēn.
Zhàn bàn yuè jiāng yǐng, xíng lè xū jí chūn.
Wǒ gē yuè pái huái, wǒ wǔ yǐng líng luàn.
Xǐng shí tóng jiāo huān, zuì hòu gè fēn sàn.
Yǒng jié wú qíng yóu, xiāng qī miǎo yún Hàn.

作者　見詩選《獨坐敬亭山》p.71

篇旨

描寫月下獨酌，歌舞自娛的情景。詩中"舉杯邀明月，對影成三人"可稱千古妙思，而人、月、影三者往復回還的結構，也很富奇趣。結尾四句道出詩人不凝滯於物的曠達，意境高絕。

This poem describes a night of drinking under moonlight, the poet entertains himself with singing and dancing without any restraint. "I raise my cup to invite the moon, with it and my shadow to make aparty of three" is a brilliant conception, and the intertwined images ofthe poet himself, the moon, and the shadow are ingeniously presented. The last four lines reveal the poet's free and easy mental outlook, free from any bond of social conventions, achieving an excellent artistic conception.

注解

1. 獨 dú 　　【副詞】獨自 alone

2. 酌 zhuó 　　【動詞】飲酒；喝酒 to drink wine

　　獨酌
　　dú zhuó 　　【動詞語】獨自喝酒 to drink alone

3. 壺 hú 　　【名詞】酒壺 a wine pot

4. 酒 jiǔ 　　【名詞】酒 wine

5. 親 qīn 　　【動詞】親近 to be imtimate with; to be close to

　　相親
　　xiāng qīn 　　【動詞語】互相親近 to be close to each other

　　　　　　　　【名詞語】互相親近的人 persons close to each other

6. 舉 jǔ 　　【動詞】舉起；舉高 to raise

7. 杯 bēi 　　【名詞】酒杯 a wine cup

8. 邀 yāo 　　【動詞】邀請 to invite

9. 明月
　　míng yuè 　　【名詞語】明亮的月亮 the bright moon

10. 對 duì 　　【動詞】面對 to face

11. 影 yǐng 　　【名詞】影子 shadow

77

12. 既 jì 【副詞】既然 already

13. 不解 bù jiě 【動詞語】不了解；不懂 do not know how

14. 徒 tú 【副詞】徒然 merely; only
白白地 vainly; in vain

15. 隨 suí 【動詞】跟隨 to follow

16. 暫 zhàn 【副詞】暫時 temporarily; for a while

17. 伴 bàn 【動詞】陪伴 to accompany

18. 將 jiāng 【連詞】與；和 and

19. 行樂 xíng lè 【動詞語】作樂；作快樂的事 to make merry;
to have fun

20. 及 jí 【動詞】趕上 to catch up

及春 jí chūn 【動詞語】趕上春天 to catch up with springtime
——→ 趁著春天 to take advantage of the spring season

21. 歌 gē 【動詞】唱歌 to sing [songs]

22. 徘徊 pái huái 【動詞】疊韻聯綿詞 a rhyming conpound
來回走動
to pace back and forth; to walk to and fro; to linger

23. 舞 wǔ 【動詞】跳舞 to dance

24. 凌亂 líng luàn 【形容詞】雙聲聯綿詞 an alliterative compound
很沒有次序；很亂 disorderly

25. 醒 xǐng 【形容詞】清醒 awake; sober

26. 交歡 jiāo huān 【動詞】交好歡樂；做好朋友覺得很快樂
to befriend each other and have fun

27. 醉 zuì 【形容詞】喝醉 drunk; inebriated

28. 分散　【動詞】分開離散　to part and separate
　　 fēn sàn

29. 永 yǒng　【副詞】永遠　forever

30. 結 jié　【動詞】結交　to tie together; to form a relationship

31. 無情遊　【名詞語】沒有感情的朋友
　　 wú qíng yóu　　　　　──→忘記感情的朋友
　　　　　　　　　　　　　emotionally detached friends

32. 相 xiāng　【副詞】指代受事 "我"　here: it stands for the object "me"
　　　　　　　　　　　See poem 3, note 17, p.11.

33. 期 qī　【動詞】約；邀約　to invite

　　相期　【動詞語】邀約我　to invite me
　　 xiāng qī

34. 邈 miǎo　【形容詞】遙(yáo)遠　far and remote

35. 雲漢　【名詞語】銀河　The Milky Way
　　 yún hàn

押韻

親、人、身	-in	春	-iun	上平聲十一真
亂	-uan	散、漢	-an	去聲十五翰

古詩可以換韻

In ancient style poems, it's allowed to change rhymes.

第二十一首

長沙過賈誼宅

唐　劉長卿

三年謫宦此棲遲，　　　Sān nián zhé huàn cǐ qī chí,

萬古惟留楚客悲。　　　wàn gǔ wéi liú Chǔ kè bēi.

秋草獨尋人去後，　　　Qiū cǎo dú xún rén qù hòu,

寒林空見日斜時。　　　hán lín kōng jiàn rì xiá shí.

漢文有道恩猶薄，　　　Hàn Wén yǒu dào ēn yóu bó,

湘水無情弔豈知。　　　Xiāng shuǐ wú qíng diào qǐ zhī.

寂寂江山搖落處，　　　Jí jí jiāng shān yáo luò chù,

憐君何事到天涯。　　　lián jūn hé shì dào tiān yí.

作者　劉長卿 (709-780 A.D.)，字文房，唐代河間（今河北河間縣）人。個性剛直，因多次觸犯權貴被貶，最後官至隨州刺史。有《劉隨州集》十一卷。

Liú Zhǎngqīng (709-780 A.D.), courtesy name Wénfáng, was a native of Héjiān, present-day Héjiān district in Héběi province. An upright and outspoken man, he frequently offended those in power and was demoted. His last official post was that of governor of Suízhōu. His work is entitled *Collected Works of Liú Suízhōu*, in eleven rolls.

篇旨

作者被貶到南方去，途經長沙，尋訪賈誼故宅，作此詩傷其有才不遇於時，憐賈誼正是自傷自憐，是典型的遷客之作。

When the poet was demoted to the south, passing by Chángshā, he visited the former residence of Jiǎ Yì and wrote this poem. Though overtly he laments for Jiǎ Yì, who was unable to give full play to his talent, covertly he is complaining for himself. This is a typical work of an official who was unduly demoted and banished to a remote place.

注解

1. 長沙 Chángshā 【名詞】地名，在今湖南
   place name, in present-day Húnán province

2. 過 guò 【動詞】前往拜訪 to visit

3. 賈誼 Jiǎ Yì 【名詞】人名；洛陽人，年少多才，文帝時為大中大夫，敢於指摘時政，為權臣所排斥，貶為長沙王太傅，三年後鬱鬱而死

   personal name; Jiǎ Yì, a native of Luòyáng, was young and talented. He once served under Emperor Wén as Superior Grand Master of the Palace. Because he was outspoken in criticizing government policies, he was ostracized by powerful courtiers and demoted to be the Tutor of Prince of Chángshā. He died in depression three years later.

4. 宅 zhái 【名詞】住宅 residence

5. 謫 zhé 【動詞】貶謫；降官 to demote

6. 宦 huàn 【動詞】作官 to serve as an official

   謫宦 zhé huàn 【動詞語】在被貶謫的情況下作官 to serve in demotion

7. 此 cǐ 【代詞】此處；這裡 this [place]; here

8. 棲遲 qī chí 【動詞】疊韻聯綿詞 a rhyming compound 停留；居住 to dwell

81

9. 萬古　【名詞語】千秋萬世　through the ages; forever
　　wàn gǔ

10. 惟　wéi　【副詞】只　only

11. 留　liú　【動詞】留下　to leave behind

12. 楚客　【名詞語】客居於楚的人，原指戰國時代楚國逐
　　chǔ kè　　　　臣屈原，此處指賈誼
　　　　　　　　the guest in Chǔ, originally it refers to Qū Yuán, an
　　　　　　　　official of Chǔ during the Warring States period,
　　　　　　　　who was exiled to this region; here it refers to Jiǎ Yì

13. 悲　bēi　【名詞】悲傷　sadness

14. 秋草　【名詞語】秋天的草　the autumnal grass
　　qiū cǎo

15. 獨　dú　【副詞】獨自　alone

16. 尋　xún　【動詞】尋覓〔賈誼的故居〕　to seek; to look for

17. 寒林　【名詞語】秋冬的樹林　chilly woods
　　hán lín

18. 空　kōng　【副詞】徒然；白白地　vainly; merely; only

　　空見　【動詞語】白白地看見；只見　to see only
　　kōng jiàn

19. 斜　xié; xiá　【動詞】傾斜　to decline; to set

20. 漢文　【名詞語】漢文帝　Emperor Wén (r. 179-157 B.C.) of Hàn
　　Hàn Wén

21. 有道　【動詞語】有治道　to have a proper way for governing
　　yǒu dào

22. 恩　ēn　【名詞】恩惠　favor; grace; kindness

23. 猶　yóu　【副詞】還　still

24. 薄 bó 　　　　【形容詞】微薄；少　little; meager

25. 湘水 　　　　　【名詞語】湘江的水　the Xiāng river
    Xiāng shuǐ

26. 無情 　　　　　【動詞語】沒有感情　without feeling or emotion
    wú qíng

27. 弔 diào 　　　　【動詞】弔祭　to lament
    指賈誼作《弔屈原賦》的事
    referring to Jiǎ's writing a rhyme prose "Lament for
    Qū Yuán"

28. 豈知 　　　　　【動詞語】怎麼知道　How could it know?
    qǐ zhī

29. 寂寂 　　　　　【形容詞】疊字　a duplicative compound
    jí jí 　　　　　　　　寂靜無聲　quiet; still

30. 江山 　　　　　【名詞】江河山岳　the mountains and the rivers
    jiāng shān

31. 搖落 　　　　　【動詞】草木搖擺零落　to shake and fall [of leaves];
    yáo luò 　　　　　　　　　　　　　to wither

32. 憐 lián 　　　　【動詞】憐憫；哀憐　to pity; to commisserate

33. 君 jūn 　　　　【名詞】您，指賈誼　you, meaning Jiǎ Yì

34. 何事 　　　　　【名詞語】何故；為何　what reason; why
    hé shì

35. 天涯 　　　　　【名詞語】天邊；極遙遠的地方　the edge of sky
    tiān yí (yá)

押韻

遲、時、知、涯　-i　　悲　-ui　　上平聲四支

第二十二首

旅夜書懷

唐　杜甫

| ｜ ｜ ― ― ｜
細草微風岸，　　Xì cǎo wēi fēng àn,

― ― ｜ ｜ ―
危檣獨夜舟。　　wéi qiáng dú yè zhōu.

― ― ― ｜ ｜
星垂平野闊，　　Xīng chuí píng yě kuò,

｜ ｜ ｜ ― ―
月湧大江流。　　yuè yǒng dà jiāng liú.

├ ｜ ― ― ｜
名豈文章著，　　Míng qǐ wén zhāng zhù,

― ― ｜ ｜ ―
官應老病休。　　guān yīng lǎo bìng xiū.

― ― ― ｜ ｜
飄飄何所似，　　Piāo piāo hé suǒ sì,

├ ｜ ｜ ― ―
天地一沙鷗。　　tiān dì yì shā ōu.

作者　杜甫(712-770 A.D.)，字子美，唐代襄陽（今湖北襄樊市）人。因長期客居少陵（在長安附近），故世稱杜少陵。他的詩抒寫個人情懷，往往結合時事。思想深厚，境界廣闊，有強烈的正義感及憂國憂時精神，後世稱他為"詩史"。他在藝術上能吸取並融合歷代詩家的長處，成為一代宗匠。中

唐以後的詩人，莫不在某種程度上或某種意義上
受到他的影響。

Dù Fǔ (712-770 A.D.), courtesy name Zǐměi, was a native of Xiāngyáng,
present-day Xiāngfán city in Húběi province. Since resided in Shàolíng,
near the capital Cháng'ān, for much of his life, he is called called Dù
Shàolíng. His poems are cherished for their depth and breadth of vision,
often expressing his personal responses to the injustice and turmoil that
threatened the nation in his own day. For that reason, he is also called a 'poet
historian' or a 'Historian among Poets'. Learning from his predecessors in
various ways, Dù Fǔ achieved a consummate synthesis of of the art of
Chinese lyricism.. Poets of later generations were all influenced by him to
one extent or another.

篇旨

詩人描述在清寂的旅途夜晚舟中，面對星垂、月
湧、江流的雄渾闊大自然景色，忽悟自己當絕意
世務，追求沙鷗似的孤獨卻自由飛翔的境界。風
格開闊峭拔，滿溢蒼勁悲壯之美。

In the night while traveling on a solitary boat down the Yángzǐ River, the poet
comes in front of a grand, magnificent scene of Nature that stars hang low by
the vastness of the plain and the moon rushes forward in the river's flow.
The poet suddenly realizes that it is time for him to cut off all worldly pursuits
to lead a lonely yet carefree life like the sea gull that hovers between earth and
sky. The style is broad and vigorous, brimming with a linguistic beauty that
is bold and heroically tragic in nature.

注解

1. 細草 xì cǎo 【名詞語】 纖 (xiān) 細的草 tiny grass

2. 微風 wēi fēng 【名詞語】 輕微的風 gentle breeze

3. 岸 àn 【名詞】 河岸 banks

4. 檣 qiáng 【名詞】 船桅；桅杆 a mast

85

危檣
wéi qiáng 　　【名詞語】高聳的船桅杆　tall mast

5. 獨夜
dú yè 　　【名詞語】孤獨的夜晚　a lonely night

6. 舟　zhōu 　　【名詞】小船　a small boat

7. 星　xīng 　　【名詞】星星　stars; star light

8. 垂　chuí 　　【動詞】低垂；垂得很低　to hang low

9. 平野
píng yě 　　【名詞語】平坦的原野　flat and open wilderness;
　　　　　　　　　　　　　　　　the level fields

10. 闊　kuò 　　【形容詞】廣闊　wide; broad; expansive

11. 湧　yǒng 　　【動詞】湧現；浮現　to surge

12. 大江
dà jiāng 　　【名詞語】大江的水　a great river; the Yángzǐ River

13. 流　liú 　　【動詞】流動　to flow

14. 名　míng 　　【名詞】名聲　reputation

15. 豈　qǐ 　　【副詞】難道…；用於反問句表肯定　Does it...?
　　　　　　　used in a rhetorical question to indicate a negative sense

16. 文章
wén zhāng 　　【名詞】詩文作品　one's written work

17. 著　zhù 　　【形容詞】顯著　eminent

18. 官　guān 　　【名詞】官職　government post or position

19. 應　yīng 　　【助動詞】應該　should; ought to

20. 老病
lǎo bìng 　　【形容詞】年老多病　old and ill

21. 休　xiū 　　【動詞】停止　to stop; to cease; here: to resign

22. 飄飄　　【形容詞】飄浮不定；行止不定　floating/drifting about
    piāo piāo

23. 所似　　【名詞語】像的N　things that resembles
    suǒ sì

    何所似　【倒裝句】像的是什麼；像什麼
    hé suǒ sì　　　　　　What does this resemble? What do I resemble?

24. 沙鷗　　【名詞語】沙鷗；海鷗　a sea gull
    shā ōu

押韻

舟、鷗　　- u;　　　流、休　-i u　　下平聲十一尤

第二十三首

登高

唐　杜甫

┠│－－││－
風急天高猿嘯哀，　　　Fēng jí tiān gāo yuán xiào āi,

┴－┠│││－
渚清沙白鳥飛迴。　　　zhǔ qīng shā bái niǎo fēi huái.

－－││－－│
無邊落木蕭蕭下，　　　Wú biān luò mù xiāo xiāo xià,

││－－││－
不盡長江滾滾來。　　　bú jìn cháng jiāng gǔn gǔn lái.

萬里悲秋長作客，　　Wàn lǐ bēi qiū cháng zuò kè,

百年多病獨登臺。　　bǎi nián duō bìng dú dēng tái.

艱難苦恨繁霜鬢，　　Jiān nán kǔ hèn fán shuāng bìn,

潦倒新停濁酒杯。　　liǎo dǎo xīn tíng zhuó jiǔ bēi.

作者　　見詩選《旅夜書懷》p.84

篇旨

唐代宗大曆二年 (767 A.D.) 秋，杜甫客居夔州（今四川省奉節縣）。扶病登高，見蕭瑟秋景，自傷潦倒，百感交集，作成此詩。全詩對仗精切，音調諧婉，情景交融，意境蒼涼。沈鬱頓挫，是杜甫的代表作。

In the fall of 767 A.D., while Dù Fǔ was residing in Kuízhōu, present-day Fèngjié district in Sìchuān province, he ascended a height, a custom, on the ninth day of the ninth month even though he was in poor health; upon seeing the desolate scene of autumn, he reflected on and mourned for his disappointed, unhappy life. All sorts of feelings welled up in his heart, and he wrote this poem. The entire poem is comprised of four precisely antithetic couplets, in which the external scene and the internal feelings are perfectly blended. Though its audial effects are harmonious and suave, its artistic conception is desolate and bleak. Profound and forceful, it is a materpiece of Dù Fǔ's poems.

注解

1. 急 jí　　【形容詞】猛烈；急烈　fierce; violent

2. 猿 yuán　　【名詞】猿　apes; gibbons

3. 嘯 xiào 【動詞】叫 to cry in a sustained voice

4. 哀 āi 【形容詞】悲哀 sad; saddening

5. 渚 zhǔ 【名詞】水中小洲 a sandy islet

6. 清 qīng 【形容詞】清晰；容易看見 clear

7. 沙 shā 【名詞】沙子；沙灘 sand; a sand beach

8. 迴 huái 【形容詞】迴旋；盤旋 circling; whirling

9. 木 mù 【名詞】樹；此處指樹葉 trees; here, leaves

   落木 luò mù 【名詞語】落葉 falling leaves

10. 蕭蕭 xiāo xiāo 【象聲詞】颯颯地 the rustling sound of falling leaves; soughingly

11. 下 xià 【動詞】落下；飄落 to fall down slowly in the air

12. 滾 gǔn 【動詞】滾動 to roll

    滾滾 gǔn gǔn 【副詞】疊字 a reduplicative compound 翻滾著；滾動著 in a rolling manner

13. 來 lai 【動詞】湧過來 to surge on approachingly

14. 萬里 wàn lǐ 【名詞語】〔遠離家鄉〕萬里之遙 a thousand li [away from home]

15. 悲秋 bēi qiū 【動詞語】對蕭瑟秋景而感到悲傷 to feel sad in front of the desolate scenes of autumn

16. 作客 zuò kè 【動詞語】在異鄉客居 to sojourn in a strange place

17. 百年 bǎi nián 【名詞語】一生 throughout one's lifetime

18. 多病　【形容詞】多於病；常常生病　often be ill
    duō bìng

19. 獨 dú　【副詞】獨自　alone

20. 登臺　【動詞語】登上高臺　to climp up a tower
    dēng tái

21. 艱難　【形容詞】疊韻聯綿詞 a rhyming compound
    jiān nán　　　　　生活困苦　in predicament

　　　　【名詞】困苦　hardship

22. 苦恨　【動詞語】痛恨　to resent bitterly
    kǔ hèn

23. 繁 fán　【形容詞】繁多；繁茂　numerous; lush

24. 霜 shuāng　【名詞】霜，比喻白色　frost, stands for white

    繁霜　【名詞語】很厚的霜；比喻白色　thick [layer of] frost;
    fán shuāng　　　　　　　　　　　white

25. 鬢 bìn　【名詞】鬢角；鬢髮　the temple; hair on the temple

    繁霜鬢　【名詞語】像繁霜一樣的白色的鬢髮　thick frost-like
    fán shuāng bìn　　　hair on the temples

    以上爲傳統的解釋　This is the traditional interpretation.

26. 苦恨　【名詞】苦惱憾恨　sufferings and regrets
    kǔ hèn

27. 繁 fán　【形容詞】繁多；繁茂　numerous; lush

　　　　【使動用法】使…繁多；增加　to make lush; to increase

    霜鬢　【名詞語】像霜一樣的鬢髮　frost-like temple hair
    shuāng bìn

90

繁霜鬢　　【動詞語】使霜一樣的白色的鬢髮更多了
fán shuāng bìn　　　　　　　to aggravate the frost-like hair on the temples

以上爲編者的新解　This is the editors' new interpretation.

28. 潦倒　　【形容詞】疊韻聯綿詞 a rhyming compound
liǎo dǎo　　　　　　窮愁衰老 old and disheartened

29. 新停　　【動詞語】新近停止 to have stopped recently
xīn tíng

30. 濁酒　　【名詞語】未過濾的酒 unstrained wine; cheap wine
zhuó jiǔ

31. 杯 bēi　　【名詞】酒杯　a wine cup; a goblet

濁酒杯　　【名詞語】盛濁酒的杯子 cups of cheap wine
zhuó jiǔ bēi

押韻

　　哀、來、臺 -ɔi　　迴、杯　　-uɔi　　上平聲十灰

第二十四首

楓橋夜泊

唐　　張繼

月落烏啼霜滿天，　　　Yuè luò wū tí shuāng mǎn tiān,
江楓漁火對愁眠。　　　Jiāng fēng yú huǒ duì chóu mián.
姑蘇城外寒山寺，　　　Gū Sū chéng wài Hán Shān Sì,

91

夜半鐘聲到客船。　　　　Yè bàn zhōng shēng dào kè chuán.

作者　張繼，字懿孫，襄州（今湖北襄陽市）人。天寶
十二年(753 A.D.)進士。他的詩清新秀逸而不事雕琢
。

Zhāng Jì, courtesy name Yìsún, was a native of Xiāngzhōu, present-day
Xiāngyáng in Húběi province. He earned his Jìnshì (Presented Scholar)
degree in 753 A.D. His poems are refreshing and delicate, without ornateness
or affectation.

篇旨

描寫旅舟孤寂，面對淒清江景，夜深不寐，聽見
遠處傳來的悠悠鐘聲，益增愁緒。意境淒迷，餘
韻深長。

This poem depicts the lonely, sleepless night of a traveler on a boat; hearing
the bell toll from a remote temple at midnight, he became even more
melancholy. The artistic atmosphere is thus contagiously despondent, and it
leaves a lasting appeal.

注解

1. 楓橋　　【名詞】也叫封橋，在今江蘇省蘇州市楓橋鎮
Fēng qiáo　　the Fēng Bridge, in present-day Sūzhōu of Jiāngsū
province

2. 泊 bó　　【動詞】使船靠岸；停船；停泊　to moor a boat

3. 烏 wū　　【名詞】烏鴉 crows

4. 啼 tí　　【動詞】叫 to caw

5. 霜 shuāng　　【名詞】霜 frost　寒霧 freezing fog

6. 滿天　　【動詞語】充滿天空；在天空中瀰漫著
mǎn tiān　　to fill the sky; to permeate in the sky

92

7. 楓 fēng 【名詞】楓樹 maple trees

江楓
jiāng fēng 【名詞語】江邊（或江岸）上的楓樹
maples on the river bank

8. 漁火
yú huǒ 【名詞語】漁船上的〔油燈的〕燈光
lamps in a fishing boat; fisherman's torch

9. 愁 chóu 【形容詞】憂愁 melancholy; sad

【名詞】憂愁 melancholiness; sadness

10. 眠 mián 【動詞】睡覺 to sleep

對愁眠
duì chóu mián 【動詞語】面對著令人憂愁的江景睡覺
[try to] sleep vis-a-vis a saddening river scene

11. 姑蘇
Gūsū 【名詞】蘇州有姑蘇山，所以蘇州也叫姑蘇
Sūzhōu was also named Gūsū because of the Gūsū
mountain there

12. 寺 sì 【名詞】廟 (miào) a temple

寒山寺
Hánshān Sì 【名詞】廟名，在楓橋鎮，始建於南朝梁時（六
世紀），相傳唐初的寒山、拾得二僧曾
居於此寺，故名寒山寺。the Hán Shān temple
in the township of Maple Bridge; it was built during the
Liáng dynasty in the 6th century. It was said that the
monks Hánshān and Shídé of the early Táng dynasty
once lived here, so the temple was called the Hánshān
Temple

13. 夜半
yè bàn 【時間詞】半夜 at midnight

14. 鐘聲
zhōng shēng 【名詞語】敲鐘的聲音 toll of a bell

15. 到 dào 【動詞】傳到 to be transmitted to

16. 客船
kè chuán 【名詞語】旅客乘的船 a traveler's boat; i.e., my boat

押韻

天、眠　　-iɛn　船　-iuɛn　　下平聲一先

第二十五首

秋夜寄丘二十二員外

唐　韋應物

懷君屬秋夜，	Huái jūn zhǔ qiū yè,
散步詠涼天。	Sàn bù yǒng liáng tiān.
空山松子落，	Kōng shān sōng zǐ luò,
幽人應未眠。	Yōu rén yīng wèi mián.

作者

韋應物(737-791 A.D.)京兆長安人，官至蘇州刺史，世稱韋蘇州。是中唐著名詩人，詩風淡雅。

Wéi Yìngwù (737-791 A.D.) was a native of Cháng'ān, and served as governor of Sūzhōu, hence he is also known as Wéi Sūzhōu. He was a famous poet of the Mid-Táng period, whose works are marked by a simple, leisurely, and elegant style.

篇旨

抒寫秋涼之夜散步詠詩懷友的心情及誠摯的情意，雅人的幽思及深情，婉曲傳出。閑淡簡遠而耐人尋味。

This poem expresses the mood of the poet's dearly thinking of his friend in an autumnal night while walking and chanting. The profound thoughts and deep affection of a refined scholar are here skillfully and subtly presented. Leisurely, succinct, and very composed, it is nevertheless thought provoking.

注解

1. 秋夜　　　【名詞語】秋天的夜晚 an autumnal night
   qiū yè

2. 寄 jì　　　【動詞】託人遞送：如寄信；此處指寄詩
   　　　　　　　　　　　to send or to mail a letter; here: to send a poem

3. 丘二十二員外　【名詞】姓丘名丹，因做過祠部員外郎，所
   Qiū èr-shí-èr yuán wài　　以稱他丘員外。二十二，是指他在
   　　　　　　　　　　弟兄中的排行。唐朝人有用排行稱
   　　　　　　　　　　人的習慣，如 "劉十九"、"元二"
   　　　　　　　　　　。丘丹辭官後，隱居在臨平山中，
   　　　　　　　　　　韋應物做蘇州刺史時，常常跟他來
   　　　　　　　　　　往唱和。

   Qiū Dān, once served as a councillor in the Ministry of Sacrifice, was here referred to as 'yuán-wài' (councillor). Twenty-second refers to his seniority among siblings. It was the custom of Táng dynasty to address people by their ranks among brothers, thus we have Liú the nineteenth, and Yuán the second. Having resigned from office, Qiū Dān led a life of recluse in Línpíng mountain; while Wéi Yìngwù was serving as the governor of Sūzhōu, he often conversed with Qiū Dān.

4. 懷 huái　　【動詞】懷念；思念　to remember with longing

5. 屬 zhǔ　　【動詞】適逢；恰遇　to happen exactly ...

6. 散步　　　【動詞語】漫步；閒步 to stroll; to go for a walk
   sàn bù

7. 詠 yǒng　　【動詞】作詩來描述　to depict in poetic form

8. 涼 liáng　　【形容詞】涼快；涼爽 (liángshuǎng) cool and comfortable

   涼天　　　【名詞語】涼爽的天氣　a cool and comfortable weather
   liáng tiān

95

9. 松 sōng 　　【名詞】松樹　pine

　　松子　　　【名詞語】松樹的種子　pine-cone; pine nuts
　　sōng zǐ

10. 幽人　　　【名詞語】隱士；遠離塵世、住在山林裡的讀書
　　yōu rén　　　　　　人　a recluse; a person who lives alone and eschews other people

11. 眠 mián 　　【動詞】睡覺　to sleep; to go to bed

押韻

天、眠　　　-iɛn　　　　　　　　　下平聲一先

第二十六首

問劉十九

唐　　白居易

綠螘新醅酒，	Lǜ yǐ xīn pēi jiǔ,
紅泥小火爐。	Hóng ní xiǎo huǒ lú
晚來天欲雪，	Wǎn lái tiān yù xuě,
能飲一杯無。	Néng yǐn yì bēi wú.

作者　白居易 (772 - 846 A.D.) 字樂天，陝西下邽（今陝西渭南縣）人，中唐著名的社會派詩人，主張"歌詩合爲事而作"，作品力求淺顯通俗，他也是詞體

96

形成期的重要作家之一。

Bái Jūyì (772-846 A. D.), courtesy name Lètiān, was a native of Xiàguī, present-day Wèinán district in Shǎnxī province. He was an important poet in the Mid-Táng period, whose works tend to focus on realistic themes. He advocated that the main function of poetry should be for social criticism. He endeavored to write poems in a simple and direct style, in tune with popular taste. He was also a major writer of 'lyric songs' during the formative years of this genre.

篇旨

天寒酒熟請好友共飲，寫得親切有趣。

The weather is cold and the wine is ready, so the poet asks a friend if he cares to share a drink. With casualness and intimacy in the tone, this poem is full of interest.

注解

1. 問 wèn 　【動詞】問 to ask

2. 劉十九　【名詞】嵩陽處士，其名不詳 a recluse living in
   Liú Shíjiǔ　　　　　 Sōngyáng, whose real name was unkown

3. 蟻 yǐ 　【名詞】酒沫；酒面浮沫 the floating froth on the surface
   　　　　　　　　　　　 of wine

   綠蟻　【名詞語】綠色酒沫
   lǜ yǐ　　　　　 the greenish froth on the surface of wine

4. 新 xīn 　【副詞】新近；剛剛 newly; recently

5. 醅 pēi 　【名詞】未過濾的酒 unstrained wine

   新醅酒　【名詞語】剛釀 (niàng) 好還沒過濾的酒
   xīn pēi jiǔ　　　　 newly brewed yet unstrained wine

6. 泥 ní 　【名詞】泥土 clay

   紅泥　【名詞語】紅色泥土 red clay
   hóng ní

97

7. 火爐
huǒ lú
【名詞】供做飯、燒水、取暖等用的器具　a stove

8. 來 lái
【副詞】以來，表示時間從過去某時持續到現在
since [a given point of time in the past]

晚來
wǎn lái
【副詞】傍晚以來；從傍晚到現在　since the dusk

9. 欲 yù
【副詞】將要；快要　to be about to

10. 雪 xuě
【名詞】雪；雪花　snow; snowflakes
【動詞】下雪　to snow

11. 飲 yǐn
【動詞】喝　to drink

12. 杯 bēi
【名詞】杯　a cup

13. 無 wú
【副詞】用在句末，和"不"、"否"相同，構成是非問句
used at the end of a sentence to form a yes-or-no type of question, it means "...or not?"

能…無
néng...wú
【疑問句】能…否？能不能…？
can or can't ...?

押韻

爐、無　　-u　　　　　　　　　上平聲七虞

第二十七首

江雪

唐　柳宗元

千山鳥飛絕，　　　Qiān shān niǎo fēi jué,

萬徑人蹤滅。　　　Wàn jìng rén zōng miè.

孤舟蓑笠翁，　　　Gū zhōu suō lì wēng,

獨釣寒江雪。　　　Dú diào hán jiāng xuě.

作者　柳宗元 (773-819 A.D.) 字子厚，河東（今山西永濟）人。卒於柳州刺史任上，世稱柳柳州，是中唐最著名的散文家及詩人之一。

Liǔ Zōngyuán (773-819 A.D.), courtesy name Zǐhòu, was a native of Hédōng, present-day Yǒngjì district in Shānxī province. He served as the governor of Liǔzhōu and died during his tenure, so he was also called Liǔ Liǔzhōu. He was one of the most famous essayists and poets in the Mid-Táng period.

篇旨

描寫漁翁寒江雪中獨釣，句句寫景也句句抒情，隱現作者的高潔孤傲，用字簡明，意境空靈峭拔，堪稱詠雪詩的絕唱。

This poem depicts a scene of a fisherman fishing alone on a small boat in a snowy night. The lines are both descritive and lyrical, revealing the poet's exalted and immaculate personality, and his aloof and proud disposition. With a diction that is simple and direct, and an artistic conception that is unworldly and vigorous, this poem on snow can be regarded as a masterpiece through the ages.

注解

1. 江 jiāng　　【名詞】江　a river

2. 雪 xuě　　【名詞】雪　snow

3. 絕 jué　　【形容詞】斷絕；淨盡；完全沒有了
　　　　　　　　ceased; completely exhausted

99

4. 徑 jìng　　　【名詞】狹窄的道路；小路　small paths

5. 蹤 zōng　　　【名詞】腳印　foot prints

6. 滅 miè　　　【動詞】隱沒；消失　to vanish; to disappear

7. 孤 gū　　　【形容詞】孤單　solitary; lonely; lone.

8. 舟 zhōu　　　【名詞】小船　a small boat

9. 蓑 suō　　　【名詞】用草或棕 (zōng)編成的衣服，用來防雨
　　　　　　　　a straw or palmbark rain cape

10. 笠 lì　　　【名詞】箬竹葉子編成的錐形寬邊帽子，用來
　　　　　　　遮雨和陽光　a wide conical bamboo hat, used
　　　　　　　to shelter from rain and sunshine

11. 翁 wēng　　　【名詞】老年人　an old man

12. 獨 dú　　　【副詞】獨自；自己一個人　alone; solitarily

13. 釣 diào　　　【動詞】釣魚　to fish with hook and line

14. 寒 hán　　　【形容詞】寒冷　cold; wintry

押韻

絕、雪　　-iuɛt　　　滅　-iɛt;　　　入聲九屑

第二十八首

遊子吟

唐　孟郊

100

慈母手中線，　　　Cí mǔ shǒu zhōng xiàn,

遊子身上衣。　　　Yóu zǐ shēn shàng yī.

臨行密密縫，　　　Lín xíng mì mì féng,

意恐遲遲歸。　　　Yì kǒng chí chí guī.

誰言寸草心，　　　Shéi yán cùn cǎo xīn,

報得三春暉。　　　Bào dé sān chūn huī.

作者

孟郊（751-814 A.D.）字東野，武康（今浙江武康縣）人。中唐詩人，跟賈島 Jiǎ Dǎo（779-843 A.D.）齊名，皆以苦吟著稱。

Mèng Jiāo (751-814 A.D.), courtesy name Dōngyě, was a native of Wǔkāng, present-day Wǔkāng district in Zhèjiāng province. He was a poet in the Mid-Táng period hose popularity matched that of Jiǎ Dǎo (779-843 A.D.). Both of them were known to compose poems laboriously.

篇旨

通過密密縫衣、恐遲遲歸描述深摯的母愛，以寸草春暉形象化的比喻說明子女難報似海親恩。頌揚母愛，情辭懇摯，動人心弦。

This poem describes the deep and earnest love of a mother who was sewing in small stitches for her son, fearing that he might not return in a long time. It figuratively likens a mother's love to sunshine and likens children to tiny grass under the sunshine, unable to repay a kindness which is as deep as the sea. It eulogizes the greatness of motherly love, rich in feelings and eloquent in expression. It plays upon the heartstrings of every reader.

注解

1. 遊子　　　【名詞語】離開家、到別處去讀書或工作的人
   yóu zǐ　　　a wanderer; one who leaves home and go to other place to study or work

2. 吟 yín　　　【動詞】吟詠(yǒng)；聲調抑揚地誦讀

101

to chant; to intone [a verse]

【名詞】古代詩歌體裁的一種，特點是音調悲淒
a type of poems that is characterized by a sad tone

遊子吟
Yóuzǐ Yín 　【名詞語】遊子之歌　A Traveller's Song

3. 慈 cí 　【形容詞】慈愛 kind and loving

慈母
cí mǔ 　【名詞語】慈愛的母親　a loving mother

4. 線 xiàn 　【名詞】棉線；絲線 cotton thread; silk thread

5. 臨行
lín xíng 　【介詞語】在快要走的時候 on the verge of a journey

6. 密密
mì mì 　【副詞】很密地 closely; densely

7. 縫 féng 　【動詞】縫〔衣服〕 to sew; to stitch

密密縫
mì mì féng 　【動詞語】很密地縫，每一針跟每一針之間離得
很近地縫
to stitch densely; to sew in small stitches

8. 意 yì 　【名詞】心意 mind; intention

9. 恐 kǒng 　【動詞】怕 to fear that; to be afraid that

10. 遲 chí 　【副詞】遲延；晚 late

遲遲歸
chí chí guī 　【動詞語】很晚回來－很久很久以後才回來
to return after a long time

11. 誰言
shéi yán 　【反問語】誰說；沒有人能說 who says; no one can say
用反問表示否定 here a rhetorical question is
used for negation

10. 寸草
cùn cǎo 　【名詞語】小草 small grass; tiny grass
比喻遊子 stands for a travelling child

11. 心 xīn 　　【名詞】草中長出來的嫩芽 a tender shoot; heart

　　寸草心 　　【名詞語】小草中長出來的嫩芽 a tender shoot; heart
　　cùn cǎo xīn 　　　　　　　比喻遊子的心 the heart of a trevelling child

12. 報 bào 　　【動詞】報答 to repay [another's kindness]

13. 三春 　　【名詞語】整個春天；一春天 the entire spring
　　sān chūn

　　三春 　　孟春：春天的第一個月 　　early spring
　　　　　　仲春：春天的第二個月 　　mid spring
　　　　　　季春：春天的第三個月 　　late spring

　　　　　　孟　夏、秋、冬
同例：　　仲　夏、秋、冬
　　　　　　季　夏、秋、冬

14. 暉 huī 　　【名詞】陽光；太陽的光 sunshine

　　三春暉 　　【名詞語】一春天的陽光 sunshine of an entire spring
　　sān chūn huī

押韻

　　衣 　-∂i 　歸、暉 　-u∂i 　　上平聲五微

第二十九首

尋隱者不遇

唐　賈島

103

松下問童子，　　　Sōng xia wèn tóng zǐ,

言師採藥去。　　　Yán shī cǎi yào qù.

只在此山中，　　　Zhǐ zài cǐ shān zhōng,

雲深不知處。　　　Yún shēn bù zhī chù.

作者　賈島(779-843 A.D.)字浪仙，范陽（今北京市）人。中唐後期詩人，與孟郊齊名，時稱"郊寒島瘦"，俱以苦吟著名。

Jiǎ Dǎo (779-843 A.D.), courtesy name Làngxiān, was a native of Fànyáng, part of present-day Běijīng metropolitan area. He was a poet in the later years of the Mid-Táng period. He name is often mentioned in tandem with Mèng Jiāo, such as 'Mèng Jiāo is shabby and Jiǎ Dǎo is lean,' for their painstaking attention to versification techniques.

篇旨

藉松下與童子問答描繪山景的清幽，隱士如閒雲野鶴般的自由生活與超逸出塵的高潔心靈。

Through a dialogue with the houseboy under a pine tree, this poem describes the quiet and secluded mountain scene, the life of a recluse freely moving like floating clouds or a wild crane, and a pure mind above worldly desires.

注解

1. 尋 xún　　　【動詞】找 to look for

2. 隱者　　　【名詞語】隱士；隱居的人 a recluse
   yǐn zhě

3. 遇 yù　　　【動詞】遇見 to meet

   不遇　　　【動詞語】沒遇見 to fail to meet; did not meet
   bú yù

4. 松 sōng 　　【名詞】松樹 pine trees

5. 童子 tóngzǐ 　　【名詞語】兒童；小孩兒 a child; a kid

6. 言 yán 　　【動詞】說 to say

7. 師 shī 　　【名詞】老師 the master

8. 採 cǎi 　　【動詞】摘取；採集 to pick; to collect

9. 藥 yào 　　【名詞】草藥 medicinal herbs; herb medicine

10. 雲 yún 　　【名詞】雲 clouds

11. 深 shēn 　　【形容詞】濃密；深厚 thick; dense

　　雲深 yún shēn 　　【描寫句】雲很濃很厚 the clouds are dense

12. 處 chù 　　【名詞】處所；地點 a place; a location

押韻

去、處　　　　-io　　　　去聲六御

第三十首

清明

唐　　杜牧

清明時節雨紛紛，　　Qīng Míng shí jié yǔ fēn fēn,

105

路上行人欲斷魂。　　Lù shàng xíng rén yù duàn hún.

借問酒家何處有？　　Jiè wèn jiǔ jiā hé chù yǒu?

牧童遙指杏花村。　　Mù tóng yáo zhǐ Xìng Huā Cūn.

作者　杜牧 (803-852 A.D.) 字牧之，京兆萬年（今陝西長安附近）人，晚唐著名唯美派詩人，文學史上稱他爲小杜，以別於杜甫。

Dù Mù (803-852 A.D.), courtesy name Mùzhī, was a native of Wànnián in Jīngzhào, in the vicinity of present-day Cháng'ān city in Shǎnxī province. He was a celebrated poet of the Late Táng period, known for his keen aesthetic sense. In histories of Chinese iterature he is often referred to as the 'Younger Dù', to distinguish him from Dù Fǔ.

篇旨

詩人以"雨紛紛"、"欲斷魂"來描繪清明時的悲傷氣氛，以牧童答問來突顯鄉村的春花爛漫、民風樸實，筆調靈活生動，很富情致。

The poet depicts a sad atmosphere on the day supposed to be Pure Brightness (Tombsweeping Day) with such lines as "It has rained profusely," and "The traveller is overpowered by grief," and then, by contrast, enfolds a magnificent view of rural beauty with apricot blossoms in full bloom and the simple and honest customs of country people through a dialogue between the enbittered traveller and a herd boy. The style is very energetic and lively, rich in emotional appeal.

注解

1. 清明　【名詞】二十四節氣之一，通常是在四月四、五
qīng míng　　　或六日，民間習俗在這天掃墓、踏青

One of the 24 seasonal periods in a year which falls on April 4, 5, or 6 when people visit their ancestral tombs, also known as tombsweeping day.

二十四節氣：即立春，雨水，驚蟄 (zhé)，春分，清明，穀雨，立夏，小滿，芒 (máng) 種，夏至，小暑，大暑，立秋

，處暑，白露，秋分，寒露，霜降，
立冬，小雪，大雪，冬至，小寒，大寒
等。二十四節氣表明氣候變化和農事季
節，在農業生產上有重要的意義，是中
國夏曆（陰曆）的特點。

The 24 seasonal periods into which the Lunar year is divided, each consisting 15 days. In temporal sequence, they are:1. the Beginning of Spring, 2. Rain Water, 3. the Waking of Insects, 4. the Spring Equinox, 5. Pure Brightness, 6. Grain Rain, 7. the Beginning of Summer, 8. Grain Full, 9. Grain in Ear, 10. the Summer Solstice, 11. Slight Heat, 12. Great Heat, 13. the Beginning of Autumn, 14. the Limit of Heat, 15. White Dew, 16. the Autumnal Equinox, 17. Cold Dew, 18. Frost's Descent, 19. the Beginning of Winter, 20. Slight Snow, 21. Great Snow, 22. the Winter Solstice, 23. Slight Cold, and 24. Great Cold. They indicate climactic changes throughout the year and serve as a practical guide for appropriate agricultural activities.

2. 時節　【名詞語】季節　time; season; a period of the year
shí jié

3. 紛紛　【形容詞】疊字 a reduplicative compound
fēn fēn　　　　　　多而雜亂；又多又亂 profuse and chaotic

4. 行人　【名詞語】走路的人 pedestrains; passers-by
xíng rén

5. 欲 yù　【副詞】將要；快要 to be about to

6. 斷魂　【動詞語】靈魂離開肉體，用來形容極度的哀傷
duàn hún　　　　the soul leaves the body; overpowered by grief

◆ 靈魂 línghún　　soul

欲斷魂　【動詞語】〔悲苦得〕將要靈魂離開肉體了
yù duàn hún　　精神恍惚 huǎnghū to be in a trance

7. 借問　【動詞語】請問　may I ask ...
jiè wèn

8. 酒家　【名詞語】酒店；酒館兒　a tavern
　　jiǔ jiā

9. 何處　【疑問詞】什麼地方；哪裡　what place; where
　　hé chù

10. 牧童　【名詞語】放牛的小孩兒　a herd boy
　　mù tóng

11. 遙 yáo　【副詞】遠遠地　remotely

12. 指 zhǐ　【動詞】指點　to point at ...

13. 杏花　【名詞】杏樹上開的花
　　xìng huā　　　　apricot blossoms

14. 村 cūn　【名詞】村莊　village

　　杏花村　【名詞語】杏花盛開的村莊；到處都開滿了杏花
　　xìng huā cūn　　　的村莊
　　　　　　　　　a village where apricot blossoms grow profusely

◎ 酒帘　【名詞】又叫酒旗 (qí) 或酒望；是酒店的幌 (huǎng)
　　jiǔ lián　　子，用布做成　a tavern sign in the form of a
　　　　　　　streamer

押韻

| 紛 | -iu n | | 上平聲十二文 |
| 魂 | -u n | 村　-n | 上平聲十三元 |

此兩韻音近通押

These two rhymes sound very closely and they are interchangeable.

第三十一首

山行

108

唐　杜牧

遠上寒山石徑斜，	Yuǎn shàng hán shān shí jìng xiá,
白雲生處有人家。	Bái yún shēng chù yǒu rén jiā.
停車坐愛楓林晚，	Tíng chē zuò ài fēng lín wǎn,
霜葉紅於二月花。	Shuāng yè hóng yú èr yuè huā.

作者　見詩選《清明》p.106

篇旨

描寫寒山楓紅的秋景，色調明麗，極富畫意。秋葉紅於春花的想法，更是新穎獨到，格調俊爽。

This poem depicts the autumnal scene of red leaves covering a cold mountain; it is picturesque and idyllic with bright color. The original conception that autumnal leaves are redder/prettier than the spring flowers is ingenious and unique, revealing a brisk and dashing style.

注解

1. 山行　【動詞語】在山路上走；在山路上驅車
   shān xíng　　to walk on a mountain path; to travel in a carriage on a mountain road

2. 遠上　【動詞語】遠遠登上
   yuǎn shàng　　to climb a long way up

3. 寒山　【名詞語】寒冷季節的山；蕭寂的山；冷清寂靜
   hán shān　　的山 chilly mountains; desolate and tranquil mountains; lonely and quiet mountains

4. 徑 jìng　【名詞】小路 a small path

5. 斜 xié, xiá　【形容詞】傾 (qīng) 斜 slanting; sloping

6. 白雲　　　【名詞語】白色的雲　white clouds
bái yún

7. 生　shēng　　【動詞】生出來；出現　to come into being; to appear

8. 處　chù　　【名詞】地方　a place

生處　　　【名詞語】生出來的地方；出現的地方
shēng chù　　　　　　　where they appear

9. 人家　　　【名詞語】人居住的宅院　human residence
rén jiā

10. 停車　　　【動詞語】停下車子　to stop the moving carriage
tíng chē

11. 坐　zuò　　【連詞】因為　due to; because

12. 愛　ài　　【動詞】愛賞；欣賞　to like; to apprecaite

13. 楓　fēng　　【名詞】楓樹　maple trees

楓林　　　【名詞語】楓樹林
fēng lín　　　　　　maple woods

14. 晚　wǎn　　【時間詞】日暮；日落時　[at] dusk; [at] sunset

15. 霜　shuāng　【名詞】frost

霜葉　　　【名詞語】經霜的葉子；被霜打過的葉子
shuāng yè　　　　　　leaves covered with frost

16. 紅　hóng　　【形容詞】紅　red

17. 於　yú　　【介詞】用在形容詞後，表示比較的意思

A 比 B 〔還〕Adj.
Used after an adjective, it indicates a comparison of the
noun before it with the noun after it, meaning "A is more
adj. than B"

18. 二月花　　【名詞語】二月間盛開的的花；春天的花
èr yuè huā　　　　　flowers blooming in March; spring flowers

110

押韻

斜　-ia　家　-a　花　-ua　下平聲六麻

第三十二首

飲湖上初晴後雨

宋　蘇軾

水光潋灩晴方好，	Shuǐ guāng liàn yàn qíng fāng hǎo,
山色空濛雨亦奇。	Shān sè kōng méng yǔ yì qí.
欲把西湖比西子，	Yù bǎ Xī Hú bǐ Xī Zǐ,
淡妝濃抹總相宜。	Dàn zhuāng nóng mǒ zǒng xiāng yí.

作者　蘇軾 (1037-1101 A.D.)字子瞻，號東坡居士，北宋眉山（今四川眉山縣）人，散文、詩、詞、書、畫都有名，著有《東坡全集》、《東坡樂府》等，是中國歷史上著名的文學家、藝術家。

Sū Shì (1037-1101 A.D.), courtesy name Zǐzhān, style name Dōngpō Jūshì, was a native of Méishān, present-day Méishān distrct in Sìchuān province. He was highly accomplished in prose writing, poetry, lyrics, calligraphy, and painting. His extant works include *Collected Works of Dōngpō, Lyrics of Dōngpō*, and other personal collections.

篇旨

以潋灩、空濛突顯西湖的景色，晴雨皆美；復以美女西子作比，想像靈巧，構思新奇。

This poem prominently describes the scene on the West Lake, using the rhyming compounds "glittering" and "drizzling" to show that the lake is always beautiful whether under sunshine or in rain. By further comparing the West Lake to the renowned beauty Xí Shī, the poet demonstates his lively and ingenious imagination and innovative conception.

注 解

1. 飲 yǐn 【動詞】喝〔酒〕to drink

2. 湖 hú 【名詞】指西湖，在今浙江杭州 the West Lake, outside present-day Hángzhōu in Zhèjiāng province

3. 初 chū 【副詞】起初；開始時 at first; in the beginning

4. 晴 qíng 【形容詞】晴朗；天空中没有雲，陽光很好 clear; sunny

5. 後 hòu 【副詞】後來 later; afterwards

6. 雨 yǔ 【動詞】下雨 to rain

7. 水光 shuǐ guāng 【名詞語】湖水的光 glitter of the lake water

8. 瀲灩 liàn yàn 【形容詞】疊韻聯綿詞 a rhyming compound 水波在陽光下閃閃(shǎn)發光 glittering

9. 方 fāng 【副詞】正 just

10. 山色 shān sè 【名詞語】山的景色 the view/scene of mountain

11. 空濛 kōng méng 【形容詞】疊韻聯綿詞 a rhyming compound 迷迷茫茫(mímáng)的；模模糊糊的 misty; drizzly

12. 奇 qí 【形容詞】奇特；不凡 outstanding; uncommon

13. 西子 Xī zǐ 【名詞】春秋時代越國的美女西施 Xīshī, the renowned beauty of Yuè in the Spring and Autumn Period

14. 淡 dàn 【副 詞】淡淡地 lightly

15. 妝 zhuāng 【動 詞】化妝 to make up; to apply cosmetics

淡妝 【動詞語】淡淡地化妝；化妝化得很淡
dàn zhuāng to make up lightly; in light make-up

16. 濃 nóng 【副 詞】濃濃地 heavily; richly

17. 抹 mǒ 【動 詞】擦抹 to rub; to apply cosmetics

濃抹 【動詞語】濃濃地擦〔脂粉〕
nóng mǒ to make up heavily; in heavy make-up

◆ 脂粉 zhī fěn rouge and face powder

18. 總 zǒng 【副 詞】都 all; in all cases; in both cases

19. 相 xiāng 【副 詞】表受事 here: it stands for the patient/receiver of action
Cf. poem 3, n. 17, p. 12

20. 宜 yí 【形容詞】宜〔於〕；適合〔於〕；〔對〕…很合適
suitable [for]; fitting...
For similar usage, see Poem 3, note 22, p.12

相宜 【形容詞】宜〔於〕她；宜〔於〕它
xiāng yí befitting her (Xī Zǐ); befitting it (Xī Hú)

押 韻

奇、宜   -i   上平聲四支

律 詩 簡 介
A Brief Introduction to Regulated Verse

律詩的格律 Rules of Versification

1. 律詩分爲五言、七言兩種。

Regulated Verse can be classified into two types: pentasyllabic and septasyllabic.

2. 每首律詩有八句，超過八句的叫作排律，句數是四的倍數。

Regulated Verse generally is compriseed of eight lines. Any longer than eight lines is called an Extended Regulated Verse, the total number of lines of which must be a multiple of four.

3. 每句律詩一定得有平仄的更迭以構成音樂性的長短高低變化及節奏。

Each line of the five or seven syllables must alternate between level and deflected tones to create a euphonic change of tonality and rhythm.

平聲：陰平、陽平，就是國語中的第一聲、第二聲。

Level tone words are pronounced in the first and second tones in modern Mandarin Chinese.

仄(zè)聲：上、去、入。上聲就是國語中的第三聲，去聲就是國語中的第四聲，入聲韻尾帶-p（如合），-t（如節），-k（如獨），僅存於方言如閩、粵、吳語中，國語已併入第一、二、三、四聲中。

Deflected tone words are pronounced in the third and fourth tones in modern Mandarin Chinese. Yet another group of deflected tone words exists; formerly called enterring tone words; these words carry a stop ending -p (hé), -t (jié), or -k (dú); such endings only exist in such dialects as Cantonese, Mǐn, or Wú dialects, but have totally disappearedin Mandarin. Words in the enterring tone are now distributed in all the four tones in Mandarin, so it is very probable that a level tone syllable is in fact a deflected one.

4. 每兩句構成一聯，一首律詩共有四聯，如下：

Every two lines make one couplet. Regulated Verse has four couplets, as follows:

首聯：第一、二句　　　　散行
Head Couplet: Lines one and two; not required to be antithetical

頷(hàn)聯：第三、四句　　　規定用對仗
Chin Couplet: Lines three and four; required to be antithetical

頸聯(jǐng)：第五、六句　　　　規定用對仗
Neck Couplet: Lines five and six; required to be antithetical

尾聯：第七、八句　　　　散行
Tail Couplet: Lines seven and eight; not required to be antithetical

5. 領聯跟頸聯應該是對句，即一聯兩句中相對應的字必須：

一、詞性相同
二、平仄相反
三、節奏一致

The Chin Couplet and the Neck Couplet must be apair of antithetical couplets, that is, of the two lines in a couplet, each corresponding syllable (or character) must:

1. belong to the same grammatical category;

2. be counterpointed by level and deflected tones; and

3. form an identical rhythm.

＿＿＿｜｜	⊢｜⊥＿＿＿｜	＿平聲	
例如： 星垂平野闊	秋草獨尋人去後		
｜｜｜＿＿	＿＿⊢｜｜＿＿	｜仄聲	
月湧大江流	寒林空見日斜時		
⊢｜＿＿｜	⊥＿｜｜＿＿｜	⊢應仄而平	
名豈文章著	漢文有道恩猶薄		
＿＿｜｜＿	⊢｜＿＿｜｜＿	⊥應平而仄	
官應老病休	湘水無情弔豈知		

6. 第二、四、六、八句諧(xié)韻，要是第一句的最後一個字也是平聲（首句入韻），也應該諧韻。一韻到底，不得換韻。

The last syllable of all even numbered lines must rhyme with each other. If the first line ends with a syllable in level tone, it must also rhyme. One rhyme runs through the entire verse; no change of rhyme is allowed.

7. 八句詩中最少有三句（三、五、七句）的最後一個字是仄聲，這三個字－如果第一句的最後一個字也是仄聲，就是四個字－應該有變化，不可完全屬於同一聲，如三個全是上聲，去聲，或入聲。

115

In the eight lines, at least three (the third, the fifth, and the seventh) end with a syllable in the deflected tone (there may be four, if the first line ends with a word in the deflected tone). These words should not be monotonous (for example: all words are in the rising tone, falling tone, or entering tone).

8. 五律的句子只有四種句式，以 A, a, B, b 來分別代表。

A pentasyllabic line may have four variatiions, represented by A, a, B, b respectively:

A   仄仄仄平平   仄起平收
Begins with the deflected tone and ends with the level tone.

a   仄仄平平仄   仄起仄收
Begins and ends with the deflected tone.

B   平平仄仄平   平起平收
Begins and ends with the level tone.

b   平平平仄仄   平起仄收
Begins with the level tone and ends with the deflected tone.

用這四個句式可組成四種不同的詩式，即：

These four types of lines can be organized into four different poetic forms:

(1)   A B b A a B b A   仄起式，首句入韻
Begins with a deflected tone word and the first line rhymes.

(2)   B A a B b A a B   平起式，首句入韻
Begins with a level tone word and the first line rhymes.

(3)   a B b A a B b A   仄起式，首句不入韻
Begins with a deflected tone word and the first line does not rhyme.

(4)   b A a B b A a B   平起式，首句不入韻
Begins with a level tone word and the first line does not rhyme.

Types (3) and (4) can be seen in poem 22, p.90, and poem 17, p.73, respectively.

五言詩以首句不入韻為主，首句入韻的以仄起式為較常見。

In pentasyllabic Regulsted Verse, types (3) and (4) in which the first line does not rhyme are predominant; of the other two, type (1) is more common.

五律第一式和第三式，第二式和第四式，都只有第一句不同。
從代表詩式的公式中，很容易看出。

Of pentasyllabic Regulated Verse, type (1) and type (2), type (3) and type (4), differ only in the first line. This can be clearly seen in the representative structures above:

9. 七律的句子也只有四式，分別用 A, a, B, b 來代表：

A   平平仄仄仄平平
Begins and ends with the level tone.

a   平平仄仄平平仄

116

Begins with the level tone and and ends with the deflected tone.

B   仄仄平平仄仄平

Begins with the deflected tone and ends with the level tone.

b   仄仄平平平仄仄

Begins and ends with the deflected tone.

用這四個句式也可以組成四種不同的詩式：

From these four line structures emerge four different forms of Regulated Verse:

(1)   A B b A a B b A   平起式，首句入韻

Begins with a level tone word and the first line rhymes.

(2)   B A a B b A a B   仄起式，首句入韻

Begins with a deflected tone word and the first line rhymes.

(3)   a B b A a B b A   平起式，首句不入韻

Begins with a level tone word and the first line does not rhyme.

(4)   b A a B b A a B   仄起式，首句不入韻

Begins with a deflected tone word and the first line does not rhyme.

Types (1) and (2) can be seen in poems 21, p.86, and poem 23, p.94, respectively.

七律以首句入韻為主。

Of septasyllabic Regulated Verses, types (1) and (2) are most common.

七律第一式和第三式，第二式和第四式，都只有第一句不同。
從代表詩式的公式中，很容易看出。

Of septasyllabic Regulated Verses, type (1) and type (3), type (2) and type (4), differ only in the first line. This is easy to see in the formulaic structure above.

用大小寫的A, a, B, b字母來代表四種不同句式是名語言學家王力先生於一九四五年創始的，其好處是簡單明瞭。凡是A型句，五言是仄起，七言是平起；B型句五言是平起，七言是仄起。凡押韻句都是大寫字母，故首句入不入韻，只看第一個字是大寫或小寫便知。每一聯的兩句各屬不同的字母，表示相對；而第二三句，四五句，六七句則屬同一字母而有大小寫的區分，表示相黏。單數詩式與雙數詩式的分別，只是第一句有大小寫即入不入韻的分別。凡此都一目瞭然，有助於學習者迅速掌握律詩的形式特點。

The renowned linguist Wáng Lì first proposed in 1945 using the letters A, a, B, and b to represent the four tonal patterns in. The beauty of this design is that it enables one to grasp the formal features at a glance. The lines 'A' or 'a' begin with words in the deflected tone if they are pentasyllabic, and words in the level tone if they are septasyllabic. Conversely, the lines 'B' or 'b' begin with words in the level tone if they are pentasyllabic, and words in the deflected tone if they are septasyllabic. All lines that rhyme are represented by capital letters, so whether the first line rhymes or not can be determined by using the upper or lower case for the first etter. Within each couplet the two lines are represented by different letters, indicating the relation of antithesis, while lines two and three, four and five, six and seven are represented by the same letter either in upper or lower cases. The poetic forms (1) and (3), (2) and (4) differ only in the first line. These overviews will help students quickly grasp the distinctive features of Regulated Verse.

10. 平仄不拘：五言律詩每句的一、三字可不受平仄的限制，即應平者可仄，應仄者可平；七言律每句的一、三、五字也可不受限。這就是平常説的"一三五不論，二四六分明。"但五律的B型句"平平仄仄平"，第一個字必須是平聲，七律的B型句"仄仄平平仄仄平"，第三個字必須是平聲，否則叫作犯孤平，即除了韻腳外，只剩了一個平聲字。這樣的句子聽起來不暢順，應該避免。至於仄收的句子（a和b型"仄仄平平仄""平平平仄仄""平平仄仄平平仄""仄仄平平平仄仄"）即使只有一個平聲字，也不算犯孤平。

Some liberty is allowed in tonal specification: pentasyllabic lines may be either level or deflected in the first and third syllables; the first, third, and fifth syllables of septasyllabic lines may be level or deflected. This is commonly recognized as "the first, the third, and the fifth do not matter, but the second, the fourth, and the sixth must be clear-cut." However, the first syllable in a pentasyllabic line and the third syllable in a septasyllabic line of a type B sentence must be in the level tone. Were it not so, it would be committing violence on a single level tone: that is, besides the rhyming words, there is only one syllable with a level tone. It will make the sounding awkward, so should be avoided. On the other hand, it matters little when there is only one syllable in the level tone for those lines ending with a syllable in the deflected tone, as in lines of types a and b.

11. 絕句：絕句是律詩的一半，可以是一、二聯，三、四聯，一、四聯，或二、三聯，但不能是一、三聯或二、四聯。

Quartrain: A Quartrain is one half of a Regulated Verse and can be formed with couplets one and two (lines one to four), three and four (lines five to eight), one and four (lines one, two, seven, and eight), or two and three (lines three to six). It may not be formed with couplets one and three (lines one, two, five, and six), or couplets two and four (lines three, four, seven, and eight).

12. 古絕：絕句中不遵守格律、押仄聲韻的叫古絕。如第二十七首"江雪"。

Ancient Quartrain: A Quartrain that does not abide by the rules of versification, or rhymes in the deflected tone, is called an Ancient Quartrain. For example: poem 27, p. 107.

13. 律詩的拗救：違反平仄規律的句子叫拗句，詩人對拗句往往用救。具體地說，就是一句中該用平聲字時用了仄聲字，然後在本句或對句的適當位置，把該用仄聲字的改用平聲來補救，合起來稱爲"拗救"。

Deviation and remedy: A line that violates the rules of versification is called a deviated line, and the poet usually take steps to remedy it. For example, a syllable that should be in the level tone but instead uses a syllable in the deflected tone creates a deviated line; the poet then will in the same line or corresponding line inserts a syllable in the level tone at the place specified for the deflected tone, thereby once again achieve the necessary balance. Together, this is called "deviation and remedy."

(1) 本句拗救：

五律第三字拗，第四字救，例如：

寒山轉蒼翠
— — — │ │
— — │ — │　　(The tones of the 3rd and the 4th syllables are reversed)

七律第五字拗，第六字救，例如：

苦恨年年壓金線
│ │ — — — │ │
│ │ — — │ — │　　(The tones of the 5th and the 6th syllables are reversed)

(2) 對句拗救：

五律的 a 型句"仄仄平平仄"，如第三或四字用了仄聲，詩人往往在對句第三個字改用平聲來救，如：

When the 3rd or 4th position of a type 'a' line in a pentasyllable Regulated Verse uses a syllable in the deflected tone, the poet often affects a remedy by inserting a syllable of the level tone in the 3rd position of the corresponding line. For example:

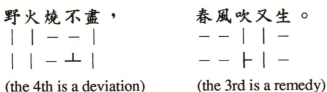

野火燒不盡，　　　春風吹又生。
│ │ — — │　　　— — │ │ —
│ │ — ⊥ │　　　— — ⊦ │ —
(the 4th is a deviation)　　(the 3rd is a remedy)

七律的 a 型句"平平仄仄平平仄"，如第五字用了仄聲，詩人往往在對句第五個字改用平聲來救，如：

When the 5th postion of a type 'a' line in a septasyllabic Regulated Verse uses a syllable in the deflected tone, the poet often affects a remedy by inserting a syllable of the level tone in the 5th position of the corresponding line. For example:

草中兩色綠堪染，　　　水上桃花紅欲燃。
— — │ │ │ — │　　　│ │ — — │ │ —
│ — │ │ ⊥ — │　　　│ │ — — ⊦ │ —

(the 5th is a deviation)   (the 5th is a remedy)

大體説，拗是因爲作者不願因一個字而傷害全句的意思而用了不合音律的字；救是補救這種缺失來保持平仄聲調的均衡，詳細的規律很多，此處只簡要地介紹一下。

Generally speaking, deviation results from the author's unwillingness to sacrifice the beauty of the poem for a single syllable, choosing instead a syllable that deviates from the general rules of versification. Remedy is an effort to rectify the defect in order to maintain an overall balance between level and deflected tones. This kinds of manneuver includes many possibilities; here we introduce just a few important ones.

14. 音頓：律詩的節奏是前面每兩個字爲一節，最後三個字自成二一或一二兩個音節。讀平聲字的時間大約是讀仄聲字的一倍，如下：

Caesura: The caesura in Regulated Verse is comprised of two syllables, with the last syllable standing alone as caesura. In chanting a poem, the level tone words take twice as long as the deflected tone words.

五言句   Pentasyllabic lines

仄－仄－| 平－－平－－| 仄－

平－－平－－| 仄－仄－| 平－－

平－－平－－| 平－－| 仄－仄－

仄－仄－| 仄－| 平－－平－－

七言句   Septasyllabic lines

平－－平－－| 仄－仄－| 平－－平－－| 仄－

仄－仄－| 平－－平－－| 仄－仄－| 平－－

仄－仄－| 平－－平－－| 平－－| 仄－仄－

平－－平－－| 仄－仄－| 仄－| 平－－平－－

15. 字音結構：每個字的音節由五部分組成，古人稱爲頭、頸、腹、尾、神，用現在的術語來説，即輔音，介音，主要元音，韻尾，及聲調。其中輔音、介音、和韻尾都可缺，主要元音及聲調則萬不可缺。

Structure of syllables: A syllable usually includes five components; traditionally, they were known as: the head, the neck, the belly, the tail, and the soul. In modern terminology, they represent the consonent initial, the medial (i, u, and ü), the main vowel, the ending (-i, -u, -m, -n, -ng, -p, -t, -k), and the tone, in that order. Of these, the initial, the medial, and the ending are optional, while the main vowel and the tone are obligatory.

16.字音演變：字音隨時間而改變，故上古音不同於中古音，中古音不同於現代音。唐以後的詩一般仍以中古音爲準。《切韻》、《廣韻》、及《平水韻》是最常用的韻書。《辭海》中的注音也多以這幾本韻書爲據。目前學者對中古音的擬構大致相近而可信，本書所注的中古音以董同龢先生的擬音爲主，間亦參用王力、李榮等語言學家的說法。

Sound change: The sound of a syllable changes constantly with time, so that archaic pronunciation differed from ancient pronunciation, and the ancient differs from the modern. Since the Táng dynasty, poets have been using such rhyme books as the *Qièyùn* (601 A.D.) by Lù Fǎyán, the *Guǎng Yùn* (1008 A.D.) by Chén Péngnián and Qiū Yōng, and the *Lǐbù Yùnlüè* (1252 A.D.) by Liú Yuān. The pronunciation given in *Cíhǎi* are mostly taken from these books. Modern linguists have reached a general consensus about the sound value of Ancient Chinese. In this book we have used the system of the late professor Dǒng Tónghé to approximate the sounds of the rhyming syllables; we have also taken into consideration some findings made by other linguists like Wáng Lì and Lǐ Róng.

第一闋

漁歌子

唐　　張志和

西塞山前白鷺飛，	Xī Sè Shān qián bái lù fēi,
桃花流水鱖魚肥。	Táo huā liú shuǐ guì yú féi.
青箬笠，綠蓑衣，	Qīng ruò lì, lù suō yī,
斜風細雨不須歸。	Xié fēng xì yǔ bù xū guī.

作者　張志和 (c.742-c.782 A.D.) ，字子同，婺州金華人，自號煙波釣徒。所作漁歌子爲最早詞調之一。

Zhāng Zhìhé (c. 742-c. 782 A.D.), courtesy name Zǐtóng, was a native of Jīnhuá in Wùzhōu, present-day Jīnhuá district in Zhèjiāng province. He adopted the style name -- "Fisherman of Mist and Waves," and his "Fisherman's Song" ranks among the earliest important works of the lyric-song genre.

篇旨

描寫春景的清麗，及漁人在斜風細雨中浮泛水上的閒適無拘。

This lyric depicts the clear and attractive scenery of Spring, and a fisherman's leisurely, unbridled life, floating on a river amidst a light wind and a drizzling rain.

注解

1. 詞 cí　　　【名詞】一種韻文形式，由五言詩、七言詩和民間歌謠發展而成，起於唐代，盛於宋代。原是配樂歌唱的一種詩體，句的長短隨著歌調而改變，因此又叫做 "長短句"

A verse form developed on the bases of penta- syllabic

poetry, hepta-syllabic poetry and folk songs that originated in the Táng Dynasty (618-907) and became fully developed in the Sòng Dynasty (960-1279). It was written to certain tunes with strict tonal patterns and rhyme schemes, in fixed number of lines and words, thus it was also known as "long-and-short-line [verse]"

2. 詞牌 cí pái 【名詞】詞調的名稱，如 "漁歌子" the verse form of "cí"; name of the tune for which a "cí" is composed

3. 漁歌子 Yú gē zǐ 【名詞】詞牌名 name of the tune for which this "cí" is composed; Fisherman's Song

4. 西塞山 Xī sè shān 【名詞】山名，在今浙江省北部吳興縣城西 name of a mountain, situated in the northern part of Zhèjiāng province, to the west of present-day Wúxīng district.

5. 鷺 lù 【名詞】鷺鷥 (sī) an egret

6. 飛 fēi 【動詞】飛 to fly

7. 桃花 táo huā 【名詞】桃樹的花 peach blossoms

8. 流水 liú shuǐ 【名詞】流動的水 flowing water

9. 鱖魚 guì yú 【名詞】鱖魚 a mandarin fish

10. 肥 féi 【形容詞】肥美 fat and delicious

11. 青 qīng 【形容詞】青色的 blue or green

12. 箬笠 ruò lì 【名詞語】箬竹葉子編成的錐形寬邊帽子，用來遮雨和陽光 a wide conical bamboo hat, used to shelter from rain and sunshine

13. 綠 lù 【形容詞】綠色的 green

14. 蓑衣 suō yī 【名詞語】用草或棕 (zōng) 編成的衣服，用來防雨 a straw or palmbark rain cape

15. 斜風　【名詞語】微風　a light wind
    xié fēng

16. 細雨　【名詞語】濛濛雨；毛毛雨　a drizzling rain
    xì yǔ

17. 須　xū　【助動詞】須　need to

18. 歸　guī　【動詞】回去；回家　to return; to go home

押韻

飛、肥　　-uəi　　衣、歸　　-əi　　上平聲五微

第二闋

憶江南

唐　白居易

江南好，	Jiāng nán hǎo,
風景舊曾諳。	Fēng jǐng jiù céng ān.
日出江花紅勝火，	Rì chū jiāng huā hóng shèng huǒ,
春來江水綠如藍。	Chūn lái jiāng shuǐ lǜ rú lán.
能不憶江南？	Néng bú yì jiāng nán?

作者　見詩選二十六《問劉十九》p.96

篇旨

描繪江南春景的明淨秀麗，及作者不能忘懷的愛
賞心情。

124

This lyric depicts the exquisite spring scene in the Jiāngnán region, and poet's nostalgic feeling.

注 解

1. **憶 江 南**
   Yì Jiāngnán
   【名詞】詞牌名 name of the musical tune for which this "cí" is composed; Reminiscing about Jiāngnán

2. **江 南**
   jiāng nán
   【名詞】指長江以南的地方，尤指江蘇、浙江兩省，山明水秀，風景秀麗。俗語說：　"上有天堂，下有蘇杭。"

   Name of a region to the south of the Yángzǐ River, especially referring to Jiāngsū and Zhèjiāng provinces where the landscapes are extremely beautiful. There is a common saying: "Above, there is the paradise, and below, there are Sūzhōu and Hángzhōu."

3. **風 景**
   fēng jǐng
   【名詞】大自然中的景色 scenery; landscape

4. **舊** jiù
   【副詞】從前 formerly; in the past

5. **曾** céng
   【副詞】曾經 once (used to indicate that something did transpire in the past at least one time)

6. **諳** ān
   【動詞】熟悉 to be familiar with; to know sb. or sth. well

7. **日 出**
   rì chū
   【敘述句】太陽出來 the sun risis

8. **江 花**
   jiāng huā
   【名詞語】江畔的花 flowers by the river bank

9. **紅** hóng
   【形容詞】紅色的 red

10. **勝** shèng
    【動詞】勝過 to surpass

11. **火** huǒ
    【名詞】火焰 fire; flame

12. **春 來**
    chūn lái
    【敘述句】春天來臨 spring time arrives

13. 江水　【名詞語】江中的水　the river water
　　 jiāng shuǐ

14. 綠 lù　【形容詞】綠色的　green

15. 如 rú　【準繫詞】像　to be like; to resemble

16. 藍 lán　【名詞】一種植物，葉子可以製藍色染料，引申
　　　　　　　　　 為藍色　indigo plant

17. 能不…　【反問句】用否定反問句表示加強的肯定
　　 néng bú　　　Here a rhetorical nagative question is used to express
　　　　　　　　　an affirmative meaning.
　　　　　　　　　能不…嗎？　Is it possible not to ...?
　　　　　　　　　不能不…　It is impossible not to....
　　　　　　　　　必定會…　Will most certainly....

18. 憶 yì　【動詞】回憶　to recall; to reminisce
　　　　　　　　　懷念　to think of ... with nostalgic longing

押韻

譜、藍、南　　　　-m　　　　下平聲十三覃

第三闋

虞美人

南唐　　李煜

　　春花秋月何時了？往事知多少？小樓昨夜又東風，故國不堪回首月明中！　　雕欄玉砌應猶在，只是朱顏改。問君能有幾多愁？恰似一江春水向東流！

Zhùyīn:

Chūn huā qiū yuè hé shí liǎo? Wǎng shì zhī duō shǎo? Xiǎo lóu zuó yè yòu dōng fēng, gù guó bù kān huí shǒu yuè míng zhōng.　　　Diāo lán yù qì yīng yóu zài, zhǐ shì zhū yán gǎi. Wèn jūn néng yǒu jǐ duō chóu? Qià sì yì jiāng chūn shuǐ xiàng dōng liú.

作者　李煜 (937 - 978 A.D.)，字重光，五代時 (907-960) 南唐後
主，降宋後被封爲違命候。後宋太宗賜藥命他自
殺，死時年僅四十二。他早期的作品純真典雅，
綺旎婉約；亡國 (975) 後所作則沈痛悲慨，感人至深
。近代文學批評家王國維推許備至，譽之爲血淚
凝聚之作。

Lǐ Yù (937 - 978 A.D.), courtesy name Chóngguāng, was the last ruler of the
state of Southern Táng during the Five Dynasties period (907 - 960 A.D.)
When his kingdom was conquered by the Sòng in 975 A.D., he was taken
captive, and made the "Marquis of Disobedience." Three years later, on his
41st birthday, he was put to death by a draught of poisoned wine presented to
him by the Sòng Emperor. The lyric-songs of his early days are graceful and
enchanting; while those of his later years are deeply tinged with a poignant
sense of tragedy, leading the modern scholar Wáng Guówéi (1877 - 1927
A.D.) to apply to him Nietzsche's famous epithet: 'written in blood'.

篇旨

春花秋月本是可以賞玩的景物，但在後主的眼中
心中都變成了愁苦的源泉。因爲回憶往昔春秋佳
日的歡樂，益發反襯出今日的凄涼。而春花秋月
是無時終止的，後主內心也就充滿像東流的江水
一樣無盡的悲愁。

Spring flowers and autumnal moon are things to be appreciated, but in the
eyes and mind of Lǐ Yù they have become the fountainhead of his remorse
and sorrow. Because recollecting the good old days will inevitably aggravate
the misery he is suffering by sharp contrast. As spring flowers and autumnal
moon last forever, so Lǐ Yù's sorrow is also endless, like a full river of spring
water that perpetually flows eastward.

注解

1. 虞美人　【名詞】詞牌名 name of the musical tune for which this "cí"
   Yú Měirén　　　　　is composed; The Beautiful Lady Yú

2. 春花　【名詞語】春天的花 spring time flowers
   chūn huā

3. 秋月　【名詞語】秋天的月 autumnal moon
   qiū yuè

4. 何時　【疑問時間詞】什麼時候 when
   hé shí

5. 了 liǎo　【動詞】終了；到盡頭 to come to an end

6. 往事　【名詞語】過去的事 things in the past
   wǎng shì

7. 知 zhī　【動詞】知道 to know; to be aware of

8. 多少　【形容詞】多少 how many
   duō shǎo

   知多少　【動詞語】用反問表否定 a rhetorical question is used
   zhī duō shǎo　　　　here to express a nagative sense
   　　　　　　　知道有多少嗎？ Do you know how many?
   　　　　　　　不知道有多少 Don't know how many.
   　　　　　　　太多了 too many!

9. 東風　【名詞語】從東方吹來的風；春風 eastern wind;
   dōng fēng　　　　　spring wind

10. 故國　【名詞語】從前的國家；已亡的國家，指南唐
    gù guó　　　　　the old home-state; a conquered nation, referring to
    　　　　　　　　the Southern Táng which he once ruled

11. 堪 kān　【動詞】承受 to bear ; to withstand

    不堪　【動詞語】不能承受；承受不了 can not bear to
    bù kān

12. 回首　【動詞語】回頭看；此處：回想 to look back; to recall
    huí shǒu

128

13. 月明
    yuè míng
【名詞語】月光 the moonlight

14. 雕 diāo
【動詞】雕刻 to engrave

15. 欄 lán
【名詞】欄杆 railings

雕欄
diāo lán
【名詞語】雕刻著花紋的欄杆 engraved railings

16. 玉 yù
【名詞】玉石 jade

17. 砌 qì
【名詞】台階 steps

玉砌
yù qì
【名詞語】玉石砌築的台階 jade steps

18. 朱顏
    zhū yán
【名詞語】年輕時美麗紅潤的容顏
the young rosy countenance of youth

19. 改 gǎi
【動詞】改變 to change; to have changed

20. 君 jūn
【代名詞】您 you

問君
wèn jūn
【動詞語】問您；此處是假想別人問作者
Here it hypothesizes someone asking the author

21. 幾多
    jǐ duō
【疑問形容詞】多少？ how much

22. 愁 chóu
【名詞】憂愁 sorrow; distress

23. 恰似
    qià sì
【準繫詞語】正像 to be just like

24. 一江
    yì jiāng
【名詞語】全江；整江 the whole river; a full river

25. 春水
    chūn shuǐ
【名詞語】春天的江水 spring water

26. 向東
    xiàng dōng
【介詞語】朝著東方 eastward

27. 流 liú 　　【動詞】流動 to flow

押韻

了、少			-iɛu		上聲十七篠
風	-iung	中	-ung		上平聲一東
在、改	-ɔi				上聲十賄
愁	-ɘu	流	-iɘu		下平聲十一尤

第四闋

生查子

宋　　歐陽修

去年元夜時，花市燈如晝。
月上柳梢頭，人約黃昏後。
今年元夜時，月與燈依舊。
不見去年人，淚濕春衫袖。

Zhùyīn:

Qù nián yuán yè shí, huā shì dēng rú zhòu.
Yuè shàng liǔ shāo tóu, rén yuē huáng hūn hòu.
Jīn nián yuán yè shí, yuè yǔ dēng yī jiù.
Bú jiàn qù nián rén, lèi shī chūn shān xiù.

作者　歐陽修 (1007-1072 A.D.) 字永叔，盧陵 (Lúlíng)（今江西
吉安縣）人，自號醉翁，又號六一居士。宋朝名

臣及文學家兼史學家。著有《新唐書》、《新五
代史》等。爲唐宋古文八大家之一，詩詞文章都
受到世人的推重。官至參知政事，卒，諡文忠。

Ouyáng Xiū (1007-1072 A.D.), courtesy name Yǒngshú, was a native of
Lúlíng (present-day Jí'ān district in Jiāngxī province). He styled himself as
"A Drunken Old Man" and also as "A Scholar of Six Ones." A well known
statesman, historian, and man of letters, he compiled the *New History of the
Táng Dynasty* and the *New History of the Five Dynasties*. One of the Eight
Great Essayists of the Táng and Sòng Period, his prose and poetic works
were highly regarded by his contemporaries and scholars of later generations.
He served as vice prime minister, and upon his death he was granted the
posthumous honorific title of "Wénzhōng" which was also used in the title of
his collected works -- *Wénzhōng jí.*

篇旨

以今昔的對比，寫景物如舊、戀人何處的悵惘之
情，低徊宛轉，感人至深。

A comparison is made between the present and the past: though the scene
remains the same, the lover is nowhere to find. The lingering sense of
disappointment is tactfully expressed, and it is extremely touching.

注解

1. 生查子　【名詞】詞牌名　name of the music tune for which this "cí"
   shēng zhā zǐ　　　　　　is composed; Raw Plum

2. 元夜　【名詞語】上元夜；陰曆正月十五夜
   yuán yè　　　　the fifteenth day of the first lunar month
   　　　　　　上元：節日名；陰曆正月十五日，民
   　　　　　　間於夜晚張設各種彩色燈籠慶祝遊樂
   　　　　　　，故也叫燈節
   　　　　　　name of a festival; in the night of the fifteenth of the
   　　　　　　first lunar month, people display colorful festive
   　　　　　　lanterns to celebrate and make merry, so it is also
   　　　　　　calleds the "Lantern Festival"

3. 花市　【名詞語】賣花的市場　a flower market
   huā shì

4. 燈　dēng　【名詞】燈籠　lanterns

131

5. 晝 zhòu 　　【時間詞】白天 daytime

6. 上 shàng 　　【動詞】上升；升到 to rise; to rise to

7. 柳 liǔ 　　【名詞】柳樹 willow trees

8. 梢頭 　　【名詞語】頂端；上頭 top
   shāo tóu

   柳梢頭 　　【名詞語】柳樹頂端 top of willow trees
   liǔ shāo tóu

9. 約 yuē 　　【動詞】預先說定在某時某地見面　to have an appointment

10. 黃昏 　　【名詞語】薄暮：傍晚 dusk
    huáng hūn

11. 依舊 　　【準繫詞語】如舊；像從前一樣
    yī jiù 　　　　　　　　　　to be as it used to be

12. 去年人 　　【名詞語】去年相約的人；愛人
    qù nián rén 　　　　　　the person of appoitment lasy year; the lover

13. 淚 lèi 　　【名詞】眼淚 tears

14. 濕 shī 　　【動詞】沾濕 to moisten; to wet

15. 衫 shān 　　【名詞】衣衫；衣服 shirts; garments

    春衫 　　【名詞語】春天穿的衣衫 the shirt worn in spring time
    chūn shān

16. 袖 xiù 　　【名詞】衣袖 sleeves

押韻

晝	-əu	舊、袖	-iəu	去聲二十六宥
後	-əu			上聲二十五有

宥、有二韻在詞中通押

These two rhymes are interchangeable in lyrics.

第五闋

水調歌頭

宋　　蘇軾

丙辰中秋，歡飲達旦，大醉，作此篇，
兼懷子由。

明月幾時有？把酒問青天。不知天上宮闕，今夕是
何年。我欲乘風歸去，惟恐瓊樓玉宇，高處不勝寒。起
舞弄清影，何似在人間！　　　轉朱閣，低綺戶，照無
眠。不應有恨，何事長向別時圓？人有悲歡離合，月有
陰晴圓缺，此事古難全。但願人長久，千里共嬋娟。

Zhùyīn:

Míng yuè jǐ shí yǒu? Bǎ jiǔ wèn qīng tiān. Bù zhī tiān shàng gōng què, jīn xī shì hé
nián? Wǒ yù chéng fēng guī qù, wéi kǒng qióng lóu yù yǔ, gāo chù bù shēng hán. Qǐ wǔ
nòng qīng yǐng, hé sì zài rén jiān! Zhuǎn zhú gé, dī qǐ hù, zhào wú mián. Bù yīng
yǒu hèn, hé shì cháng xiàng bié shí yuán? Rén yǒu bēi huān lí hé, yuè yǒu yīn qíng yuán
quē, cǐ shì gǔ nán quán. Dàn yuàn rén cháng jiǔ, qiān lǐ gòng chán juān.

作　者　見詩選《飲湖上初晴後雨》p.111

篇　旨

這闋詞作於宋神宗熙寧九年 (1076 A.D.)，蘇軾時任密

州知府。望月懷人，詞中反映了作者既願出世又
熱愛人間的矛盾心情，但全詞的基調是樂觀的。

This lyric was written on the Mid-Autumn night (the fifteenth of the eighth lunar month) of 1076, while Sū Shì was the prefect of Mìzhōu. Looking at the moon, he missed his brother very much. The tone is ambivalent: he wanted to break away from the mundane world, but he also cared too much about people to do so. However, the keynote of this lyric remained optimistic.

注解

1. 水調歌頭 【名詞】 詞牌名 name of the musical tune for which this "cí"
   Shuǐ diào gē tóu   is composed; Prelude to Water Melody

2. 丙辰 【名詞】 宋神宗熙寧九年（1076A.D.），依干支紀
   Bǐng chén   年為丙辰 the year of Bǐng Chén, i.e. 1076 A.D.

3. 中秋 【名詞】 舊曆八月十五日為中秋 the Mid-Autumn Day;
   zhōng qiū   the fifteenth day of the eighth lunar month

4. 歡 huān 【副詞】 歡樂地 happily

5. 飲 yǐn 【動詞】 喝酒 to drink wine

6. 旦 dàn 【時間詞】 天明時 daybreak

   達旦 【動詞語】 到天明 to reach daybreak; till daybreak
   dá dàn

7. 醉 zuì 【形容詞】 酒醉 drunk with too much wine

8. 兼 jiān 【副詞】 同時 concurrently

9. 懷 huái 【動詞】 懷念；想念 to think of; to miss

10. 子由 【名詞】 蘇軾之弟蘇轍 (Chè or Zhé)，字子由。當時
    Zǐ yóu   在濟南作官，兄弟分別已有七年 the coutesy
    name of Sū Shì's younger brother Sū Chè, who was then serving in Jǐnán; the brothers had parted for 7 years.

11. 幾時 【疑問時間詞】 何時；什麼時候 when
    jǐ shí

12. 把 bǎ 【動詞】拿 to hold

把酒
bǎ jiǔ 【動詞語】拿著酒；端著酒 to hold wine [cup]

13. 問 wèn 【動詞】問 to ask; to question

14. 青天
qīng tiān 【名詞語】青色的天 to blue/azure sky

15. 宮 gōng 【名詞】宮殿 palaces

16. 闕 què 【名詞】宮門兩側的崗樓
two watch towers outside of the palace gate

17. 夕 xī 【名詞】夜；晚上 night

今夕
jīn xī 【名詞語】今晚；今夜 this night; tonight

18. 何年
hé nián 【名詞語】哪一年 what year

19. 欲 yù 【動詞】想要 to want; to intend

20. 乘風
chéng fēng 【動詞語】駕風 to ride on winds

21. 歸去
guī qù 【動詞語】回去；此處指回到天上宮闕去
to return; meaning to return to palaces in heaven

22. 惟 wéi 【副詞】只 only

23. 恐 kǒng 【動詞】怕 to fear

24. 瓊 qióng 【名詞】美玉 precious jade

瓊樓
qióng lóu 【名詞語】美玉建成的樓
storied building made of or decorated with jade

25. 玉宇
yù yǔ 【名詞語】玉建成的宮殿 a jewelled palace

135

瓊樓玉宇【名詞語】神話中月宮裡的亭臺樓閣
qióng lóu yù yǔ   [Chines mythology] the palace of the moon

26. 高處 【名詞語】高的地方；指天上宮闕 a high place;
gāo chù   palace in the sky

27. 勝 shēng 【動詞】承受 to bear; to withstand

不勝 【動詞語】不能承受；承受不了
bù shēng   can't bear

28. 寒 hán 【名詞】寒冷 chill; coldness

29. 舞 wǔ 【動詞】舞蹈；跳舞 to dance

起舞 【動詞語】起身舞蹈；站起來跳舞 to rise and dance
qǐ wǔ

30. 弄 nòng 【動詞】玩賞 to enjoy; to amuse by view

31. 清影 【名詞語】清晰的身影 a clear shadow
qīng yǐng

32. 似 sì 【準繫詞】像 to be like; to be the equal of

何似 【準繫詞語】哪比得上 How can it compare with...;
hé sì   How could it be equal to ...

33. 人間 【名詞語】塵世 the human world; the world of mortals
rén jiān

34. 轉 zhuǎn 【動詞】轉過 to turn round

35. 朱閣 【名詞語】朱紅的樓閣 a red chamber
zhū gé

36. 低 dī 【形容詞】低 low

【使動用法】使…低 to make ...low; to lower

37. 綺戶 【名詞語】雕花的門窗 doors or windows with engraved
qǐ hù   patterns

38. 照 zhào 【動 詞】照射 to shine upon

39. 無眠 wú mián 【動 詞 語】不眠；失眠 to be sleepless

【名 詞 語】失眠的人 a sleepless person

40. 應 yīng 【助 動 詞】應該 should; ought to

41. 恨 hèn 【名 詞】遺憾；不滿 regret or grudge

有恨 yǒu hèn 【動 詞 語】有遺憾；有不滿 to have regrets or grudges

42. 何事 hé shì 【名 詞 語】什麼事；為什麼 what; for what; why

43. 向 xiàng 【動 詞】朝向 to face toward

44. 別時 bié shí 【名 詞 語】分別的時候 time of separation

45. 圓 yuán 【動 詞】變圓 to wax; to become full

43. 有 yǒu 【動 詞】有；有…的時候 to have; to have occasions when it is ...

46. 悲 bēi 【形 容 詞】悲傷 sad; grieved

47. 歡 huān 【形 容 詞】歡樂 happy

48. 離 lí 【形 容 詞】離別；離散 separated

49. 合 hé 【形 容 詞】會合；聚合 joined together; united

※ 悲歡離合 bēi huān lí hé 【成 語】悲傷、歡樂、離別、會合 sorrows and joys, partings and reunions--vicissitudes of life

50. 陰 yīn 【形 容 詞】陰晦 cloudy; gloomy

51. 晴 qíng 【形 容 詞】晴朗 fair; clear

52. 圓 yuán 　　【形容詞】圓滿 round; full

53. 缺 quē 　　【形容詞】殘缺；不圓滿 waning [of moon]

※ 陰晴圓缺 【成語】陰晦、晴朗、圓滿、殘缺
　 yīn qíng yuán quē 　　overcast, clear up, wax and wane -- inconstant

54. 此事 　　【名詞語】這種事；指人的悲歡離合與月的陰晴
　 cǐ shì 　　　　　　　　圓缺 these things; such things

55. 古 quán 　　【名詞】古代；自古以來 ancient times; since ancient times

56. 難 quán 　　【形容詞】不易 not easy;

57. 全 quán 　　【形容詞】齊全；完美 nothing missing; perfect

58. 願 yuàn 　　【動詞】願意；希望 to hope; to wish

59. 長久 　　【形容詞】〔壽命〕很長 to live long
　 cháng jiǔ

60. 千里 　　【名詞語】〔相隔〕一千里
　 qiān lǐ 　　　　　　　a thousand li [apart/away]

61. 共 gòng 　　【動詞】共享；共賞 to share; to enjoy together

62. 嬋娟 　　【形容詞】姿態美好 beautiful; graceful
　 chán juān 　　　　　　月色明媚 the moon is bright and charming
　　　　　　　　　　　　此處指代明月或月光
　　　　　　　　　　　　here it stands for the bright moon or moonlight

押 韻

天、年、眠	-iɛn	圓、全、娟 -iuɛn	下平聲一先
寒	-ɑn		上平聲十四寒
間	-an		上平聲十五刪

此三韻音近，詞中通押
These three rhymes are very close and interchangeable in lyrics.

第六闋

臨江仙

宋　蘇軾

夜飲東坡醒復醉，	Yè yǐn Dōng Pō xǐng fù zuì,
歸來髣髴三更。	Guī lái fǎng fú sān gēng.
家童鼻息已雷鳴，	Jiā tóng bí xí yǐ léi míng,
敲門都不應，	Qiāo mén dū bú yìng,
倚杖聽江聲。	Yǐ zhàng tīng jiāng shēng.
長恨此身非我有，	Cháng hèn cǐ shēn fēi wǒ yǒu,
何時忘卻營營？	Hé shí wàng què yíng yíng?
夜闌風靜縠紋平，	Yè lán fēng jìng hú wén píng,
小舟從此逝，	Xiǎo zhōu cóng cǐ shì,
江海寄餘生。	Jiāng hǎi jì yú shēng.

作者　見詩選《飲湖上初晴後雨》p.111

篇旨

描述夜飲歸來靜聽江水流逝而興逃離塵世，追求
自由之心情。《莊子‧列禦寇》：「巧者勞而智者
憂，無能者無所求，飽食而遨遊，汎若不繫之舟
。」可為此詞注腳。

Returning from a long night's drinking, listening to the murmuring flow of
the river, the poet was suddenly struck by the desire of escaping the turmoil
world. Zhuāngzǐ's words: "The clever man wears himself out, the wise man

worries. But the man of no ability has nothing he seeks. He eats his fill and wanders idly about, drifting along like an unmoored boat." (Lièyùkòu) can aptly express the sentiment of the author.

注 解

1. 臨江仙　【名詞】詞牌名 name of the musical tune for which this "cí"
   Lín jiāng Xiān　　　　is composed; Immortal at the River

2. 髣髴　【副詞】同"仿佛"、"彷彿"，好像 as if
   fǎng fú

3. 三更　【時間詞】晚上十一點到一點；半夜
   sān gēng　　　　the third watch --11:00 p.m. - 1:00 a.m.; mid-night

4. 家童　【名詞語】年輕的男用人 a young male domestic servant
   jiā tóng

5. 鼻息　【名詞語】打鼾 (hān)的聲音 sound of snore
   bí xí

6. 雷鳴　【動詞語】雷一般地響 to sound thunderously
   léi míng

7. 敲 qiāo　【動詞】叩打 to tap; to knock

   敲門　【動詞語】叩門；打門 to knock at the door
   qiāo mén

8. 應 yìng　【動詞】回答 to respond; to answer

9. 倚杖　【動詞語】靠著拐杖 leaning on a cane
   yǐ zhàng

10. 恨 hèn　【動詞】遺憾 to regret

11. 此身非我有【判斷句】這個身體不是我（自己）所有的，
    cǐ shēn fēi wǒ yǒu　　意指：被世事束縛失掉自由與自主
    the body is not what I own, meaning that being restrained by worldly affairs, I have lost my freedom and can not keep the initiative in my own hands

140

12. 忘卻　　　　【動詞】忘掉　to forget
　　wàng què

13. 營營　　　　【形容詞】東奔西跑、忙忙碌碌地〔求名求利〕
　　yíng yíng　　　　　　　to be hustling and bustling about [seeking wealth and fame]

14. 夜闌　　　　【時間詞】夜深　late at night
　　yè lán

15. 靜　jìng　　【動詞】靜止下來　to stop; to calm down

16. 縠　hú　　　【名詞】皺紗 (zhòu shā) crepe

17. 縠紋　　　　【名詞語】像皺紗似的細微的波紋
　　hú wén　　　　　　　　the crepe-like ripple

18. 平　píng　　【動詞】平靜下來　to calm down; to become quiet

19. 舟　zhōu　　【名詞】船　a boat

20. 逝　shì　　　【動詞】往；到別的地方去 to go away

21. 江海　　　　【名詞】江海　river and sea
　　jiāng hǎi

22. 寄　jì　　　　【動詞】寄託　to consign; to place on

23. 餘生　　　　【名詞語】餘下的生命 the remaining of one's life
　　yú shēng

押韻

更、聲、生	-əng;	
鳴、營、平	iəng	下平聲八庚

第七闋

鵲橋仙

宋　秦觀

纖雲弄巧，飛星傳恨，銀漢迢迢暗度；

金風玉露一相逢，便勝卻人間無數。

柔情似水，佳期如夢，忍顧鵲橋歸路？

兩情若是久長時，又豈在朝朝暮暮！

Zhùyīn:

Xiānyún nòngqiǎo, fēixīng chuán hèn, Yínhàn tiáotiáo àndù;
Jīnfēng yùlù yì xiāngféng, biàn shèngquè rénjiān wúshù.
Róuqíng sì shuǐ, jiāqī rú mèng, rěn gù quèqiáo guīlù?
Liǎngqíng ruòshì jiǔcháng shí, yòu qǐzài zhāozhāo mùmù!

作者　　秦觀 (1049 -1100 A.D.)，字少游，一字太虛，號淮海居士，揚州高郵人。曾舉進士，然仕官不得意，早卒。其詩、詞甚得蘇軾稱賞，著有《淮海詞》。

Qín Guàn (1049 - 1100 A.D.), courtsy name Shàoyóu or Tàixū, style name 'Retired Scholar of Huáihǎi', was a native of Gāoyóu at Yángzhōu, in present-day Jiāngsū province. He succeeded in the civil service examinations, but was frustrated in his official career and died young. His poems and lyrics were highly esteemed by Sū Shì. His extant work includes the *Collected Lyrics of Huáihǎi*.

篇旨

根據中國神話，織女星與牛郎星被銀河阻隔，不

能相見，但織女星被允許在每年陰曆七月七日的
夜晚，經由喜鵲搭成的橋，到銀河南岸和牛郎相
會一夜，天明前回到北岸。本詞即描述這浪漫、
淒美的一夜，並藉以說明愛情的真諦。

According to Chinese mythology, the stars Weaving Maid (Vega) and Herd
Boy (Altair) were separated by the Milky Way, unable to live together as
lovers. Only once a year in the evening on the seventh day of the seventh
lunar month was the Weaving Maid allowed to cross a bridge formed by
migpies to the south of the Milky Way to join the Herd Boy for the night.
She must return to the north of the Milky Way before dawn. This lyric
artistically describes the rather romantic, sad, and beautiful legend; in the
mean time, it expounds on the true meaning of love.

注解

1. 鵲 què 　【名詞】喜鵲 magpies

2. 橋 qiáo 　【名詞】橋 a bridge

3. 仙 xiān 　【名詞】仙人 an immotal

4. 鵲橋仙 Quèqiáoxiān 　【名詞】詞牌名 Name of the musical tune for which this "cí"
is composed; Immortal on Magpie Bridge

5. 纖 xiān 　【形容詞】輕薄的 light and thin

　纖雲 xiān yún 　【名詞語】輕薄的雲 thin clouds

6. 弄 nòng 　【動詞】顯現 to manifest

7. 巧 qiǎo 　【形容詞】巧妙 ingenious

　　　【名詞】巧妙的形狀 ingenious shape

8. 飛星 fēi xīng 　【名詞語】快速移動的星；指織女星 a shooting star;
a quickly moving star; here: the Weaving Maid

9. 傳 chuán 　【動詞】傳達 to convey

143

10. 恨 hèn 　　【名詞】憾恨；怨恨 regrets; resentment

11. 銀漢 yín hàn 　　【名詞語】銀河；天河 the Silver River; the Milky Way

12. 迢迢 tiáo tiáo 　　【形容詞】疊字 a reduplicative compound
　　　　遙遠 far and remote
　　　　此處意為寬廣 here: vast; broad; wide

13. 暗度 àn dù 　　【動詞語】在暗中度過 to cross over secretly/imperceptibly

14. 金風 jīn fēng 　　【名詞語】秋風；西風；西方在五行中屬金，故稱西風為金風
　　　　the west wind; the autumnal wind
　　　　Among the five primary elements--metal, wood, water, fire, and earth, the metal represents the west, so west wind is also called "metal wind"

15. 玉露 yù lù 　　【名詞語】像玉一樣光潤的露
　　　　the jade-like dew drops

16. 逢 féng 　　【動詞】會面 to meet

　　 一相逢 yì xiāng féng 　　【動詞語】會面一次 to meet once

17. 便 biàn 　　【副詞】就 then

18. 勝卻 shèng què 　　【動詞語】勝過 to surpass; to be better than

19. 人間 rén jiān 　　【名詞語】人世間〔的男女相逢〕
　　　　[the meeting between lovers of] the human world

20. 無數 wú shù 　　【形容詞】許多；許多次 innumerable times

21. 柔情 róu qíng 　　【名詞語】溫柔的情意
　　　　the tender feelings; the affection

22. 似 sì 　　【準繫詞】好像 as if; to be the same as

23. 水 shuǐ 　【名詞】水；無窮無盡的水 water, soft and inexhaustible

24. 佳期 jiā qí 　【名詞語】美好的約會
the happy rendezvous

25. 如 rú 　【準繫詞】好像 to be like

26. 夢 mèng 　【名詞】夢；似真似幻的夢 a dream

27. 忍 rěn 　【形容詞】忍心 to be able to bear

28. 顧 gù 　【動詞】回看 to look back at

忍顧 rěn gù 　【動詞語】忍心回頭看嗎？
Can one bear to look back at ...?
怎麼忍心回頭看？
How could one have the heart to look back at ...?

29. 鵲橋 què qiáo 　【名詞語】由喜鵲搭成的橋
the bridge built by magpies

30. 歸路 guī lù 　【名詞語】回到天河以北的路
the road leading back to the north of the Milky Way

31. 兩情 liǎng qíng 　【名詞語】彼此的情意
the feelings on both sides; the mutual affection

32. 久長 jiǔ cháng 　【形容詞】長久；永恆 long-lasting; eternal

33. 豈 qǐ 　【副詞】哪裡 how; how could ...
用在反問句中強調否定的意思
It is used in a rhetorical question to emphasize a negative meaning.

34. 在 zài 　【動詞】依靠 to rest upon; to rely on

豈在 qǐ zài 　【動詞語】哪裡依靠 How could it depend on ...
不依靠 It doesn't depend on ...

35. 朝 zhāo 　【名詞】早晨 morning

36. 暮 mù　　【名詞】傍晚　evening

　　朝朝暮暮【名詞】疊字　a reduplicative compound
　　zhāo zhāo mù mù　　天天從早到晚〔廝守〕
　　　　　　　　　　　　[staying together] day and night; from morning till evening

押韻

　　度、數、路、暮　　　　-u　　　　去聲七遇

第八闋

如夢令

宋　李清照

| | | — — |
昨夜雨疏風驟，　Zuó yè yǔ shū fēng zòu,

| | | — — |
濃睡不消殘酒。　Nóng shuì bù xiāo cán jiǔ.

| | | — —
試問捲簾人，　Shì wèn juǎn lián rén,

| | | — — |
卻道海棠依舊。　Què dào hǎi táng yī jiù.

— | — |
知否？知否？　Zhī fǒu? Zhī fǒu?

├ | | — — |
應是綠肥紅瘦。　Yīng shì lǜ féi hóng shòu.

146

作者　李清照 (1084 A.D.- 1151? A.D.)，號易安居士，山東濟南人。她常被認爲中國成就最高的女詞人，其晚年作品反映出北宋到南宋之間戰亂中個人與國家的不幸遭際。

Lǐ Qīngzhào (1084-1151 A.D.), style name Yìān Jūshì, was a native of Jǐnán, in present-day Shāndōng province. She is often considered to be China's most accomplished woman poet, whose works reflect both her own personal tragedy and that of the nation during the upheavals of the Northern and Southern Sòng transition.

篇旨

悼惜海棠花爲風雨摧殘，兼有自傷青春易逝之意。

The author mourns for the crabapple blossoms wrecked by the wind and rain, and also laments for her beauty being faded away as time goes by.

注解

1. 如夢令　【名詞】詞牌名 Name of the musical tune for which this "cí"
   Rú mèng Lìng　　　is composed; As in a Dream: a Song

2. 疏 shū　【形容詞】稀疏；不密 sparse; off and on

3. 驟 zòu　【形容詞】急驟；猛烈 heavy; strong

4. 濃睡　【名詞語】很沈很舒服地睡 sound sleep; sleep soundly
   nóng shuì

5. 消 xiāo　【動詞】消除 to get rid of ; to clear up; to dispel

   不消　【動詞語】沒消除掉 did not dispel
   bù xiāo

6. 殘 cán　【形容詞】剩餘的 remnant

   殘酒　【名詞語】剩餘的酒意；剩下來的喝過酒以後的
   cán jiǔ　　　　感覺 a hangover

7. 試問
shì wèn
【動詞語】試著問 try to ask

8. 捲 juǎn
【動詞】把東西彎轉裹成圓筒形 to roll up

9. 簾 lián
【名詞】用竹、布、葦等做成的遮蔽門窗的幕
screen curtain

捲簾人
juǎn lián rén
【名詞語】正在捲簾的丫頭
the young maid who is rolling up the curtain

10. 海棠
hǎi táng
【名詞】海棠樹 Chinese flowering crabapple

11. 依舊
yī jiù
【準繫詞語】如舊；像從前一樣
as usual; as it used to be

12. 否 fǒu
【副詞】不，用在句末，構成是非問句 not, used at
the end of a sentence to form a yes-or-no question

知否
zhī fǒu
【動詞語】知道不？知道不知道？
Do you kow or not? Do you realize ...

13. 應 yīng
【助動詞】應該 should; ought to

14. 綠 lǜ
【名詞】指葉 green, stands for leaves

15. 肥 féi
【形容詞】 fat; lush; growing

16. 紅 hóng
【名詞】指花 red, stands for flowers

17. 瘦 shòu
【形容詞】 thin; frail; fading

押韻

驟、瘦	əu	舊	-iəu	去聲二十六宥
酒	-iəu	否、否	əu	上聲二十五有

宥、有二韻在詞中通押
These two rhymes are interchangeable in lyrics.

148

第九關

醜奴兒

宋　辛棄疾

少年不識愁滋味，	Shào nián bù shí chóu zī wèi,
愛上層樓，愛上層樓，	Aì shàng céng lóu, ài shàng céng lóu,
為賦新詞強說愁，	Wèi fù xīn cí qiǎng shuō chóu.
而今識盡愁滋味，	Ér jīn shí jìn chóu zī wèi,
欲說還休，欲說還休，	Yù shuō huán xiū, yù shuō huán xiū,
卻道天涼好個秋。	Què dào tiān liáng hǎo gè qiū.

作者　辛棄疾(1140-1207A.D.)字幼安，號稼軒，南宋初山東濟南人。少年時曾組織義軍抵抗金兵，是南宋著名的愛國詞人。他的詞題材廣闊，風格豪放，不拘守一定的格律，在文學史上跟蘇軾齊名。

Xīn Qìjí (1140-1207 A.D.), courtesy name Yòuān and style name Jiàxuān, was a native of Jǐnán in Shāndōng province. In his youth he organized a volunteer army to fight the Jurchens, for which he gained eternal renown as the leading patriotic poet of Southern Sòng dynasty. His lyrics cover a broad range of subject matter and manifest a free style that does not strictly abide by the rules of versification. His lyric-songs are usually ranked as equal to those of Sū Shì.

篇旨

以強說愁來描寫少年的不識愁，以欲說還休來描寫年華老大者的識盡愁，用對比的方式來突顯如今強烈的悲涼之感。

149

The gloomy mood is what youngsters don't understand but like to talk about. However, when one is really caught in that mood, one gets so overwhelmed and doesn't want to speak about it any more. By way of contrast the present sadness is made even more acute.

注解

1. 醜奴兒　【名詞】詞牌名 name of the musical tune for which this "cí"
   Chǒu nú ér　　　　is composesd; An Ugly Slave

2. 少年　【名詞】年輕人　youth
   shào nián

3. 識　shí; shì　【動詞】知道；了解 to know; to understand

4. 愁　chóu　【名詞】憂愁　melancholy; grief; sorrow

5. 滋味　【名詞】滋味；味道 taste; flavor
   zī wèi

   愁滋味　【名詞語】憂愁的味道 the taste of grief/sorrow
   chóu zī wèi

6. 層樓　【名詞語】有很多層的樓 a storeyed building
   céng lóu

7. 賦　fù　【動詞】作詩、詞等 to compose ...

8. 新詞　【名詞語】新作的詞
   xīn cí　　　　　newly composed lyrics

9. 強　qiǎng　【副詞】勉力　to make efforts to
   　　　　　努力　to exert oneself to

10. 說　shuō　【動詞】述說；描述　to talk about; to describe

11. 而今　【副詞】現在 now; at present
    ér jīn

12. 盡　jìn　【副詞】到極限；徹底 to reach the extremity; thoroughly

識盡 shí jìn	【動詞語】	了解到極限；徹底了解 to understand thoroughly/completely	
13. 欲 yù	【動詞】	想要 to want to; to intend to	
14. 休 xiū	【動詞】	停 to cease; to stop	
15. 卻 què	【副詞】	反而 contrarily; instead	
16. 道 dào	【動詞】	說 to say	
17. 天 tiān	【名詞】	天氣 the weather	
18. 涼 liáng	【形容詞】	涼爽 cool and comfortable	
19. 好個 hǎo gè	【形容詞】	好一個N；多麼好的一個N what a wonderful [N].	
20. 秋 qiū	【名詞】	秋天 autumn; an autumn day	

押韻

味、味	-uəi	去聲五未
樓、樓、愁	-əu	
休、休、秋	-iəu	下平聲十一尤

兩片首句自相押去聲五未，其餘押下平聲十一尤

The first line of the two stanzas rhyme to each other in going tone; the rest rhyme with each other in level tone.

曲選

天淨沙　秋思

元　馬致遠

151

枯藤老樹昏鴉，　　　Kū téng lǎo shù hūn yā,

小橋流水人家，　　　Xiǎo qiáo liú shuǐ rén jiā,

古道西風瘦馬，　　　Gǔ dào xī fēng shòu mǎ,

夕陽西下，　　　　　Xī yáng xī xià,

斷腸人在天涯。　　　Duàn cháng rén zài tiān yá.

作者　馬致遠 (1250-1324 A.D.)，號東籬，元朝大都（今北京）人。曾在浙江省做過官，後來歸隱山林。他是元朝最有名的散曲作家。

Mǎ Zhìyuǎn (1250-1324 A.D.), style name Dōnglí, was a native of the Yuán capital of Dàdū, present-day Běijīng. He once served as an official in Zhèjiāng province, but soon resigned and lived in seclusion. He was the most famous Yuán dynasty writer of *sǎnqǔ*, a genre of verses akin to the Táng and Sòng lyric-songs, but more colloquial in their use of language.

篇旨

以淒清衰颯的秋暮景色，襯托出天涯羈客的愁思。

A dreary, desolate scene of an autumnal evening is used here to foil the sad, nostalgic feeling of a wanderer staying long at a remote place.

注解

1. 天淨沙　【名詞】曲牌名　name of the musical tune for which this
   Tiān jìng shā　　　　　　　"qǔ" is composed; Sky-Clear Sand

2. 秋思　【名詞語】秋日愁思　autumn thoughts; a lonesome and
   qiū sī　　　　　　　　　　desolate mood in autumn

3. 枯 kū 【形容詞】乾枯的 withered

4. 藤 téng 【名詞】一種蔓（màn）生的植物；藤子 vines; rattan

   枯藤 kū téng 【名詞語】乾枯的藤子 withered vines/rattan

5. 昏 hūn 【時間詞】黃昏的時候兒 dusk

6. 鴉 yā 【名詞】烏（wū）鴉 crows

   昏鴉 hūn yā 【名詞語】黃昏時的烏鴉 crows at dusk

7. 橋 yā 【名詞】橋 a bridge

8. 流水 liú shuǐ 【名詞語】流動的水 flowing water

9. 人家 rén jiā 【名詞語】人居住的宅院 human dwellings

10. 古 gǔ 【形容詞】古舊的；古老的 old; ancient

11. 道 dào 【名詞】道路 a road

    古道 gǔ dào 【名詞語】古舊的道路 an ancient road

12. 西風 xī fēng 【名詞語】從西面吹來的風；秋風 the west wind

13. 瘦 shòu 【形容詞】瘦弱 lean; thin

14. 馬 mǎ 【名詞】馬 a horse

    瘦馬 shòu mǎ 【名詞語】很瘦弱的馬 a lean horse

15. 夕陽 xī yáng 【名詞語】傍晚的太陽 the sun at dusk; the setting sun

16. 西下　【動詞語】向西邊落下去 to set wastward
　　xī xià

17. 斷 duàn　【動詞】斷裂 to break

18. 腸 cháng　【名詞】腸 the intestine; the bowels

　　斷腸　【動詞語】猶 "心碎"，形容悲痛到極點
　　duàn cháng　　　　　　heart-broken

※ 心碎腸斷、柔腸寸斷、腸斷心碎：都用來形容極度的
　　　　　　　　　　　　　　　　悲痛 in extreme sorrow

19. 斷腸人　【名詞語】極度悲痛的人 a heart-broken person
　　duàn cháng rén

20. 天涯　【名詞語】天邊；極遠的地方
　　tiān yá　　　　　　the end of the world; the remotest corner of the earth

押韻

| 鴉、涯 | -ia | 家 | -a | 下平聲六麻 |
| 馬 | -a | 下 | -ia | 上聲二十一馬 |

下平聲六麻與上聲二十一馬同音不同調，曲中通押

These two rhymes differ only in tones, and they are interchangeable in song-poems.

第一篇

漁父

戰國　　屈原

作者

屈原 (343-290 B.C.) 姓屈，名平，字原，是楚國的王族。他博聞強記，品德高潔，文學才華極高，也有治國的才能及興趣，楚懷王很賞識信任他，任命他做三閭大夫。後來由於同僚嫉妒進讒，漸受疏遠，終遭放逐。他在被放逐的期間創作了《離騷》、《哀郢》等詩篇來抒發憂國憂民及自傷懷才不遇的情懷。最後他對腐敗的政治、污濁的人世徹底絕望，終於投入汩羅江自殺了。他是中國南方文學《楚辭》最重要的作家。

Qū Yuán (343-290 B.C.), surnamed Qū, named Píng, courtesy name Yuán, was a clansman of the royal family of the ancient state of Chǔ. He had broad learning and a powerful memory. Endowed with a noble character and great literary talent, he was an able government administrator, appreciated by King Huái of Chǔ (r. 328-299 B.C.) and appointed to the post of Grandee of the Three Households. Later, however, he was slandered by envious colleagues and lost the King's favor. While living in exile, he wrote the Lísāo (On Encountering Sorrow), Aīyǐng (A Lament for Yǐng), and other poetic works expressing his deep concern over the fate of the nation and the people, as well as his personal frustration over the waste of his own talents. According to tradition, he eventually threw himself into the Mìluó River out of despair over the corruptness of the world of mortal men. He was the most important writer in the Chǔcí genre.

篇旨

屈原藉與漁父的問答表明他不願同流合污，寧願"伏清白以死直"的高尚情操。篇幅短，寓意深，是楚辭中的精品。

Through a dialogue between a fisheman and himself, Qū Yuán firmly asserts his unswerving will -- he would rather die to preserve his purity than wallow in the mire within a corrupt world. A short piece with profound implications, this is generally recognized as a gem in the *Chǔ Cí* collection.

屈原既放，遊於江潭，行吟澤畔；顏色憔悴，形容枯槁。漁父見而問之曰：“子非三閭大夫與？何故至於斯？”

屈原曰：“舉世皆濁我獨清，眾人皆醉我獨醒，是以見放。”

漁父曰：“聖人不凝滯於物，而能與世推移。世人皆濁，何不淈其泥而揚其波？眾人皆醉，何不餔其糟而歠其醨？何故深思高舉，自令放為？”

Zhùyīn:

Qū Yuán jì fàng, yóu yú jiāng tán, xíng yín zé pàn; yán sè qiáo cuì, xíng róng kū gǎo. Yúfù jiàn ér wèn zhī yuē: “Zǐ fēi sānlú Dàifū yú? Hé gù zhì yú sī?”

Qū Yuán yuē: “Jǔ shì jiē zhuó wǒ dú qīng, zhòng rén jiē zuì wǒ dú xǐng, shì yǐ jiàn fàng.”

Yúfù yuē: “Shèng rén bù níng zhì yú wù, ér néng yǔ shì tuī yí. Shì rén jiē zhuó, hé bù gǔ qí ní ér yáng qí bō? Zhòng rén jiē zuì, hé bù bū qí zāo ér chuò qí lí? Hé gù shēn sī gāo jǔ, zì lìng fàng wéi?”

注 解

1. 漁父　【名詞】漁翁；打漁的老頭兒。“父”是對老年人的尊
   yú fù　　　　　稱。此處為篇名

   an old fisherman; "fù" is an honorific term for someone of an advanced age; here, it is the title of one of Qū Yuán's writing.

2. 屈原　【名詞】人名。姓屈名平，字原，戰國時代楚國的大臣
   Qū Yuán　　　及著名的作家

   a personal name. Surnamed Qū, named Píng, and courtesy name Yuán (343-290 B.C.), was a minister in the state of Chǔ

156

during the Warring States period, and also a famous writer.

3. 既 jì 【副詞】已經 to have...; already

4. 放 fàng 【動詞】放逐；被放逐 to exile; to be exiled

5. 遊 yóu 【動詞】漫遊 to wander

6. 潭 tán 【名詞】深水池 a deep pool

江潭 jiāng tán 【名詞語】泛指有很多河、很多湖的地區 generally referring to a region with many rivers and lakes

7. 吟 yín 【動詞】吟詠；聲調抑揚、很有節奏地誦讀詩文 to chant or intone; to sing or recite verses in a melodious way

◆ 聲調 shēngdiào   tone; voice
◆ 抑揚 yìyáng   cadence; rise and fall
◆ 節奏 jiézòu   rhythm
◆ 誦讀 sòngdú   to read aloud; to recite

8. 行吟 xíng yín 【動詞語】一邊走一邊吟詠 to chant while walking

9. 澤 zé 【名詞】沼澤 a marsh; a swamp

澤畔 zé pàn 【名詞語】澤邊 marsh side

10. 顏色 yán sè 【名詞】面色 complexion

11. 憔悴 qiáo cuì 【形容詞】灰黃 sallow

12. 形 xíng 【名詞】形體 shape of a body; figure

13. 容 róng 【名詞】面容 face

14. 枯槁 kū gǎo 【形容詞】乾枯 haggard

157

15. 三閭大夫【名詞】楚國官名，主管楚國屈、景、昭 (Zhāo) 三姓
    sān lú dài fū　　　　王族的事務 Grandee of Three Households

　　　　◆ 主管 zhǔguǎn　　　be responsible for; be in charge of
　　　　◆ 王族 wángzú　　　persons of royal lineage

16. 與 yú　【疑問語氣語】表示自己以為是…，但不能十分確
　　　　　　　　　　　定，要求証實時的疑問語氣，可以譯
　　　　　　　　　　　作 " 嗎 " 或 " 呢 "
　　　　　　　　　　　此處 "N1非…N2與" 應譯作 "N1不是
　　　　　　　　　　　…N2嗎？"

　　　　　　　　　　a particle indicating an interrogative tone when one
　　　　　　　　　　thinks something is so but not quite sure, and asks
　　　　　　　　　　for confirmation. Depending on the context, it can
　　　　　　　　　　be rendered in modern Chinese as " 嗎 " or " 呢 ".
　　　　　　　　　　Here "N1非 N2 與 ?" should be translated as " Isn't
　　　　　　　　　　N1 N2?" -- " Aren't you the Grandee of Three
　　　　　　　　　　Households?"

17. 至 zhì　【動詞】到；到達 to reach; to come to

18. 斯 sī　【指示代詞】此；這個地步 this; this situation

19. 舉 jǔ　【形容詞】全 entire; whole

　　舉世　【名詞語】全世界；整個人世 the whole world
　　jǔ shì

20. 濁 zhuó　【形容詞】混濁 muddy; turbid
　　　　　　　　　　卑污 despicable and filthy

21. 獨 dú　【副詞】獨自 alone

22. 清 qīng　【形容詞】清潔；潔淨 clean; spotless
　　　　　　　　　　高潔 noble and pure

23. 眾人　【名詞語】大家 the masses
　　zhòng rén

24. 醉 zuì　【形容詞】沈醉 drunken

昏憒；糊塗 muddle-headed

25. 醒 xǐng 【形容詞】清醒 awake; sober

26. 見 jiàn 【結構助詞】相當於 " 被 " ；是表示被動的助詞
like "bèi", it's a passive marker; to be V-ed

◆ 結構助詞　　　　　a structural particle
jiégòu zhùcí

見放　【動詞語】被放逐　to be exiled
jiàn fàng　　　⟶ 受到放逐 to suffer an exile

27. 聖人 【名詞語】具有最高智慧、深通事理的人
shèng rén　　　a sage; a man of great wisdom and resourcefulness

◆ 智慧 *zhìhuì*　　　wisdom
◆ 深通 *shēntōng*　　to understand profoundly and thoroughly

28. 凝 níng 【動詞】凝結 to freeze; to congeal

29. 滯 zhì 【動詞】停滯；不流通 to stagnate

凝滯 【動詞】水凝結不流通，此處比喻觀念、想法固執不
níngzhì　　　變或堅持己見、不肯改變

[For water] to congeal and stagnate, here used to liken to a state
of mind that refuses to change or to adapt; to be inflexible

◆ 比喻 *bǐyù*　　　to liken
◆ 觀念 *guānniàn*　　concepts
◆ 固執 *gùzhí*　　　stubborn; obstinate

30. 物 wù 【名詞】存在於天地間的一切事物，此處指外在的時
勢 things in the world; here: the external circumstances within
his time

◆ 外在 *wàizài*　　objective; external

31. 世 shì 【名詞】時代 time; age; epoch

32. 推 tuī 　【動詞】推動 to move on; to move forward

33. 移 yí 　【動詞】轉移 to shift; to change course

　推移 　【動詞】推動轉移 to move and shift
　tuī yí 　　　──→改變 to change

　與世推移【動詞語】跟時代〔情況〕一起改變
　yǔ shì tuī yí 　　　　　　to change along with the entire world

34. 淈 gǔ 　【形容詞】混 (hùn) 濁 muddy; turbid

　　　　　【使動用法】使混濁 to make ... turbid; to muddy
　　　　　　　　──→把…弄混濁 to cause ... to be turbid
　　　　　　　　──→把…弄髒 to cause ... to be filthy

35. 泥 ní 　【名詞】濕土 mud

36. 揚 yáng 　【動詞】揚起 to raise

37. 波 bō 　【名詞】波浪 waves

38. 餔 bū 　【動詞】吃 to eat; to feed on

39. 糟 zāo 　【名詞】酒糟 distillers' grains; residue of fermented grains after the alcoholic contents have been distilled; dregs

40. 歠 chuò 　【動詞】同"啜"，喝 to drink

41. 醨 lí 　【名詞】薄 (bó) 酒；味道很淡的劣 (liè)酒 weak wine; wine of low quality

42. 深 shēn 　【副詞】深深地 deeply

43. 思 sī 　【動詞】思考 to ponder over; to deliberate

　深思 　【動詞語】深深地思考；思考得很深，指憂(yōu)國憂民
　shēn sī 　　　　　to ponder deeply and profoundly; here referring to being concerned about the country and the people

44. 高 gāo 【副詞】高尚地 in a noble attitute; exaltedly

45. 舉 jǔ 【動詞】行動 to act

高舉 【動詞語】高尚地行動；行動得很高尚；指行為超過
gāo jǔ 一般人，表現得與眾不同
to act or behave in a lofty way, unlike the general public

◆ 超過 chāoguò to surpass
◆ 與眾不同 different from other people;
yǔzhòngbùtóng to be extraordinary

淈其泥、揚其波、餔其糟、歠其醨：意思是跟世人同流
gǔ qí ní yáng qí bō bū qí zāo chò qí lí 合污，一起做不正
當的事 to wallow in the
mire with others and together
do improper things

46. 自 zì 【代名詞】自己 self

47. 令 lìng 【動詞】使 to cause; to make ... happen

自令 【動詞語】自己使自己 to cause oneself ...
zì lìng

在"自＋V"的結構中，"自"兼有副詞和反身代名詞的
作用。"自令"意思是"自己使自己"或"自己讓自己"
In the grammatical construction "自＋V," the word "自" functions both as an
adverb and a reflexive personal pronoun. "自令" means "one makes onself" or
"one causes oneself..."

自令放 【動詞語】自己使自己被放逐 to cause oneself to be exiled
zì lìng fàng

48. 為 wéi 【語氣詞】用於句末，表示疑問，可譯成"呢？"
used at the end of an interrogative sentence, functioning as a
question mark.

屈原曰："吾聞之：'新沐者必彈冠，新浴者必振
衣'，安能以身之察察，受物之汶汶者乎？寧赴湘流，

161

葬身於江魚之腹中，安能以皓皓之白，而蒙世俗之塵埃乎？"

漁父莞爾而笑，鼓枻而去。歌曰："滄浪之水清兮，可以濯吾纓；滄浪之水濁兮，可以濯吾足。"遂去，不復與言。

Qū Yuán yuē: "Wú wén zhī: 'Xīn mù zhě bì tán guān, xīn yù zhě bì zhèn yī.' ān néng yǐ shēn zhī chá chá, shòu wù zhī mén mén zhě hū? Nìng fù Xiāng liú, zàng shēn yú jiāng yú zhī fù zhōng, ān néng yǐ hào hào zhī bái, ér méng shì sú zhī chén āi hū?"

Yúfù wǎněr ér xiào, gǔ yì ér qù. Gē yuē: "Cāngláng zhī shuǐ qīng xī, kě yǐ zhuó wú yīng; cāngláng zhī shuǐ zhuó xī, kě yǐ zhuó wú zú." Suì qù, bú fù yǔ yán.

49. 新 xīn 【副詞】不久前；剛 recently; newly

50. 沐 mù 【動詞】洗頭髮 to wash hair; to shampoo

51. 彈 tán 【動詞】用手指輕敲 to flip with [one's] fingers

52. 冠 guān 【名詞】帽子 a hat

彈冠 tán guān 【動詞語】彈彈帽子〔把上面的灰塵彈掉〕 to flip [the dust off] a hat

◆ 灰塵 huīchén dust; dirt

53. 浴 yù 【動詞】洗澡 (zǎo) to bathe; to take a bath

54. 振 zhèn 【動詞】抖 (dǒu) 動 to shake

振衣 zhèn yī 【動詞語】抖抖衣服〔把上面的灰塵抖掉〕 to shake [the dust off] one's clothes

55. 察察 chá chá 【形容詞】清潔；乾淨 clean

162

身之察察【名詞語】"身之察察"就是"察察之身";清潔的
shēn zhī chá chá   身體;乾乾淨淨的身體 'my clean body'
This is a case of modifier postposition, here used for
emphatic purpose. See n. 57 below.

56. 受 shòu 【動詞】接受 to accept; to be influenced by

57. 汶汶 【形容詞】污濁;蒙塵垢 dirty; muddy
mén mén

物之汶汶者【名詞語】汶汶之物;污濁的東西;骯骯髒髒
wù zhī mén mén zhě   (āng āng zāng zāng) 的東西 'dirty things'

形容詞後置 Modifier Postposition:
文言中的名詞語通常是定語在前,被修飾的中心詞
在後,但若作者要突顯中心詞,往往把中心詞提前
而把定語放到中心詞後面去,然後再加一個"者"
字來複指那個中心詞。

In classical Chinese, a noun phrase usually comprises an adjectival
modifier and the noun it modifies, with the modifier preceding the noun.
However, if the writer wishes to highlight the noun in the sentence, he
will often place the modified noun in front of the adjectival modifier. In
such cases, the modified pronoun "zhě" is attached to te adjectival
modifier to reiterate the modified noun. As in this phrase:
"mén mén zhī wù" ---> "wù zhī mén mén zhě"

58. 赴 fù 【動詞】奔 (bēn) 赴;很快地到…去,此處是投 (tóu) 入的意
思 to go straight toward; to head for. here: 'to throw into'

59. 湘 Xiāng【名詞】湘江,也叫湘水,在湖南省 River Xiāng, in Húnán
province

60. 流 liú 【名詞】流水 water; current

湘流 【名詞語】湘江的流水 the current of the Xiāng River
Xiāng liú

61. 葬 zàng 【動詞】埋葬 to bury

62. 江魚 【名詞語】江中的魚 river fish
jiāng yú

163

63. 腹 fù　　【名詞】肚子　abdomen; belly

64. 皓皓　　【形容詞】明亮　bright; luminous; shining
　　hào hào

65. 白 bái　　【形容詞】純潔　white; pure

　　　　　　　【用作名詞】意思是 "純白的本質"
　　　　　　　　　　　　　　whiteness; purity

66. 蒙 méng　【動詞】蒙受　to sustain

67. 世俗　　【名詞】社會上流傳的風俗習慣　customs and traditions;
　　shì sú　　　　　　　　　　　social conventions; secular; worldly

68. 塵埃　　【名詞】塵土　dust and dirt
　　chén āi

69. 莞爾　　【副詞】微笑著　smilingly
　　wǎn ěr

　　莞爾而笑【動詞語】微微地笑了一笑　to smile engagingly
　　wǎn ěr ér xiào

70. 鼓 gǔ　　【動詞】拍打　to row

71. 枻 yì　　【名詞】槳 (jiǎng)　oars

　　鼓枻　　【動詞語】打槳；用槳打水使船前進　to move a boat with oars
　　gǔ yì　　　　　　　　——→ 划船　to row a boat

72. 歌 gē　　【動詞】唱歌　to sing

73. 滄浪　　【名詞】水名　name of a river
　　Cāng láng

74. 可以　　【動詞語】可用它來；可用來　can be used to …
　　kě yǐ

75. 濯 zhuó　【動詞】洗滌 (dí)　to wash; to cleanse

164

76. 纓 yīng 【名詞】帽帶子 chin strap for holding a hat

77. 足 zú 【名詞】腳 foot; feet

78. 去 qù 【動詞】離開 to leave; to depart

79. 復 fù 【副詞】再 again; any more

80. 言 yán 【動詞】說話 to speak

補充生字

◎ 1. 執著 【形容詞】堅持一種觀念、態度、理想而不放棄
　　　 zhí zhuó　　　　　　　　persistent in upholding a concept, attitude, or ideal

◎ 2. 豁達 【形容詞】性格開朗；氣量大 generous or magnanimous
　　　 huò dá

◎ 3. 灑脫 【形容詞】〔性情、胸懷〕自然、脫俗 casual and care-free
　　　 sǎ tuō　　　　　　　　　[usually said of **a person's character**]

◎ 4. 瀟灑 【形容詞】〔神情舉止〕自然文雅 natural and elegant; dashing
　　　 xiāo sǎ　　　　　　　　 and refined [usually said of **a man's manner**]

第二篇

蘭亭集序

晉　　王羲之

作者　王羲之 (321-379 A.D.) 字逸少，會稽人。曾做過右軍
　　　參軍，故又稱王右軍。他是東晉最傑出的書法家

165

，胸懷曠達，愛好山水。

Wáng Xīzhī (321-379 A.D.), courtesy name Yìshào, was a native of Kuàijī, present-day Shàoxīng in Zhèjiāng province. He served as Consultant to General of the Right, hence he is also known as Wang Yòujūn. He was the most outstanding calligrapher of the Eastern Jìn period, known for his breadth of vision and sensitivity to the beauties of nature.

篇旨

人世美景、美情、美境，瞬息即逝，與之相應的欣悅與悵惘，也飄忽如風；詩文卻能以定格的方式爲時、事、情留下鮮明深刻的痕跡，使不同時代的讀者同感共鳴。作者爲蘭亭集作序，指出此點，堪稱要言不繁，古今獨步。王羲之以行書寫的蘭亭集序，筆勢矯健靈動，豪放瀟灑，公認爲中國書史上無可超越的傑作，摹本流傳不絕，至今仍爲書法愛好者寶愛。

In our mundane world, beautiful scenery, wonderful feelings, and splendid circumstances are all transient, fleeting by in an instant; the corresponding personal joy and sorrow also fluctuate like unstable winds. Through literary works, however, one can capture a precise moment and make a penetrating and distinct impression of times, events, and feelings, which arouse the sympathy of readers for generations to come. The author succinctly makes such an argument while writing a preface for the Lántíng gathering, and it is unique in this regard. Wáng Xīzhī wrote the preface in his famous running hand calligraphy, which was vigorous and flexible, bold yet natural, commonly recognized as an unsurpassable masterpiece. Even to this day versions of it in rubbings and tracings are still treasured by lovers and collectors of Chinese calligraphy

　　永和九年，歲在癸丑，暮春之初，會於會稽山陰之蘭亭，修禊事也。群賢畢至，少長咸集。此地有崇山峻嶺，茂林修竹，又有清流激湍，映帶左右，引以爲流觴曲水，列坐其次，雖無絲竹管絃之盛，一觴一詠，亦足以暢敘幽情。是日也，天朗氣清，惠風和暢，仰觀宇宙之大，俯察品類之盛，所以游目騁懷，足以極視聽之娛，信可樂也。

Zhùyīn:

Yǒnghé jiǔ nián, suì zài guǐ chǒu, mù chūn zhī chū, huì yú Kuàijī Shānyīn zhī Lán Tíng, xiū xì shì yě. Qún xián bì zhì, shào zhǎng xián jí. Cǐ dì yǒu chóng shān jùn lǐng, mào lín xiū zhú, yòu yǒu qīng liú jī tuān, yìng dài zuǒ yòu, yǐn yǐ wéi liú shāng qū shuǐ, liè zuò qí cì, suī wú sī zhú guǎn xián zhī shèng, yì shāng yì yǒng, yì zú yǐ chàng xù yōu qíng. Shì rì yě, tiān lǎng qì qīng, huì fēng hé chàng, yǎng guān yǔ zhòu zhī dà, fǔ chán pǐn lèi zhī shèng, suǒ yǐ yóu mù chéng huái, zú yǐ jí shì tīng zhī yú, xìn kě lè yě.

注 解

1. 蘭亭　【名詞】在紹興縣西南，有亭名蘭亭
   Lán tíng　　Orchid Pavilion, to the southeast of present-day Shàoxīng district of Zhèjiāng province

2. 集 jí　【名詞】把詩文等編在一起形成的書
   a collection of literary works

3. 序 xù　【名詞】書前的介紹文　a preface; an introduction

4. 永和　【名詞】晉穆帝年號 (345-361)；永和九年為公元三五三年
   Yǒnghé　　the reign title of Emperor Mù of Jìn (345-361 A.D.); the ninth year of Yǒnghé was 353 A.D.

5. 癸丑　【名詞】用干支紀年法計算，永和九年是癸丑年
   guǐ chǒu　　Using the ten Celestial Stems along with the twelve Terrestrial Branches to designate years, the ninth year of the Yǒnghé reign was the year of Guǐ Chǒu.

6. 暮春　【名詞語】陰曆春季的第三月為暮春
   mù chūn　　late Spring; the third lunar month of the year

7. 初 chū　【名詞】起始；開端 (duān) beginning

暮春之初【名詞語】三月初上巳日，即陰曆三月三日
mù chūn zhī chu　　the first day of Sì (one of the 12 Terrestrial Branches) in the third lunar month, i.e., the third day of the third lunar month

167

8. 會 huì 　【動詞】集會；聚會 to gather; to get together

9. 會稽 　【名詞】郡名，包括今江蘇東部、浙江西部一帶地區
Kuàijī 　name of a commandery encompassing the territory from the eastern parts of present-day Jiāngsū province to the western parts of present-day Zhèjiāng province.

10. 山陰 　【名詞】今浙江紹興縣
Shānyīn 　place name; present-day Shàoxīng district in Zhèjiāng province

11. 修 xiū 　【動詞】舉行某種活動
to hold or to perform a certain ceremony/activity

12. 禊 xì 　【名詞】祭名，古人祓 (fú) 除不祥的祭祀
name of a sacrifice; a purification sacrifice

修禊事【動詞語】舉行禊祭之事；指三月上巳臨水洗濯、祓 (fú)
xiū xì shì 　　除不祥的祭祀活動
to hold a purification ceremony; [among the old Chinese literati] to hold a drinking party on the third day of the third lunar month at some scenic spot to eliminate evil influence

13. 群賢 　【名詞語】成群的賢士；眾多才德之士
qún xián 　　a group of worthies and scholars

14. 畢 bì 　【副詞】完全 totally; completely

15. 至 zhì 　【動詞】到達 to arrive; to attend

16. 少長 　【名詞】年少的、年長的
shào zhǎng 　　the young and the old

17. 咸 xián 　【副詞】皆；都 all

18. 集 jí 　【動詞】集聚；聚在一起 to assemble; to get together

19. 崇 chóng【形容詞】高聳 (sǒng) 的；巍峨 (wéi é) 的 tall; lofty

20. 峻 jùn 　【形容詞】險峻；危險難行的 precipitous

21. 嶺 lǐng 　【名詞】山脊 (jǐ) mountain ridges

22. 茂 mào 　【形容詞】茂盛　dense; luxuriant

茂林　【名詞語】茂盛的樹林　dense woods; luxuriant forests
mào lín

23. 修 xiū 　【形容詞】修長；高　long; tall

修竹　【名詞語】高大挺秀的竹子　tall and straight bamboos
xiū zhú

24. 清流　【名詞語】清澈的河水　crystal-clear stream
qīng liú

25. 激 jī 　【形容詞】急速　swift and torrential

激湍　【名詞語】急速流動的水　swift torrents; a large amount of water
jī tuān 　　　　　　　　moving very quickly

26. 映帶　【動詞】…互相襯托；…把兩岸景物映現襯托出來
yìng dài 　　　　to highlight each other; [said of a beautiful natural scene] mountains, lakes, tress, flowers, etc. in their perspective that merge together to form an enchanting sight

27. 引 yǐn 　【動詞】引導　to lead; to drench

28. 流觴　【動詞語】使酒杯流動；用漆製的酒杯盛酒，放在彎曲
liú shāng 　　　　小溪的水面上，使它從上游漂浮下來，止於
　　　　　　　　某地，坐在該地近處的人即取飲，故稱流觴
　　　　　　　　to float a lacqerware wine cup down the current of a winding creek, so that whoever sitting nearby can pick up the cup and partake of the wine

29. 曲水　【名詞語】引導河水使它成為一條彎曲流動的小溪
qū shuǐ 　　　　a curve stemming from the main course of water flow to form a tributary stream [near which people can sit]

30. 列坐　【動詞語】排列地坐；一個挨一個地坐
liè zuò 　　　　to sit side by side in a line

31. 其次　【名詞語】其旁；此處指曲水水邊
qí cì 　　　　its side; along the loop/curve by the river

169

32. 絲竹　【名詞】絃樂器及管樂器，如琴瑟簫(xiāo)笛(dí)之類
sī zhú　　　　　silk and bamboo; stringed music and piped music

33. 管絃　【名詞】竹管和絲絃，即絲竹
guǎn xián　　　　pipes and strings

34. 一觴　【動詞語】喝一觴酒　to drink a cup of wine
yì shāng

35. 一詠　【動詞語】詠一首詩　to chant a poem
yì yǒng

36. 足以　【合成詞】足夠用來　sufficient to be used to ...
zú yǐ

　　　　　　　這是由形容詞 "足" 和介詞 "以" 結合而成的 "合成詞"
　　　　　　　，譯成白話是 "足夠用來…"。因 "足以" 基本上用在表
　　　　　　　示被動性的主語之後，故最準確的譯法應該是 "足夠被用
　　　　　　　來…"。由於句子的被動性很明顯，儘管省去被字，聽的
　　　　　　　人還能了解，所以習慣上還是譯成 "足夠用來…"

　　　　　This is a **composite word** comprised of the adjective "zú" and the
　　　　　preposition"yǐ"; it can be rendered into spoken Chinese as "Zú gòu yòng lái ...".
　　　　　Since this expression is almost always used after a subject conveying a passive
　　　　　sense, it should be rendered more precisely as "zú gòu bèi yòng lái ...". Because
　　　　　the passive nature of such sentence is obvious to the reader or listener whether the
　　　　　word "bèi" is expressed or not, the sense of this **composite word** is usuaally
　　　　　translated into spoken Chinese as "zú gòu yòng lái ..."

37. 暢 chàng　【副詞】暢快地　happily; heartily

38. 敘 xù　　【動詞】敘談；發抒　to chat; to express

39. 幽情　【名詞語】幽深的情懷；內心深處真實的感情
yōu qíng　　　　　deep feelings

　　　一觴一詠，　亦　　足 以　暢 敘 幽 情。
　　　s/o.　　　adv　adj. prep adv v　　o

40. 天朗　【描寫句】天色晴朗
tiān lǎng　　　　　the sky is fair and clear

41. 氣清　【描寫句】空氣清新
qì qīng　　　　　the air is pure and refreshing

42. 惠風　【名詞語】輕柔的風
　　huì fēng　　　　　　　gentle breezes

43. 和暢　【形容詞】和暖舒暢
　　hé chàng　　　　　　　warm and pleasant

是日也，天 朗 氣 清，惠風　和暢。
adv.　 s　pa　s　pa　s　　　pa

44. 仰觀　【動詞語】抬頭觀賞
　　yǎng guān　　　　　　to lift the head to observe and enjoy

45. 宇宙　【名詞】天地　the universe
　　yǔ zhòu

46. 俯察　【動詞語】低頭察看
　　fǔ chá　　　　　　　to lower the head to observe and examine

47. 品類　【名詞語】萬物
　　pǐn lèi　　　　　　　all kinds of things

48. 盛 shèng　【形容詞】眾多　numerous

〔人〕，仰　觀 宇宙之大 俯察 品類之盛。
[s].　adv　v　 o　　adv v　 o

49. 以 yǐ　【介詞】用；憑藉　with; to use; to depend on

所以 v-o【名詞語】以之 v-o 之物；憑藉它來 v-o 之物
suǒ yǐ v-o　　　　　　　　that which one depends on to v-o
　　　　　所＋介詞＋動詞＋賓語＝名詞語
　　　　　所＋preposition＋verb＋object＝noun phrase
　　　　　所＋以＋游目騁懷＝用來游目騁懷的方法
　　　　　Here the word "suǒ" stands for the object of the preposition "yǐ" (to use) and
　　　　　indicates the means by which a certain thing is/was/will be done.

50. 游目　【動詞語】使目光游動；放眼流覽
　　yóu mù　　　　　　　to roam with one's eyes; to look around

51. 騁懷　【動詞語】使胸懷馳騁；使心神縱遊
　　chěng huái　　　　　　to free up one's mind; to let one's imagination roam

〔二者〕〔皆〕〔為〕〔人〕〔之〕 所以 游目騁懷〔者〕
[s].　[adv]　[l.v]　[s]　[conj]　o-prep　v　o　v　o　[pron]

"游目騁懷"中的"游"和"騁"都是動詞的使動用法，
把一般的使動式"使目游使懷騁"中兼語後的動詞移放在
兼語之前而省去"使"字，其目的在使句子簡練。

The verbs "yóu" and "chěng" in the phrase "yóu mù chěng huái" are used causatively. When the verb that would usually follow the **pivotal element** in a typical **causative construction** is transposed in front of the **pivotal element**, it functions as a causative verb, and there is no need to add another verb to express a causative meaning. The object of this type of construction is to create a more compact sentence with a laconic tone.

52. 極 jí　　【動詞】窮盡 to exhaust

53. 視聽
　　shì tīng　　【動詞】看、聽 to look and to listen

　　　　　　　　【名詞】視覺、聽覺 the senses of sight and hearing; ears and eyes

54. 娛 yú　　【名詞】娛樂 joy; amusement; entertainment

55. 信 xìn　　【副詞】誠然；確實 really; indeed

56. 可樂
　　kě lè　　【動詞語】讓人快樂 enjoyable

　　夫人之相與，俯仰一世，或取諸懷抱，晤言一室之內；或因寄所托，放浪形骸之外。雖取捨萬殊，靜躁不同，當其欣於所遇，暫得於己，快然自足，曾不知老之將至。及其所之既倦，情隨事遷，感慨系之矣。向之所欣，俯仰之間，已為陳跡，猶不能不以之興懷，況修短隨化，終期於盡。古人云："死生亦大矣。"豈不痛哉！

Fú rén zhī xiāng yǔ, fǔ yǎng yí shì, huò qǔ zhū huái bào, wù yán yí shì zhī nèi; huò yīn jì suǒ tuō, fàng làng xíng hái zhī wài. Suī qǔ shě wàn shū, jìng zào bù tóng, dāng qí xīn yú suǒ yù, zhàn dé yú jǐ, kuài rán zì zú, zēng bù zhī lǎo zhī jiāng zhì. Jí qí suǒ zhī jì juàn, qíng suí shì qiān, gǎn kǎi xì zhī yǐ. Xiàng zhī suǒ xīn, fǔ yǎng zhī jiān, yǐ wéi chén jī, yóu bù néng bù yǐ zhī xīng huài, kuàng xiū duǎn suí huà, zhōng qī yú jìn. Gǔ rén yún: "Sǐ shēng yì dà yǐ." Qǐ bú tòng zāi!

57. 相與　【動詞語】互相交往　to associate; to befriend each other
　　xiāng yǔ

58. 俯仰　【動詞】俯察、仰觀　to look up and down
　　fǔ yǎng

59. 一世　【名詞語】一代〔之人、之事〕
　　yí shì　　　　　　　　　a whole generation [of persons and things]

60. 或　huò　【代名詞】有的　someone

61. 取諸　【動詞語】取之於　to take things from ...
　　qǔ zhū

62. 懷抱　【名詞語】胸中蘊 (yùn) 藏的想法；心懷；心意
　　huái bào　　　　　　　what is cherished in one's mind; the ideas one entertains

63. 晤言　【動詞】會晤談話；對面談話
　　wù yán　　　　　　　to meet and talk

64. 因寄　【動詞】憑依；依靠　to rely on
　　yīn jì

65. 所託　【名詞語】所 +V= N;　V 的 N　　cf. p. 49, n. 10
　　suǒ tuō　　　　　〔心神〕寄託的對象：如志趣；理想；人生
　　　　　　　　　　觀等　what the heart rests on, such as one's aspiration,
　　　　　　　　　　ideal, outlook on life, etc.

66. 放浪　【形容詞】放蕩；不受〔禮法的〕拘束
　　fàng làng　　　　　　to be dissolute; to be unconventional and unbriddled

67. 形骸　【名詞】形體　the human body; one's physical appearance
　　xíng hái

形骸之外【名詞語】形體的外面；外面的形體
xíng hái zhī wài　　　　　external, physical body

173

※ 放浪形骸 【成語】 過一種放蕩的生活
fàng làng xíng hái   to lead a Bohemian life;
                         to abandon oneself to Bohemianism

或　因寄　〔情之〕所託，放浪　〔於〕形骸之外
s   v   o   v   [prep]   o

68. 取舍　【動詞語】採取、捨棄　to take or to give up; to accept or to reject
   qǔ shě
         【名詞語】採取的、捨棄的　what one accepts or rejects
                 處世的態度　the way one behaves oneself

69. 殊 shū　【形容詞】殊異；不同　to be different

   萬殊　【形容詞】有萬種殊異；有種種不同
   wàn shū   to be different in myriad ways

70. 靜 jìng　【形容詞】安靜　quiet

71. 躁 zào　【形容詞】急躁　irritable; restless; impetuous

72. 欣 xīn　【形容詞】欣喜　joyful; happy; delighted
         【用作動詞】感到欣喜　to feel joyful/ happy/ delighted

73. 所遇　【名詞語】所 + V= N; V 的 N　Cf. poem 2, n. 10, p. 49
   suǒ yù   遇到的人、事、或情況
                    what one encounters: persons, things, or circumstances

74. 暫得於己 【動詞語】暫時在自己心中感到非常滿意
   zhàn dé yú jǐ   temporarily feeling fully satisfied with one's self

75. 快然　【副詞】快慰地　happily; self-contently
   kuài rán

76. 自足　【動詞語】自以為足；自己感到很滿足
   zì zú   to be self-sufficient; to be self-content

       "足"字在此是形容詞用作動詞，意動用法。

       The word "zú" is an adjective that functions here as a **putative verb** (i.e., to
       think or feel N (oneself) Adj (content))

77. 曾 zēng　【副詞】竟；簡直，強調某種說法　simply; surprisingly, used to

emphasize a statement

78. 老之將至 【主謂短語】老年即將來臨
    lǎo zhī jiāng zhì   old age is approaching

79. 及 jí   【介詞】到 until; by the time

80. 之 zhī   【動詞】往；到…去；嚮往 to go to; to aspire

    所之   【名詞語】所 + V= N; V 的 N
    suǒ zhī   之的事情；嚮往的事物、情境
                      what one aspires; one's aspiration or longings

81. 倦 juàn   【形容詞】厭倦 to be tired of

82. 遷 qiān   【動詞】遷移；改變 to shift; to change

83. 感慨   【名詞語】感傷慨歎 laments and sighs; regrets; painful recollections
    gǎn kǎi

84. 系 xì   【動詞】聯繫；隨之而起 to come along; to be attached to

※ 感慨系之 【成語】感傷慨嘆跟隨著這情況發生
    gǎn kǎi xì zhī   laments and sighs come along with this situation
                      對某事不勝感慨（現在一般的解釋）
                      to feel deeply touched about something

        〔人於〕   〔人之〕   〔人之〕   情事俱遷
        及 其 所之 既倦，   情 隨 事 遷，   感慨 繫 之 矣。
        comj . o   v   s v-o v   s   v o   part

85. 向 xiàng 【副詞】往昔；不久之前 previously; not long ago

86. 所欣   【名詞語】感到欣喜的事物情境
    suǒ xīn   things and circumstances one feels delighted in

87. 俯仰之間 【副詞】在一俯一仰的時間內；在很短的時間內
    fǔ yǎng zhī jiān   as soon as one raises or lowers one's head; within a short
                      while

88. 陳跡   【名詞語】過去了的痕跡 traces from the past
    chén jī

89. 以之　【介詞語】因之；為它　for it; because of it
　　yǐ zhī

90. 興懷　【動詞語】發生感慨　to have regretful feelings [well up]
　　xīng huái

91. 況 kuàng　【連詞】何況　let alone; not to mention...

92. 修短　【形容詞】〔壽命〕長短　long or short [of one's life span]
　　xiū duǎn

93. 化 huà　【名詞】自然的變化或規律　the change or law of nature

94. 期 qī　【動詞】會合　to meet; to converge
　　　　　　　　　到達　to reach

95. 盡 jìn　【名詞】盡頭　the end; the extremity

　　每覽昔人興感之由，若合一契，未嘗不臨文嗟悼，不能喻之於懷。固知一死生為虛誕，齊彭殤為妄作，後之視今，亦猶今之視昔。悲夫！故列敘時人，錄其所述。雖世殊事異，所以興懷，其致一也。後之覽者，亦將有感於斯文。

　　Měi lǎn xí rén xīng gǎn zhī yóu, ruò hé yí qì, wèi cháng bù lín wén jiē dào, bù néng yù zhī yú huái. Gù zhī yī sǐ shēng wéi xū dàn, qí Péng Shāng wéi wàng zuò, hòu zhī shì jīn, yì yóu jīn zhī shì xí. Bèi fū! Gù liè xù shí rén, lù qí suǒ shù. Suī shì shū shì yì, suǒ yǐ xīng huái, qí zhì yī yě. Hòu zhī lǎn zhě, yì jiāng yǒu gǎn yú sī wén.

96. 覽 lǎn　【動詞】閱覽；讀　to read

97. 昔人　【名詞語】往昔的人；古代的人　the ancient people
　　xí rén

98. 由 yóu　【名詞】原由；原因　the cause; the reason

99. 若 ruò　【準繫詞】好像　to be like

100. 合 hé 　【動詞】拼合 to tally

101. 契 qì 　【名詞】符節、憑證、字據等信物；古代契分為左右兩半，雙方各執其一，用時將兩半合對，以作徵信
a tally, a credential, or a contract that consisting of two halves, carried for identification, as a warrant

若合一契【準繫詞語】像把分為兩半的契合起來一樣
ruò hé yí qì 　to be like uniting the two halves of a tally
完全相同
completely identical

※ 若合符節【成語】像把分為兩半的符節合起來一樣
ruò hé fú jié 　as similar as the two halves of a tally--to tally perfectly

102. 未嘗不【副詞】從來沒有不…；總是 to have never not...ved; always
wèi cháng bù

"未嘗不"是用雙否定來表示肯定，意思是"從來沒有不"或"總是"

A **double negative construction** is used here to indicate affirmation. It means "never once not..." or "always...".

103. 臨文 　【動詞語】面對〔昔人的〕文章 to face the articles of ancients
lín wén

104. 嗟悼 　【動詞】嗟歎哀傷 to sigh and to grieve
jiē dào

105. 喻 yù 　【動詞】明白 to comprehend；解釋 to explain

106. 固 gù 　【副詞】"固"通"故"，因此 therefore

◆ 通 tōng 　to be interchangeable with

107. 一 yī 　【形容詞】相同；一樣 same; identical

【形容詞意動】認為…一樣 　Cf. n. 76, p.174
to think ...as same or identical

一死生【動詞語】以死生為一；認為死生一樣
yī sǐ shēng 　to think that life and death are same

177

108. 虛誕　【形容詞】虛假荒誕　unreal and absurd
　　　xū dàn
　　　　　　　【名詞語】虛假荒誕的言論　unreal and absurd opinion

109. 齊 qí　【形容詞】齊一；等同；相等　even in length; equal
　　　　　　　【形容詞意動】認為…相等　to think ... as equal

110. 彭 Péng【名詞】彭祖，傳說中的人物，因封於彭，故稱。傳說
　　　　　　　他善養生，有導引之術，活到八百高齡

　　　　　Péngzǔ, a legendary figure, so called because he was once
　　　　　enfeoffed at Péng. It was said that he excelled in preserving
　　　　　good health, practiced beathing exercises, and lived to the
　　　　　advanced age of eight hundred years.

111. 殤 shāng【名詞】殤子；未成年而死的人　a child who died young

　　　齊彭殤【動詞語】以彭祖與殤子為同壽；
　　　qí Péng Shāng　　　認為彭祖和殤子的壽命相等
　　　　　　　　　　　　to think that the long lived Péngzǔ and a child who died
　　　　　　　　　　　　young are equal

112. 妄 wàng【形容詞】沒有根據的；不合理的　groundless; unreasonable

　　　妄作　【名詞語】沒有根據的、不合理的述作
　　　wàng zuò　　　　　　a groundless, unreasonable writing

113. 後 hòu　【名詞】後世〔的人〕　people of later generations

114. 視 shì　【動詞】看　to look at

115. 今 jīn　【名詞】現在〔的人和事〕　the present [people and things]

116. 猶 yóu　【準繫詞】如同　to be like

117. 昔 xí　【名詞】往昔〔的人和事〕　the past

118. 敍 xù　【動詞】記述　to record and narrate

　　　列敍　【動詞語】一一記述　to list one by one; to record one by one
　　　liè xù

178

119. 時人　【名詞語】此時參加蘭亭集會的人
　　　shí rén　　　　　　　people taking part at this gathering

120. 錄 lù　【動詞】記錄；記載　to record; to write down

121. 所述　【名詞語】記述的 N；作品
　　　suǒ shù　　　　　　what was written; the writings

122. 世 shì　【名詞】世代　times and generations

123. 殊 shū　【形容詞】殊異；不同　different

124. 異 yì　【形容詞】不同　not the same; different

125. 以 yǐ　【連詞】因為　bacause

　　　所以　【名詞語】所 + prep.= N; prep. 的 N　　Cf. n. 49, p. 171
　　　suǒ yǐ　　　　　　因之而…的事物
　　　　　　　　　　　　因為它而…的事物
　　　　　　　　　　　　things beacuse of which one ...

126. 興 xīng【動詞】觸動；引起　to touch upon; to arouse

127. 懷 huái【名詞】感懷　emotional response

128. 致 zhì　【動詞】招致　to bring about

　　　其致　【名詞語】其〔所〕致；它招致的結果；它產生的影響
　　　qí zhì　　　　　　what they bring about; the results or influences that they
　　　　　　　　　　　　bring about
　　　　　　　　　　　　"其"指"殊世異事"；不同的時代和事情
　　　　　　　　　　　　"Qî" stands for different times and different things/events

　　　故　〔予〕列敍時人，　錄　其所述，
　　　comj [s]　adv v o　　　v
　　　　　　　　　　　〔殊世異事〕〔皆　為〕
　　　雖　世殊事異，然，　　　　　　　　〔人之〕所以興懷〔者〕，
　　　comj s pa s pa　conj　　[s]　　[adv l.v]　　　　　n
　　　　　　　　　　其〔所〕致 一 也。
　　　　　　　　　　s　　pa part

179

129. 覽 lǎn 　【動詞】 閱覽 to read; to browse

130. 有感 　【動詞語】 發生感觸 to have feelings [about/aroused by]
　　 yǒu gǎn

131. 斯文 　【名詞語】 這些詩文 these writings
　　 sī wén

第三篇

五柳先生傳

晉　陶潛

作者　見詩選《歸園田居》 P. 34

篇旨

五柳先生是陶淵明的自畫像。他不慕榮利，好讀
書，愛喝酒，喜著述，貧而不以為苦。他的灑脫
自得的人生態度千百年來飽受讀書人的敬慕與讚
佩。他也是隱士的典型。

Master Five Willows is the self-portrait of Táo Yuānmíng. He does not long
for fame and wealth, he is fond of reading, he likes to drink, and he keeps
writing. He does not mind being impoverished and remains carefree and self-
content. For thousand of years he has lived in the hearts of literati and been
admired and praised. He is also an exemplary model of recluses.

先生不知何許人也，亦不詳其姓字。宅邊有五柳樹
，因以為號焉。閒靜少言，不慕榮利。好讀書，不求甚
解；每有會意，便欣然忘食。

Zhùyīn:

180

Xiānshēng bù zhī hé xǔ rén yě, yì bù xiáng qí xìng zì. Zhái biān yǒu wǔ liǔ shù, yīn yǐ wéi hào yān. Xián jìng shǎo yán, bú mù róng lì. Hào dú shū, bù qiú shèn jiě; měi tǒu huì yì, biàn xīn rán wàng shí.

注 解

1. 柳 liǔ 　【名詞】柳樹 the willow tree

   五柳 　【名詞語】五棵柳樹 five willow trees
   wǔ liǔ

2. 傳 zhuàn 　【名詞】傳記，記錄某人生平事跡的文字　a biography; the story of a person's life written by someone else

   ◆ 生平 shēngpíng 　　all one's life; life time
   ◆ 事跡 shìjī 　　deeds; achievements

3. 許 xǔ 　【名詞】處 a place

   何許人 【名詞語】何處人；甚麼地方的人 a man of what place
   hé xǔ rén

4. 詳 xiáng 　【動詞】知悉 (xī)；知道 to know

   不詳 　【動詞語】不知道 do not know
   bù xiáng

5. 宅 zhái 　【名詞】住宅；居住的房子 residence

6. 號 hào 　【名詞】別號。中國人的姓名包括姓、名、字、號及別號 an alias; a style. The name of a Chinese scholar includes a surname, a given name, a courtesy name, and an alias or style

7. 閒靜 　【形容詞】安靜 quiet; taciturn
   xián jìng

8. 慕 mù 　【動詞】羨慕；思慕；嚮往 to aspire for; to long for

9. 榮 róng 　【名詞】榮名 honor and fame

181

10. 利 lì 　　【名詞】利祿　wealth and position

不慕榮利【動詞語】不羨慕榮名利祿　do not long for fame and wealth
bú mù róng lì

11. 不求甚解【動詞語】不尋求過度的解釋　do not seek far-fetched
bù qiú shèn jiě 　　　　　　　　　interpretations; do not over-interpret

12. 會意 　　【名詞語】領會了的意思　something comprehended
huì yì

13. 欣然 　　【形容詞】欣喜的；高興的　rejoiceful
xīn rán

　　性嗜酒，家貧不能常得；親舊知其如此，或置酒而招之。造飲輒盡，期在必醉；既醉而退，曾不吝情去留。環堵蕭然，不蔽風日，短褐穿結，簞瓢屢空，晏如也。常著文章自娛，頗示己志，忘懷得失，以此自終。

　　Xìng shì jiǔ, jiā pín, bù néng cháng dé; qīn jiù zhī qí rú cǐ, huò zhì jiǔ ér zhāo zhī. Zào yǐn zhé jìn, qī zài bì zuì; jì zuì ér tuì, zēng bú lìn qíng qù liú. Huán dǔ xiāo rán, bú bì fēng rì, duǎn hé chuān jié, dān piáo lǚ kōng, yàn rú yě. Cháng zhù wén zhāng zì yú, pō shì jǐ zhì, wàng huái dé shī, yǐ cǐ zì zhōng.

14. 嗜 shì 　　【動詞】愛好　to be fond of

15. 親舊 　　【名詞】親戚故舊；親戚朋友　relatives and old friends
qīn jiù

16. 置酒 　　【動詞語】設置酒；預備酒　to prepare wine
zhì jiǔ

17. 招 zhāo 　　【動詞】邀請　to invite

18. 造 zào 　　【動詞】到　to attend

19. 輒 zhé 　　【副詞】就　then

20. 盡 jìn 【動詞】〔飲〕盡；〔喝〕光 to finish up [drinks]

21. 期 qī 【動詞】期望；希望 to wish

22. 醉 zuì 【形容詞】喝醉 to be drunken; inebriated

23. 曾 zēng 【副詞】表示事實出人意外，語氣帶誇張，可譯作"竟然"，"簡直" somewhat to one's surprise ...; simply

　　◆ 語氣 yǔqì　　　　tone (of speech)
　　◆ 誇張 kuāzhāng　　exaggeration

24. 吝 lìn 【動詞】吝惜；捨不得 to grudge

25. 情 qíng 【名詞】情感 emotion; feeling

不吝情去留 【動詞語】不吝情〔於〕去留
bú lìn qíng qù liú 　　won't grudge his feeling toward leaving or staying;
　　　　對於離去或留下不吝惜情感
　　　　not care whether he leaves or stays
　　　　──→覺得離去或留下都很好
　　　　──→離去〔就離去〕，留下〔就留下〕都覺得很好 to feel all right either leaving or staying

26. 堵 dǔ 【名詞】牆 walls

27. 蕭然 【形容詞】冷清；空 empty; bleak
xiāo rán

※ 環堵蕭然【成語】在四面的牆內冷冷清清的，甚麼家具都沒有
huán dǔ xiāo rán 　──→屋子裡僅有四壁，空空的、甚麼家具都沒有
　　　　a bleak room barely decorated or furnished

28. 褐 hé 【名詞】粗布衣服 coarse clothes

短褐 【名詞語】短的粗布衣服 short coarse clothes
duǎn hé

29. 穿 chuān 【動詞】洞穿；破了 torn; worn out

30. 結 jié 　【動詞】連結　to join together
　　　　　　　　──→縫補 (féng bǔ)　to mend [clothes]

31. 簞 dān 　【名詞】竹子做的圓形的盛飯器　a round bamboo ware for
　　　　　　　　holding cooked rice

32. 瓢 piáo 　【名詞】瓜瓢 a gourd；舀 (yǎo)水的用具　a ladle

33. 屢 lǚ 　【副詞】屢次；多次　frequently; often

　　屢空 　【形容詞】屢次空著；很多次空著
　　lǚ kōng 　　　　　　　──→常常空著　often empty

※ 簞瓢屢空【成語】時常沒飯吃，沒水喝
　　dān piáo lǚ kōng 　　　　[lit.] The basket and gourd are frequently empty--with no
　　　　　　　　food and water; stark poverty

34. 晏如 　【形容詞】晏然；安樂；安適快樂　at ease; happy
　　yàn rú

35. 著 zhù 　【動詞】作；寫　to write; to compose

36. 文章 　【名詞】指詩、文等文學作品
　　wén zhāng 　　　　　　a writting; a composition

　　著文章【動詞語】作詩、寫文章 to compose poems and prose
　　zhù wén zhāng

37. 娛 yú 　【動詞】娛樂；使…快樂　to entertain

　　自娛 　【動詞語】〔自己〕娛樂自己；〔自己〕使自己快樂
　　zì yú 　　　　　　　　to entertain oneself

38. 頗 pō 　【副詞】很；相當地　rather; relatively

39. 示 shì 　【動詞】表示；顯示　to express; to reveal

40. 志 zhì 　【名詞】內心深處真實的願望；志願 intention; aspiration

己志　【名詞語】自己內心深處真實的願望；自己的志願
jǐ zhì　　　　　　　　deeply rooted, heartfelt ambition or aspiration

41. 忘懷　【動詞】不介意；不放在心上　do not mind
wàng huái

42. 得失　【名詞】所得或所失　gain or loss
dé shī　　　　　　——→成功或失敗　success or failure

43. 終 zhōng　【動詞】終結　to end
　　　　　　　——→到終點；到盡頭；到最後　to live to the end

自終　【動詞語】自己使自己〔活〕到〔生命的〕盡頭
zì zhōng　　　　　　to make oneself live to the end of one's life

以此自終【動詞語】用這種態度來使自己活到生命的盡頭
yǐ cǐ zì zhōng　　　——→用這種態度來過完自己的一生
　　　　　　　　In this way he led his entire life.

　　贊曰：黔婁有言：“不戚戚於貧賤，不汲汲於富貴。”其言茲若人之儔乎！銜觴賦詩，以樂其志，無懷氏之民歟！葛天氏之民歟！

　　Zàn yuē: "Qiánlóu yǒu yán: "Bù qī qī yú pín jiàn, bù jí jí yú fù guì." qí yán zī ruò rén zhī chóu hū! Xián shāng fù shī, yǐ lè qí zhì, Wúhuái shì zhī mín yú? Gětiān shì zhī mín yú?

44. 贊 zàn　【名詞】傳記的結尾部分，等於是傳中人一生的總評
　　　　　　　a general comment at the end of a biography

45. 黔婁　【名詞】戰國時齊國隱士，修身清節，不求仕進。魯共
Qián lóu　　　公(r.376-355 B.C.) 欲以為相，齊威王 (r. 358-320 B.C.)
　　　　　　　聘為卿，均不就。見皇甫謐《高士傳》。
　　　　　　　name of a recluse of Qí during the Warring States period. Qián Lóu cultivated a stainless moral integrity and did not pursue an official career. Duke Gōng of Lǔ (r. 376-355 B.C.) wanted to have him as the Prime Minister, and King Wēi of Qí (r. 358-320 B.C.) appointed him a high minister; he rejected both.
　　　　　　　See *Biographies of Noble Scholars* written by Huángfǔ Mì of the Jìn dynasty.

46. 戚戚　【形容詞】憂愁；悲傷　distressed; weighed down with sorrow
    qī qī

47. 汲汲　【形容詞】心情急切的　anxious; avid
    jí jí
    ───→ 心情急切地努力追求 to pursue avidly
    ───→ 渴望得到 to crave

48. 其…乎　【固定結構】大概…吧　perhaps...; probably...
    qí　　hū
    用推測的語氣委婉地表示肯定的意思
    A tone of supposition is used here to express an affirm-
    ative meaning indirectly

49. 茲 zī　【代詞】此 this

50. 若 ruò　【代詞】此 this

    茲若　【代詞】此 this
    zī ruò

51. 儔 chóu　【名詞】同類　of the same kind/class; peer

52. 銜 xián　【動詞】含 to hold in the mouth

53. 觴 shāng 【名詞】酒杯　a general name for all sorts of wine vessels

54. 賦詩　【動詞語】作詩　to write poems
    fù shī

55. 樂 lè　【形容詞】快樂；愉快 happy; cheerful

    【使動用法】使…快樂 to make ... happy
    cf. Prose 2, n. 51, p. 184

56. 志 zhì　【名詞】心情；心意 the frame of one's mind

57. 無懷氏【名詞】上古之帝　name of a ruler of a remote age
    Wú huái shì

58. 民 mín 【名詞】人民 the people; the subjects; the populace

59. 葛天氏 【名詞】上古之帝　name of a ruler of a remote age
Gě tiān shì

60. 與 yū　【疑問詞】用在並列選擇疑問句的末尾，可譯成白話的
"呢"

an interrogative particle used at the end of parallel clauses in an Alternative Compound Sentence, can be rendered as "nē" in modern Chinese.

第四篇

桃花源記

晉　陶潛

作者　見詩選《歸園田居》 P. 34

篇旨

生活在戰亂頻仍的時代中，陶淵明通過《桃花源記》描述出一個安定、樸實、和諧、快樂的社會——他的理想寄託的地方，也是世世代代的人所追求的美好的生活環境。中國的"桃花源"，有如西方的"烏托邦"，是人人都嚮往，但還達不到的理想境界。

Living at a time of chaos and social upheavals brought about by frequent wars, Táo Yuānmíng, through his fictional "Record of the Peach Blossom Spring" depicts a peaceful, unsophisticated, harmonious, and happy society -- a place where his ideals rest, and a perfect envirnment that was pursued by Chinese for generation after generation. The "Peach Blossom Spring" in China is like "Utopia" in the West; both of them standing for an ideal world where everybody aspires to live, yet fails to find or create.

晉太元中，武陵人捕魚為業，緣溪行，忘路之遠近
。忽逢桃花林，夾岸數百步，中無雜樹，芳草鮮美，落
英繽紛；漁人甚異之。復前行，欲窮其林。林盡水源，
便得一山。山有小口，髣髴若有光；便捨船從口入。

Zhùyīn:

Jìn Tàiyuán zhōng, Wúlíng rén bǔ yú wéi yè, yuán xī xíng, wàng lù zhī yuǎn jìn, hū féng táo huā lín, jiā àn shù bǎi bù, zhōng wú zá shù, fāng cǎo xiān měi, luò yīng bīn fēn; yú rén shèn yì zhī. Fù qián xíng, yù qióng qí lín. Lín jìn shuǐ yuán, biàn dé yì shān. Shān yǒu xiǎo kǒu, fǎng fú ruò yǒu guāng; biàn shě chuán, cóng kǒu rù.

注 解

1. **桃花源**【名詞語】桃花溪的源頭；桃花溪開始流之處
   Táohuāyuán   the Peach Blossom Spring

2. **記** Jì   【名詞】文體名   name of a literary genre; a record

3. **晉** Jìn   【名詞】朝代名 (265-419 A.D.)，晉武帝司馬炎(Yán)所建
                     name of a dynasty (265-419 A.D.) founded by Sīmǎ Yán, known as Emperor Wǔ of Jìn.

4. **太元**【名詞】晉孝武帝司馬曜(Yào) 的年號 (376-396 A.D.)
   Tàiyuán   reign (376-396 A.D.) title of Emperor Xiàowǔ of Jìn -- Sīmǎ Yào.

   ◆ **年號** *nián hào*   a reign title

5. **武陵**【名詞】郡名，在今湖南省常德縣
   wǔlíng   name of a prefecture, located in present-day Chángdé district in Húnán province

   ◆ **郡** *jùn*   a prefecture
   ◆ **縣** *xiàn*   a county; a district

6. **捕魚為業**【動詞語】以捕魚為業；把捕魚當作職業
   bǔ yú wéi yè   to take fishing as a career; to make a living on fishing

7. 緣 yuán　【動詞】順著；沿著　to follow; to go along

8. 溪 xī, qī　【名詞】小河　a brook; a stream

9. 夾 jiā　【動詞】從兩面夾住　to sandwich from both sides

10. 岸 àn　【名詞】河邊；河岸　a bank

　　夾岸　【名詞語】水流的兩岸；堤岸的兩邊　on both banks
　　jiā àn

11. 雜樹　【名詞語】雜色的樹；開不同顏色的花的樹
　　zá shù　　　　　　──→別種的樹　other kinds of trees

12. 芳 fāng　【形容詞】芳香　fragrant

　　芳草　【名詞語】芳香的草　fragrant grass
　　fāng cǎo

13. 鮮美　【形容詞】新鮮、美麗　fresh and luxuriant
　　xiān měi

14. 英 yīng　【名詞】花　flowers; petals

　　落英　【名詞語】落花；落下的花　fallen flowers or petals
　　luò yīng

15. 繽紛　【形容詞】繁多雜亂；又多又亂　in riotous profusion
　　bīn fēn

16. 異 yì　【形容詞】奇異；奇怪　strange

　　　　【形容詞意動】以…為異　to think ... strange

　　異之　【動詞語】以之為異；覺得這情形很奇怪　think it strange
　　yì zhī　　　　　　　Cf. prose 2, n. 76, p. 174

17. 窮 qióng　【動詞】窮盡　to exhaust

189

窮其林 【動詞語】窮盡那座桃林
qióng qí lín ——→ 走到那座桃林的盡頭
to walk through the forest of peach trees

18. 盡 jìn 【動詞】完；終結 exhausted; to come to an end

19. 水源 【名詞語】水開始流的地方 the source of the water
shuǐ yuán

20. 口 kǒu 【名詞】裂口 a breach; a gap; an opening

21. 髣髴 【副詞】同"仿佛"、"彷彿"；似乎
fǎng fú as if

22. 捨 shě 【動詞】放棄 to give up; to leave behind

捨船 【動詞語】放棄船
shě chuán ——→ 離開船 to leave the boat behind
——→ 下船 to get off the boat

初極狹，纔通人；復行數十步，豁然開朗。土地平
曠，屋舍儼然；有良田、美池、桑竹之屬；阡陌交通，
雞犬相聞。其中往來種作，男女衣著，悉如外人；黃髮
垂髫，並怡然自樂。

Chū jí xiá, cái tōng rén; fù xíng shù shí bù, huò rán kāi lǎng. Tǔ dì píng kuàng, wū
shè yǎn rán; yǒu liáng tián, měi chí, sāng zhú zhī shǔ; qiān mò jiāo tōng, jī quǎn xiāng wén.
Qí zhōng wǎng lái zhòng zuò, nán nǚ yī zhuó, xī rú wài rén; huáng fǎ chuí tiáo, bìng yí rán zì
lè.

23. 初 chū 【副詞】起初；開始 at first; in the beginning

24. 狹 xiá 【形容詞】狹窄；窄 narrow

25. 纔 cái 【副詞】同"才"；僅僅 only; merely

26. 通 tōng 【動詞】通過 to pass; to allow to pass

27. 行 xíng 【動 詞】 走；前進 to walk; to advance

復行 【動 詞 語】 再向前走 to walk on forward; to go straight on
qián xíng

28. 豁然 【副 詞】 開闊的樣子；開闊地 openly and clearly
huò rán

29. 開朗 【形 容 詞】 寬大明亮 spacious and bright
kāi lǎng

豁然開朗【形 容 詞】 形容山的裂口（山洞）中由昏暗窄小突
huò rán kāi lǎng 然變得很寬敞、很明亮，這是本文所採
用的意思
[said of a place] to become extensive and bright all of a
sudden; this is what is meant in this context

※ 豁然開朗 【成 語】 比喻〔人〕經過別人的提醒或自己的學習、
huò rán kāi lǎng 思索，突然明白了一種道理。這是一種引申
的用法 metaphorically, suddenly see the light; to become
clear or visible all of a sudden

30. 曠 kuàng 【形 容 詞】 廣大；空闊 vast

平曠 【形 容 詞】 平坦空闊；又平坦又空闊 smooth and vast
píng kuàng

31. 儼然 【形 容 詞】 整齊 neat; orderly
yǎn rán

32. 屬 shǔ 【名 詞】 類 a kind; a sort

…之屬 【名 詞 語】 …之類；…一類的〔N〕 the kind of ...
zhīshǔ

33. 阡陌 【名 詞】 田間縱橫的小路，南北叫阡，東西叫陌
qiān mò the vertical and horizontal paths in the field

◆ 縱 zōng vertical or north-south
◆ 橫 héng horizontal or east-west

34. 交通　【動詞語】〔路跟路〕相交〔人可以〕通過
　　 jiāo tōng　　　　　criss-cross and leads to all directions

　　　　　　◆ 相交 xiāngjiāo　　 to cross each other

35. 種作　【動詞】耕作；在田裡耕種 to do farming
　　 zhòng zuò

36. 衣著　【名詞】穿戴的衣帽；穿的衣服，戴的帽子
　　 yī zhuó　　　　　clothes; costumes

37. 悉 xī　【副詞】完全 fully; entirely

38. 黃髮　【名詞語】老年人。因為老年人的頭髮發黃，所以用
　　 huáng fǎ　　"黃髮"代表老年人 the yellow-haired elders;
　　　　　　because old people's hair turn yellowish, thus represent old
　　　　　　folks with "yellow hair"

39. 垂髫　【名詞語】小孩子。因為小孩子披著頭髮，不把頭髮
　　 chuí tiáo　　梳到頭頂上去束成髻，所以用"髻"代表
　　　　　　兒童 the tufted children; because children's hair are
　　　　　　hanging down loosely, not bound into a coiffure with a top
　　　　　　knot, thus represent children with "tufted hair"

　　　　　　◆ 束 shù　　　　　to bind
　　　　　　◆ 髻 jì　　　　　a coiffure with a top knot

40. 怡然　【形容詞】愉快的　pleasant and contented; satisfied and happy;
　　 yí rán　　　　　cheerful

41. 樂 lè　【形容詞】快樂 happy

　　　　　【形容詞意動】覺得快樂 to feel happy　Cf. prose 2, n. 76, p. 188

　　 自樂　【動詞語】自以為樂；覺得自己很快樂
　　 zì lè　　　　　to feel oneself very happy; to be self-content

※ 怡然自樂【成語】很愉快地感到自己很快樂
　　 yí rán zì lè　　　　cheerfully feeling oneself very happy and content

見漁人，乃大驚，問所從來；具答之。便要還家，
設酒殺雞作食。村中聞有此人，咸來問訊。自云先世避
秦時亂，率妻子邑人來此絕境，不復出焉；遂與外人間
隔。問今是何世，乃不知有漢，無論魏、晉。此人一一
為具言所聞，皆歎惋。餘人各復延至其家，皆出酒食。
停數日，辭去。此中人語云："不足為外人道也。"

Jiàn yú rén, nǎi dà jīng, wèn suǒ cóng lái; jù dá zhī. Biàn yāo huán jiā, shè jiǔ shā jī
zuò shí. Cūn zhōng wén yǒu cǐ rén, xián lái wèn xùn. Zì yún xiān shì bì Qín shí luàn, shuài
qī zǐ yì rén lái cǐ jué jìng, bú fù chū yān; suì yǔ wài rén jiàn gé. Wèn jīn shì hé shì, nǎi bù zhī
yǒu Hàn, wú lùn Wèi, Jìn. Cǐ rén yī yī wèi jù yán suǒ wén, jiē tàn wǎn. Yú rén gè fù yán
zhì qí jiā, jiē chū jiǔ shí. Tíng shù rì, cí qù. Cǐ zhōng rén yù yún: "Bù zú wèi wài rén dào
yě."

42. 大驚　【形容詞】非常驚異　greatly surprised
dà jīng　　　　　──→ 大吃一驚　to be greatly surprised; to be startled

43. 所從來【名詞語】所＋介＋V＝N　Cf. prose 2, n. 49, p.171
suǒ cóng lái　　　從那兒來的地方
the place where he came from

問所從來【動詞語】問〔其〕所從來〔為〕〔何〕
wèn suǒ cóng lái　　──→ 問〔他之〕所從來〔為〕〔何處〕
　　　　　　　　　　──→ 問他從那兒來的地方〔是〕〔甚麼地方〕
　　　　　　　　　　──→ 問他〔是〕從哪兒來〔的〕
to ask where he came from

44. 具 jù　【副詞】完備地；詳盡地　in detail

45. 要 yāo　【動詞】邀請　to invite

46. 設酒　【動詞語】設置酒；預備酒　to prepare wine
shè jiǔ

193

47. 咸 xián　【副詞】皆；都　all

48. 訊 xùn　【名詞】消息　tidings; news; information

問訊
wèn xùn　【動詞語】問消息；打聽消息　to inquire

49. 先世
xiān shì　【名詞語】先代；祖先　ancestors

50. 避 bì　【動詞】躲避　to evade; to flee from

51. 秦時亂　【名詞語】秦朝時的戰亂，指秦朝末年(209 B.C.) 陳勝
Qín shí luàn　　　(Chén Shèng)、吳廣(Wú Guǎng)、劉邦(Liú Bāng)、項
羽(Xiàng Yǔ)等人起兵反抗殘暴的秦朝的事

the great turmoil of the Qín time, referring to the last year of
Qín (209 B.C.) when Chén Shèng, Wú Guǎng, Liú Bāng
and Xiàng Yǔ revolted against the imperial court

52. 率 shuài　【動詞】率領；帶領　to lead

53. 邑人
yì rén　【名詞語】同鄉的人　countrymen; fellow villagers

54. 絕境　【名詞語】跟外邊交通斷絕的地方
jué jìng　　　　——→沒有路可以進來、出去的地方
a secluded place; a cut-off place

55. 間隔　【動詞】隔離；隔絕；分開　to separate; separated
jiàn gé

56. 今 jīn　【名詞】現代　now; at present

57. 何世
hé shì　【名詞語】甚麼朝代　what dynasty; what age

58. 乃 nǎi　【副詞】竟　unexpectedly; surprisingly

59. 漢 Hàn　【名詞】朝代名 (B.C.206-220 A.D.)，漢高祖劉邦所建
the Hàn dynasty founded by Liú Bāng, Emperor Gāo of Hàn

60. 無論　　【動詞語】〔更〕不必説；〔更〕不要説　not to mention;
　　　wú lùn　　　　　　　　　　　　　　　　　　　　let alone

61. 魏　Wèi　【名詞】朝代名 (220-265 A.D.)；魏文帝曹丕 (pī) 所建
　　　　　　　　the Wèi dynasty (220-265 A.D.) founded by Cáo Pī, Emperor
　　　　　　　　Wén of Wèi

62. 晉　Jìn　【名詞】朝代名 (265-419 A.D.)，晉武帝司馬炎 (Yán) 所建
　　　　　　　　the Jìn dynasty (265-419 A.D.) founded by Sīmǎ Yán, Emperor
　　　　　　　　Wǔ of Jìn

63. 具　jù　【副詞】詳盡地　in great detail

64. 所聞　　【名詞語】聽到的事　what he has heard
　　　suǒ wén

65. 歎惋　　【動詞語】嗟 (jiē) 歎惋 (wàn) 惜　to sigh and to feel regret at
　　　tàn wǎn

66. 延　yán　【動詞】邀請　to invite

67. 此　cǐ　【指示代詞】這個；這個村子　this; this village

　　　此中人【名詞語】此村中人；這個村子裡的人
　　　cǐ zhōng rén　　　　　　the villagers

68. 足　zú　【形容詞】足夠；值得　enough; to be worth ...ing

69. 道　dào　【動詞】説　to mention

　　　不足道【動詞語】不值得説　not worth mentioning
　　　bù zú dào

　　　既出，得其船，便扶向路，處處誌之。及郡下，詣
太守，説如此。太守即遣人隨其往。尋向所誌，遂迷不
復得路。南陽劉子驥，高尚士也。聞之，欣然規往，未
果，尋病終。後遂無問津者。

　　　Jì chū, dé qí chuán, biàn fú xiàng lù, chù chù zhì zhī. Jí Jùn xià, yì Tàishǒu, shuō rúcǐ. Tàishǒu jí qiǎn rén suí qí wǎng. Xún xiàng suǒ zhì, suì mí, bú fù dé lù. Nányáng Liú Zǐjì, gāo shàng shì yě. Wén zhī, xīn rán guī wǎng,wèi guǒ, xún bìng zhōng. Hòu suì wú wèn jīn zhě.

70. 扶 fú 【動詞】沿著 to follow; to go along

71. 向 xiàng 【時間詞】同 "嚮" ，以前 previous; formerly

向路 【名詞語】從前的路；舊路；老路 the old route
xiàng lù ——→來時經過的路 the way he came

72. 處處 【名詞】每個地方 every place; everywhere
chù chù

73. 誌 zhì 【動詞】作記號 to mark

74. 及 jí 【動詞】到達 to arrive at

75. 郡 jùn 【名詞】古代行政區畫名 a political division in ancient China; a commandery; but by this time, a prefecture

郡下 【名詞語】郡的首府 the capital city of a prefecture where the
jùn xià magistrate resides

76. 詣 yì 【動詞】至；到 to arrive at; to visit

77. 太守 【名詞】官名；一郡的首長；郡守 the prefect; the magistrate
tàishǒu

78. 迷 mí 【動詞】迷失 to get lost
——→找不著 unable to find

79. 復 fù 【副詞】再 again

80. 南陽 【名詞】郡名；今河南省南陽縣
Nányáng name of a prefecture; present-day Nányáng of Hénán province

81. 劉子驥【名詞】人名；好遊山玩水，採集藥草
Liú Zǐjì a personal name. He liked to roam about and to collect medicinal herbs

82. 高尚士 【名詞語】品德高尚的讀書人
    gāo shàng shì　　　——→清高的讀書人 a noble-minded scholar

83. 欣然　【副詞】欣喜地；高興地　happily; cheerfully
    xīn rán

84. 規 guī　【動詞】計劃；打算 to plan

85. 未果　【動詞語】未能實現；還沒結果 to have not realized [his wish];
    wèi guǒ　　　　　　to have not achieved a result

86. 尋 xún　【副詞】不久；沒多久 before long; shortly thereafter

87. 病終　【動詞語】病死 to die of an illness
    bìng zhōng

88. 津 jīn　【名詞】河岸渡口；可以從那兒坐船過河的地方
    　　　　　　　　a ford

    問津　【動詞語】問渡口 to ask about a ford
    wèn jīn　　　——→問路 to ask for direction
    　　　　　　——→打聽路 to ask for direction

    問津者【名詞語】問路的人 one who asks for direction
    wèn jīn zhě　　——→打聽〔到桃源去的〕路的人

※ 無人問津【成語】沒有人問渡口 No one asks about a ford.
    wú rén wèn jīn　　　引申的意思是：沒有人對…有興趣
    　　　　　　　　the extended meaning: No one cares about it;
    　　　　　　　　No one is interested in ...

197

第五篇

世說新語選讀

宋　劉義慶

作者　劉義慶 Liú Yìqìng (403-444 A.D.)，南朝宋臨川王。

Liú Yìqìng (403-44 A.D.) was the Prince of Línchuān of the Sòng dynasty, one of the so-called 'Southern Dynasties' during the Six Dynasties period.

篇旨

《世說新語》記錄了東漢後期到晉末 (c. 180-400 A.D.) 二百餘年間士大夫的嘉言、懿行、與風采，簡練雋永，深爲歷代讀者喜愛。此處所選四則，約略顯示當時人重視語言藝術，愛賞自然，尊崇佛學，及特重感情的心態。

A New Account of the Tales of the World records the witty words, exemplary conduct, and elegant demeanour of scholar-officials from the latter part of the Eastern Hàn dynasty to the end of Jìn dynasty, a period spanning over two hundred years. Its language is terse and succinct, its content thought-provoking and full of meaning, which explains why it has been treasured by generations of scholars. The four selections below reveal the literati's care of linguistic arts, their love of nature, their esteem for Buddhism, and their attitude toward affection.

一

詠絮

世說新語・言語

謝太傅寒雪日內集，與兒女講論文義，俄而雪驟，公欣然曰：“白雪紛紛何所似？”兄子胡兒曰：“撒鹽空中差可擬。”兄女曰：“未若柳絮因風起。”公大笑樂。即公大兄無奕女，左將軍王凝之妻也。

Zhùyīn:

Xiè Tàifù hán xuě rì nèi jí, yǔ ér nǚ jiǎng lùn wén yì, é ér xuě zòu, gōng xīnrán yuē: "Bái xuě fēnfēn hé suǒ sì?" Xiōng zǐ Húér yuē: "Sǎ yán kōng zhōng chā kě nǐ." Xiōng nǚ yuē: "Wèi ruò liǔ xù yīn fēng qǐ." Gōng dà xiào lè. Jí gōng dà xiōng Wúyì nǚ, Zuǒ Jiāngjūn Wáng Níngzhī qī ye.

注 解

1. 世說新語【名詞】書名；劉義慶著
   Shìshuō Xīnyǔ — Title of a book written by Liú Yìqìng; *A New Account of the Tales of the World.*

2. 詠 yǒng 【動詞】吟詠；作詩來描述 to chant [a poem]; to create/compose [a poem] to describe

3. 絮 xù 【名詞】柳絮 willow catkins

   詠絮 yǒng xù 【動詞語】吟詠柳絮；用柳絮作成詩句 to create a line with "willow catkins"

4. 言語 Yányǔ 【名詞】《世說新語》中的篇名 Heading of a chapter in *A New Account of the Tales of the World*; 'Speeches and Dialogues'

5. 太傅 Tài fù 【名詞】官名 an official title; Grand Mentor

   謝太傅 Xiè tài fù 【名詞語】東晉謝安，字安石 Xiè Ān of the Eastern Jìn dynasty, courtesy name Ānshí.

6. 寒雪日 hán xuě rì 【名詞語】寒冬下雪的日子 a cold snowing day in the winter

7. 內集 nèi jí 【動詞語】家人集會 to have a family gathering

199

8. 兒女　　【名詞語】兒子、女兒；孩子們 sons and daughters; children
　　ér nǚ

9. 講論　　【動詞】講談論述 to discuss and expound
　　jiǎng lùn

10. 文義　　【名詞詞】文章中的意義 the meaning of certain books/articles
　　wén yì

11. 俄而　　【副詞】不久；過了一會兒 shortly afterwards; in a short while
　　é ér

12. 驟 zòu　【形容詞】急驟；大 heavy [said of rain or snow fall]

13. 紛紛　　【形容詞】又多又亂 profuse and disorderly; thick and fast
　　fēn fēn

14. 兄子　　【名詞語】哥哥的兒子；姪兒 a nephew
　　xiōng zǐ

15. 胡兒　　【名詞】謝安次兄謝據之長子，名朗，字長度，小字
　　Húér　　　　胡兒 Xiè Lǎng, courtesy name Chángdù, also known by a
　　　　　　　pet-name Húér, was a son of Xiè Ān's second elder brother
　　　　　　　Xiè Jù.

16. 撒 sǎ　【動詞】播撒 to scatter

17. 鹽 yán　【名詞】鹽 salt

18. 差 chā　【副詞】差不多 approximately; nearly; almost

19. 擬 nǐ　【動詞】比擬 to liken; to compare to

20. 兄女　　【名詞語】哥哥的女兒；姪女，此處指謝道蘊
　　xiōng nǚ　　　　a niece, here referring to Xiè Dàoyùn

21. 因 yīn　【介詞】憑藉 to rely on; with

22. 起 qǐ　【動詞】飛起；飄揚 to flutter

23. 無奕　【名詞】謝安長兄（最大的哥哥）名奕，字無奕
    Wú yì　　　　　Xiè Ān's eldest brother Xiè Yì, courtesy name Wúyì.

24. 左將軍【名詞】官名 an official title; General of the Left Army
    Zuǒ Jiāngjūn

25. 王凝之【名詞】字叔平，右軍將軍王羲之之次子
    Wáng Níngzhī　　　Wáng Níngzhī, courtesy name Shúpíng, the second son of General of Right Army Wáng Xīzhī.

26. 妻 qī　【名詞】妻子 wife

二
山陰道上

世說新語・言語

顧長康自會稽還。人問山川之美，顧云：“千巖競秀，萬壑爭流，草木蒙籠其上，若雲興霞蔚。”

Zhùyīn:

Gù Chángkāng zì Kuàijī huán.　Rén wèn shān chuān zhī měi, Gù yún: "Qiān yán jìng xiù, wàn hè zhēng liú, cǎo mù ménglóng qí shàng, ruò yún xīng xiá wèi."

注解

1. 山陰　【名詞】地名，今浙江省紹興縣
   Shānyīn　　　　a place name; present-day Shàoxīng district in Zhèjiāng province

2. 道 dào　【名詞】道路 roads

   道上　【名詞語】路上 on the roads
   dào shàng

3. 顧長康 【名詞】人名；姓顧名愷之，字長康
   Gù Chángkāng   a personal name. Surnamed Gù, named Kǎizhī, courtesy name Chángkāng.

4. 會稽 【名詞】郡名，在浙江省，治山陰（今紹興縣）
   Kuàijī   name of a prefecture, in present-day Zhèjiāng province. Its government site is in Shānyīn, present-day Shàoxīng district.

5. 巖 yán 【名詞】山峰 peaks

6. 競 jìng 【動詞】競爭；比賽 to compete; to vie with each other

7. 秀 xiù 【形容詞】秀麗 to be beautiful and splendid

8. 壑 huò 【名詞】山谷；山溝 gullies

9. 蒙籠 【形容詞】草木茂盛 luxuriant [said of plants]
   méng lóng

10. 興 xīng 【動詞】湧起 to rise up; to surge

11. 霞 xiá 【名詞】〔日出及日落時的〕彩色的雲；紅雲
    colored and low-hanging clouds [at sunrise and sunset]

12. 蔚 wèi 【動詞】蔚薈 to grow luxuriantly
    ——→瀰漫 to permeate

王子敬云：“從山陰道上行，山川自相映發，使人應接不暇；若秋冬之際，尤難為懷。”

     Wáng Zǐjìng yún: "Cóng Shānyīn dào shàng xíng, shān chuān zì xiāng yìngfā, shǐ rén yìngjiē bù xiá; ruò qiū dōng zhī jì, yóu nán wéi huái."

13. 王子敬 【名詞】人名；姓王名獻之，字子敬
    Wáng Zǐjìng   a personal name, Wáng Xiànzhī, courtesy name Zǐjìng

14. 山陰 【名詞】地名，今浙江省紹興縣
    Shānyīn   a place name; present-day Shàoxīng district in Zhèjiāng province

15. 行 xíng 【動詞】走 to walk; to travel

16. 川 chuān 【名詞】河 a river

17. 映 yìng 【動詞】映襯 to set off

18. 發 fā 【動詞】顯現；顯露 to reveal

19. 應接 yìng jiē 【動詞語】反應接受 to respond and absorb/appreciate

20. 暇 xiá 【名詞】閒暇；空閒 leisure; free time; spare time

　　不暇 bù xiá 【動詞語】沒有足夠的時間；來不及 there is not enough time to...;

※ 應接不暇 yìng jiē bù xiá 【成語】來不及反應接受；來不及看；來不及欣賞 there is not enough time to observe and appreciate

21. 若 ruò 【連詞】至若；至於 as for

22. 際 jì 【名詞】間；指先後交接的時期 in the middle of; between

　　秋冬之際 qiū dōng zhī jì 【名詞語】秋冬交接的時期 between autumn and winter

23. 尤 yóu 【副詞】尤其 especially

24. 懷 huái 【名詞】情懷；內心的感受 feelings

　　為懷 wéi huái 【動詞語】描述內心的感受 to express/describe one's feelings

三
遠公講學

世說新語·規箴

遠公在盧山中，雖老，講論不輟。弟子中或有惰者，遠公曰：“桑榆之光，理無遠照；但願朝陽之暉，與時並明耳！”執經登坐，諷誦朗暢，詞色甚苦。高足之徒，皆肅然增敬。

Zhùyīn:

Yuǎngōng zài Lúshān zhōng, suī lǎo, jiàng lùn bú chuò. Dìzǐ zhōng huò yǒu duò zhě, Yuǎngōng yuē: "Sāng yú zhī guāng, lǐ wú yuǎn zhào; dàn yuàn zhāo yáng zhī huī, yǔ shí bìng míng ěr!" Zhí jīng dēng zuò, fěng sòng lǎng chàng, cí sè shèn kǔ. Gāo zú zhī tú, jiē sùrán zēng jìng.

注解

1. 規箴　【名詞】《世說新語》中的篇名 Heading of a chapter in *A New*
   Guīzhēn　　　　　　*Account of the Tales of the World*; 'Advices and Exhortations'

2. 遠公　【名詞】慧遠，晉代高僧
   Yuǎn Gōng　　　　Huì Yuǎn, a famous Buddhist master of the Jìn dynasty

3. 盧山　【名詞】在江西省九江市南 Mt. Lú, situated to the south of
   Lú Shān　　　　　present-day Jiǔjiāng city in Jiāngxī province

4. 講論　【動詞】講談論述 to discuss and expound
   jiǎng lùn

5. 輟 chuò　【動詞】停 to halt; to stop

6. 弟子　【名詞】門徒 disciples
   dì zǐ

7. 或 huò　【副詞】間或；偶爾；有時候 occasionally

8. 惰 duò　【形容詞】懶惰；懈怠 (xiè dài) lazy; idle

   惰者　【名詞語】懈怠的人 one who is idle/lazy
   duò zhě

9. 桑榆 【名詞】桑樹榆樹 mulberry and elm trees
   sāng yú 　　　　日落時光照桑榆，因以指日暮，比喻老年
   As the setting sun shines on top of mulberry or elm trees, these trees are commonly used to stand for sunset, which in turn is a metaphor for old age

   桑榆之光 【名詞語】日落時的光 the beams of a setting sun
   sāng yú zhī guāng 　　比喻老年人衰退的的精力
   standing for the declining energy of an old man

10. 理 lǐ 【名詞】按照道理 in principle; by reason

11. 無 wú 【副詞】不 not

12. 遠照 【動詞語】照得很遠 to shine very far
    yuǎn zhào

13. 願 yuàn 【動詞】願望；希望 to wish

14. 朝陽 【名詞語】朝陽；早晨的太陽 the morning sun; the rising sun
    zhāo yáng

15. 暉 huī 【名詞】光暉 lights; beams

    朝陽之暉 【名詞語】朝陽的光暉 the lights of a rising sun
    zhāo yáng zhī huī 　　比喻年輕人旺盛的的精力
    standing for the brimful energy of youngmen

16. 時 shí 【名詞】時間 time

17. 並 bìng 【副詞】一起 together; along with

18. 明 míng 【形容詞】明亮 bright

    並明 【形容詞】一起明亮 to be bright along
    bìng míng

    與時並明 【形容詞】跟時間一起明亮 bright along with time
    yǔ shí bìng míng 　　隨著時間變得越來越明亮

205

to brighten along with time; to become brighter as time goes by

19. 耳 ěr 　【助 詞】而已；罷了 [and] that's all

20. 執 zhí 　【動 詞】拿 to hold

21. 經 jīng 　【名 詞】經書；佛經 scriptures

22. 登坐 　【動 詞 語】登上座位 to go to one's seat
　　 dēng zuò

23. 諷 fěng; 　【動 詞】誦讀 to read aloud; to recite
　　 fèng

24. 朗暢 　【形 容 詞】響亮暢順 resonant and smooth
　　 lǎng chàng

25. 詞色 　【名 詞】言詞神色 the words and the expression
　　 cí sè

26. 苦 kǔ 　【形 容 詞】懇切 earnest

27. 高足 　【名 詞 語】門徒中品學優秀的人 accomplished disciples
　　 gāo zú

28. 肅然 　【副 詞】恭敬地；肅穆地 reverently; solumnly
　　 sù rán

29. 增敬 　【動 詞 語】增加敬意 to increase their respect/reverence
　　 zēng jìng

※ 肅然起敬 【成 語】肅穆地產生敬佩的態度或心情
　　 sù rán qǐ jìng 　　　　　great respect rising in one's heart

四
王戎喪兒

世說新語・傷逝

王戎喪兒萬子，山簡往省之。王悲不自勝。簡曰：
"孩抱中物，何至於此？"王曰："聖人忘情，最下不
及情；情之所鍾，正在我輩。"

Zhùyīn:

　　Wáng Róng sàng ér Wànzǐ, Shān Jiǎn wàng xǐng zhī. Wáng bēi bú zì shēng. Jiǎn
yuē: "Hái bào zhōng wù, hé zhì yú cǐ?" Wáng yuē: "Shèngrén wàng qíng, zuì xià bù jí
qíng, qíng zhī suǒ zhōng, zhèng zài wǒ bèi."

注解

1. **傷逝** 　【名詞】《世說新語》中的篇名 Heading of a chapter in *A New*
   Shāng shì 　　　*Account of the Tales of the World*; 'Lament for the Dead'

2. **王戎** 　【名詞】人名。姓王名戎，字濬沖，竹林七賢之一
   Wáng Róng 　　a personal name. Surnamed Wáng, named Róng, and courtesy
   name Ruìchōng, he was one of the Seven Masters in the
   Bamboo Groves.

3. **喪** sàng 　【動詞】喪失；死掉 to lose; to have...died; to suffer the death of...

4. **兒** ér 　【名詞】兒子 a son

5. **萬子** 　【名詞】人名。姓王，名綏，字萬子，是王戎之子
   Wànzǐ 　　a personal name. Surnamed Wáng, named Suí, courtesy name
   Wànzǐ, he was the son of Wáng Róng.

6. **山簡** 　【名詞】人名。姓山名簡，山濤之子，山濤亦為竹林七
   Shān Jiǎn 　　賢之一 a personal name. Surnamed Shān and named Jiǎn,
   he was the son of Shān Tāo, who was also one of the Seven
   Masters in the Bamboo Groves.

7. **省** xǐng 　【動詞】探望；拜望 to visit; to pay a visit to

8. **悲** bēi 　【形容詞】悲痛；傷心 to be grieved

9. **勝** shèng 　【動詞】克制；克服 to overcome; to keep ... under control

207

不自勝 【動詞語】〔自己〕克制不住自己
bú zì shèng　　　　　　　　unable to restrain one's grief; to be overcome with grief

※ 悲不自勝 【成語】悲傷得自己克制不住自己
bēi bú zì shèng　　　　　　so grieved as to be unable to control oneself

10 孩抱中物 【名詞語】抱在懷中的小東西；小孩兒
hái bào zhōng wù　　　　　something small cuddled in one's arms; a child

11. 何至於此 【動詞語】為什麼…到這個地步
hé zhì yú cǐ　　　　　　　why ... to such a degree?

12. 聖人　　【名詞語】聰明睿(ruì)智，於事無不通的人
shèng rén　　　　　　　　a man of great wisdom and resourcefulness; a sage

13. 情 qíng　【動詞】情感　feelings; affection; sentiments; emotions

　　忘情　【動詞語】忘掉情感；超越情感
wàng qíng　　　　　　　　to be unmindful of all emotions; to transcend emotions

14. 最下　【名詞語】最愚笨的人
zuì xià　　　　　　　　　a fool; an imbecile

15. 及 jí　　【動詞】達到　to reach; to be up to

　　不及情 【動詞語】達不到情；不知情為何物
bù jí qíng　　　　　　　　isn't up to feelings; doesn't understand what feelings are

16. 鍾 zhōng【動詞】聚集　to concentrate; to accumulate

　　所鍾　【名詞語】所＋V＝V之 N；聚集之處
suǒ zhōng　　　　　　　　where ... concentrate(s)

17. 正 zhèng【副詞】正好；恰好　just; happen to

18. 我輩　【名詞語】我等；我們這類的人
wǒ bèi　　　　　　　　　we folks; people like us

第六篇

說馬

唐　韓愈

作者　韓愈 (Hán Yù, 768-824 A.D.) 字退之，唐昌黎（今河北通縣東）人。博通五經、百家之言，崇尚儒家學說，駁斥佛教及老子的思想。提倡古文，反對駢文，是唐宋兩代最著名的八大散文家之一。官至吏部侍郎。卒諡文。著有《韓昌黎集》。

Hán Yù (768-824 A.D.) courtesy name Tuìzhī, was a native of Chānglí, to the east of present-day Tōng district in Héběi province. With an extensive knowledge of the Five Confucian Classics as well as the doctrines of various schools of thought, he upheld Confucian teachings and repudiated those of Buddhism and Taoism. He promoted the ancient style of prose and rejected vehemently the 'parallel prose' style that had been prevalent since the time of the Southern Dynasties. He was one of the 'eight prose masters' of the Táng and Sòng. Having reached the rank of Vice-president of the Department of Civil Personnel, he was granted the posthumous honorific title 'Wén.' His written works are preserved in the *Collected Works of Hán Chānglī*.

篇旨

作者以千里馬難遇伯樂為喻，來慨嘆人即使讀書人懷有美好的才幹，若遇不到人賞識、愛惜、重用，也只能鬱鬱以終，無由發揮而浪費了他的才能。

The author uses the fact that steeds rarely find a good appraiser as a metaphor for those scholars of extraordinary ability who are not appreciated, let alone cherished, and who, failing to find appropriately employment, are bound to die in obscurity and disappointment, their remarkable talents totally wasted.

世有伯樂，然後有千里馬；千里馬常有，而伯樂不常有。故雖有名馬，祇辱於奴隸人之手，駢死於槽櫪之間，不以千里稱也。

Zhùyīn:

    Shì yǒu Bólè, rán hòu yǒu qiān lǐ mǎ; qiān lǐ mǎ cháng yǒu, ér Bólè bù cháng yǒu. Gù suī yǒu míng mǎ, zhǐ rù yú nú lì rén zhī shoǔ, pián sǐ yú cáo lì zhī jiān, bù yǐ qiān lǐ chēng ye.

注 解

1. 世 shì　　【名詞】天下；世界上；世間　the world; in society

2. 伯樂　　【名詞】周代善於相馬的人，姓孫名陽，伯樂是他的
   Bó lè　　　　　　字。 Sūn Yáng, a famous horse appraiser in Zhōu dynasty, Bólè was his coutesy name

   ◆ 相 xiàng　　　　　　to examine the appearance and judge

3. 里 lǐ　　【名詞】長度單位，等於三分之一英里　a unit of length (=1/3 mile)

4. 馬 mǎ　　【名詞】馬　horses

   千里馬【名詞語】日行千里之駿(jùn)馬；每天能跑一千里的好
   qiān lǐ mǎ　　　　　馬　a horse that covers a thousand li a day; a winged steed

5. 辱 rǔ　　【動詞】侮(wǔ)辱　to insult; to humiliate

6. 奴隸　　【名詞】供人役使而身體不能自由的人　a bond servant;
   nú lì　　　　　　a slave

   奴隸人【名詞語】做奴隸的人　slaves
   nú lì rén

7. 駢 pián　　【動詞】並列　to stand side by side; to place side by side

8. 槽 cáo　　【名詞】馬槽；喂牲畜（牛、馬等）盛飼(sì)料的器具
   　　　　　　a manger; a trough

210

9. 櫪 lì 　【名詞】養馬的地方；馬棚(péng) a stable

10. 稱 chēng 　【動詞】叫 to name; to call

　　馬之千里者，一食或盡粟一石；食馬者不知其能千里而食也。是馬也，雖有千里之能，食不飽，力不足，才美不外見；且欲與常馬等不可得，安求其能千里也。

Mǎ zhī qiān lǐ zhě, yí shí huò jìn sù yí dàn; sì mǎ zhě, bù zhī qí néng qiān lǐ ér sì yě. Shì mǎ yě, suī yǒu qiān lǐ zhī néng, shí bù bǎo, lì bù zú, cái měi bú wài xiàn; qiě yù yǔ cháng mǎ děng ér bù kě dé, ān qiú qí néng qiān lǐ yě.

11. 馬之千里者 【名詞語】千里馬（形容詞後置）　a winged steed
　　mǎ zhī qiān lǐ zhě 　　　　For modifier postposition, see prose 2, n. 57, p. 163

　　"千里馬"是個名詞語。"千里"是定語，"馬"是被修飾的中心詞。為了突顯中心詞"馬"，把它提到前面來，而把定語"千里"放在它後面，再加一"者"複指中心詞"馬"，寫成"馬之千里者"。中心詞"馬"與定語"千里"間的關係好樣是分母（馬）與分子（千里）的關係。"馬之千里者"一字一字地譯成白話應為"馬裡的每天能跑一千里的"，聽起來很囉嗦。為求通順自然，仍然可以譯成"每天能跑一千里的馬"。

"Qiān lǐ mǎ" (a thousand li horse) is a noun phrase in which "mǎ", the modified noun, is modified by "qiānlǐ". If a writer wishes to highlight the word "mǎ", he could move it in front of the adjectival modifier "qiānlǐ" and add the pronoun "zhě" immediately after the the adjectival modifier to reiterate the modified noun "mǎ". This construction would yield the following phrase: "mǎ zhī qiānlǐ zhě". In the noun phrase "mǎ zhī qiānlǐ zhě", the relation between the adjectival modifier and the noun is comparable to that between a general class or genus "mǎ" and a sub-class or species "qiānlǐ"; that is, the modifier defines or delimits a class or group inside the general category defined by the noun. Translated into spoken Chinese, the noun phrase "mǎ zhī qiānlǐ zhě" literally means "mǎ lǐ dē měitiān néng pǎo yìqiānlǐ dē" (of horses the can run one thousand lǐ every day ones). It sounds very awkward and wordy. For the sake of smoothness, it can be simply rendered in spoken Chinese as "měitiān néng pǎo yìqiānlǐ dē mǎ" (horses that can run one thousand lǐ every day).

12. 食 shí 　【動詞】吃 to eat

一食　【動詞語】吃一次；吃一頓(dùn)　to eat one meal
yì shí

13. 盡 jìn　【動詞】窮盡；吃完　to exhaust; to eat up

14. 粟 sù　【名詞】小米　millet
　　　　　　　糧(liáng)食　grain

15. 石 dàn　【名詞】容量單位，等於一公石。它在古書中讀作 shí
　　　　　　　a unit of dry measure for grain (=1 hectolitre). It was
　　　　　　　pronounced "shí" in ancient books

16. 食 sì　【動詞】給…吃；餵(wèi)　to bring food to; to feed

　　食馬者　【名詞語】餵馬的人　the person who feeds the horses
　　sì mǎ zhě

17. 是 shì　【指示代詞】此；這　this

18. 能 néng　【名詞】能力　ability; capability

19. 飽 bǎo　【形容詞】飽足　to have eaten one's fill; to be full

20. 力 lì　【名詞】力量；氣力　the strength

21. 足 zú　【形容詞】充足；夠　sufficient; enough; ample

22. 才 cái　【名詞】才力；才能　talent; ability

23. 美 měi　【形容詞】美好　perfect; excellent

　　才美　【描寫句】才能美好　[endowed with] perfect ability;
　　cái měi　　　　　　　the excellence of its ability

24. 見 xiàn　【動詞】同"現"，顯(xiǎn)現　to show; to manifest

　　外見　【動詞語】在外面顯現；顯現到外面來
　　wài xiàn　　　　　　to manifest outwardly

25. 欲 yù　【動詞】想要　to desire; to want

26. 常 cháng 【形容詞】平常；普通 common; general; ordinary

27. 等 děng 【形容詞】相等；相同；一樣 to equal; to be the same

28. 求 qiú 【動詞】要求 to demand; to require

策之不以其道，食之不能盡其材，鳴之而不能通其意，執策而臨之，曰：“天下無馬。”嗚呼！其真無馬邪？其真不知馬也？

Cè zhī bù yǐ qí dào, sì zhī bù néng jìn qí cái, míng zhī ér bù néng tōng qí yì, zhí cè ér lín zhī yuē: "Tiānxià wú mǎ." Wū hū! Qí zhēn wú mǎ yé? Qí zhēn bù zhī mǎ yě?

29. 策 cè 【名詞】竹製的馬鞭 (biān) 子 a whip made of bamboo

【動詞】鞭打 to whip

30. 道 dào 【名詞】規律；道理 proper ways; principle

31. 材 cái 【名詞】通 “才”，資質、才能、能力
natural endowment; talents; ability

盡其材【動詞語】使其才能窮盡 to exhaust its ability
jìn qí cái ——→使牠的才能完全發揮出來
to bring its ability into full play

32. 鳴 míng 【動詞】吆喝 (yāo hè)；大聲驅趕 to shout at [the horse] and urge it on

33. 通 tōng 【動詞】通曉 (xiǎo)；徹底明瞭 (liǎo) to understand thoroughly

34. 意 yì 【名詞】意願；願望 inclination; wish; desire

35. 執 zhí 【動詞】拿 to hold in the hand

36. 臨 lín 【動詞】走近 to appoach

37. 嗚呼　【感嘆詞】唉　alas!
　　wū hū

◆ **感嘆詞**　　　　　　an exclamation
　　gǎntàncí

38. 其 qí　【連詞】用在選擇問句句首，可譯為 " 是… "
　　　　　　　used at the beginning of an alternative interrogative sentence,
　　　　　　　it can be rendered as "shì …" in modern Chinese

◆ **選擇問句**　　　　an alternative interrogative sentence
　　xuǎnzéwènjù

39. 邪 yé　【助詞】用在選擇問句句末，可譯為 " 呢 "
　　　　　　　used at the end of an alternative interrogative sentence, it can be
　　　　　　　rendered as "nē?" in modern Chinese

40. 也 yě　【助詞】用如 " 邪 "　here it is used as the interrogative particle "yé"

　　其…邪？其…也【選擇問句】是…呢？還是…呢？
　　qǐ … yé　　qí … yě　　　　　　　　Is it …, or is it …?

第七篇

陋室銘

唐　劉禹錫

作 者　劉禹錫 (772-842 A.D.) 字夢得，爲唐代彭城（今江蘇省徐州市）人。早年官至監察御史。後因黨爭長期被貶。828 A.D.方回朝爲主客郎中，晚年任太子賓客。秉性剛介傲岸，長於詩文。著有《劉賓客文集》。

Liú Yǔxí (772-842 A.D.), courtesy name Mèngdé, was a native of Péngchéng, present-day Xúzhōu in Jiāngsū province. In his early years he served as a censor, but as a result of factional politics, he was demoted for a long period of time, before being called back to the court in 828 A.D. to serve in the Board of Rites. In his last years he was the Tutor of the Crown Prince. He was a great writer in both the poetry and essay modes, esteemed for his upright, outspoken, and proud character. His work was entitled *Literary Collections of Tutor Liú*.

篇旨

作者強調所居陋室簾外景色清幽、室內情調高雅，擺脫俗務的君子居於其中，滿室自有道德芳香，可與古代賢人的居所相比，簡陋而不鄙陋！

The author stresses that although his abode is crude, the scenery outside the curtain of his dwelling is serene and charming, and even the sentiment and atmosphere within his room have a nobility and elegance. Where a true gentleman resides without any worldly cares is comparable to the dwellings of ancient worthies, for both are permeated with the fragrance of virtue. It may be crude, but it's not rude at all!

　　山不在高，有仙則名。水不在深，有龍則靈。斯是陋室，唯吾德馨。苔痕上階綠，草色入簾青。談笑有鴻儒，往來無白丁。可以調素琴，閱金經。無絲竹之亂耳，無案牘之勞形。南陽諸葛廬，西蜀子雲亭。孔子曰："何陋之有？"

Zhùyīn:

　　Shān bú zài gāo, yǒu xiān zé míng. Shuǐ bú zài shēn, yǒu lóng zé líng. Sī shì lòu shì, wéi wú dé xīng. Tái hén shàng jiē lǜ, cǎo sè rù lián qīng. Tán xiào yǒu hóng rú, wǎng lái wú bái dīng. Kě yǐ tiáo sù qín, yuè jīn jīng. Wú sī zhú zhī luàn ěr, wú àn dú zhī láo xíng. Nányáng Zhūgé lú, Xīshǔ Zǐyún tíng. Kǒngzǐ yuē: "Hé loù zhī yǒu?"

注解

1. 陋 lòu 　　【形容詞】 簡陋 humble and crude; lack of refinement

215

陋室 【名詞詞】簡陋的居室 a humble room; a crude abode
lòu shì

2. 銘 míng 【名詞】〔刻在器物上的〕記述文字，通常押韻 inscriptions; words cut in stone or metal as a record, usually in rhyme

3. 在 zài 【動詞】在於；決定於；依靠 to rest on; to be decided by ...

4. 仙 xiān 【名詞】仙人，神話中長生不老並有種種超自然力量的人 immortals with supernatural power

5. 名 míng 【形容詞】有名；著名 famous; noted

6. 龍 lóng 【名詞】龍 dragons

7. 靈 líng 【形容詞】靈驗；〔對祈禱〕有神奇的反應或效果 efficacious; effective; miraculously responsive [to prayers]

8. 斯 sī 【指示代詞】此；這個 this

9. 德 dé 【名詞】道德；品行 moral character

10. 馨 xīng; 【形容詞】芳香 fragrant
xīn

11. 苔 tái 【名詞】青苔 moss

苔痕 【名詞語】青苔的痕跡 the trace of moss; mossy traces
tái hén

12. 上 shàng 【動詞】爬上，向上蔓延 to creep up; to extend upward

13. 階 jiē 【名詞】台階 steps leading up to a building

上階 【動詞語】上台階；蔓延到台階上 to creep up the flight of
shàng jiē steps

14. 綠 lù 【形容詞】綠 green

15. 草色 cǎo sè 【名詞語】草的顏色 the color of grass

16. 簾 lián 【名詞】竹簾 a bamboo curtain

入簾 rù lián 【動詞語】透入竹簾內 to go through/penetrate the bamboo curtain

17. 青 qīng 【形容詞】綠 green

18. 談笑 tán xiào 【動詞】談論、說笑 to chat and laugh

19. 鴻儒 hóng rú 【名詞語】博學之士；學識淵博的讀書人 erudite scholars

20. 往來 wǎng lái 【動詞】彼此訪問；交往 to visit or associate with each other

21. 白丁 bái dīng 【名詞語】無學識的人 ignorant persons

22. 調 tiáo 【動詞】彈奏 to play [a musical instrument]

23. 素 sù 【形容詞】樸素 simple and plain

24. 琴 qín 【名詞】樂器，有五弦或七弦 a Chinese lute having five or seven strings

素琴 sù qín 【名詞語】樸素的、沒有雕飾的琴 a plain Chinese lute

25. 閱 yuè 【動詞】讀 to read

26. 金經 jīn jīng 【名詞語】用泥金書寫的佛經 a Buddhist Sutra written with ink made of gold powder

27. 絲竹 sī zhú 【名詞】絲弦和竹管；指琴簫(xiāo)等樂器 strings and pipes; musical instruments

28. 亂 luàn 【動詞】擾亂 to confuse; to bother

亂耳
luàn ěr　　【動詞語】擾亂耳朵 to bother the ears; cacophonous to the ears

29. 案牘
àn dú　　【名詞語】官府文書 official correspondence or documents

30. 勞 láo　　【形容詞】勞累 fatigued; tired

【形容詞使動用法】使…勞累 to cause ... to be fatigued

勞形
láo xíng　　【動詞語】使形體勞累 to tire out the body

"使形勞"是個使動結構，其中"形"是兼語，若把兼語
後的形容詞"勞"移放到兼語"形"之前，就會有使動的
作用，不再需要"使"字。其目的在求文句簡練。

"shǐ xíng láo" is a typical causative construction, where "xíng" is the pivotal
element. If the adjective "láo" which follows the pivotal element is transposed in
front of the pivottal element, it assumes a causative meaning and the original "shǐ"
is no long necessary. The object of this type of construction is to create a more
compact sentence with a laconic tone. Cf. prose 2, n. 51, p. 172

31. 南陽
Nán yáng　　【名窗語】地名，在今湖北襄陽縣西
　　　　　　　a place name, to the west of present-day Xiāngyáng district
　　　　　　　in Húběi province

32. 諸葛
Zhūgé　　【名詞】諸葛亮，字孔明(181-234 A.D.)，三國時代蜀國
　　　　　的丞相，曾隱居南陽躬耕
　　　　　Zhūgé Liàng (181-234 A.D.), courtesy name Kǒngmíng, was
　　　　　the prime minister of the Shǔ state during the Three Kingdoms
　　　　　period. He once led a reclusive, farming life in Nányáng.

33. 廬 lú　　【名詞】茅廬；草頂的房子 a thatched hut or cottage

34. 西蜀
Xī shǔ　　【名詞語】地名，四川西部
　　　　　place name; the western part of Sìchuān province

35. 子雲
Zǐyún　　【名詞】揚雄，字子雲(B.C. 53 - 18 A.D.)，西漢末著名的
　　　　　文學家和學者
　　　　　Yáng Xióng (B.C. 53-18 A.D.), courtesy name Zǐyún, was a
　　　　　famous scholar and man of letters at the end of the Western Hàn
　　　　　dynasty.

36. 亭 tíng 【名詞】亭子 a pavilion

37. 孔子 【名詞】姓孔名丘，字仲尼 (B.C. 551 - 479)，儒家創始人
    Kǒng zǐ   Surnamed Kǒng and named Qiū (B.C. 551-479), courtesy name Zhòngní, he was the founder of the Confucian school, also known in the West as Confucius.

38. 曰 yuē 【動詞】說 to say

39. 之 zhī 【助詞】"之"有把賓語提到動詞前的作用，表示強調
    As a structural particle, the word "zhī" has a function of transposing the object in front of the verb, to indicate emphasis.

何陋之有【疑問句】有何陋？有什麼陋呢？
Hé lòu zhī yǒu   Where is the lacking of refinement? What rudeness will there be?

《論語・子罕》子欲居九夷。或曰："陋如之何？"子曰："君子居之，何陋之有？"

The Matser was wishing to go and live among the nine wild tribes of the east. Someone said, 'They are rude. How can you do such a thing?' The Master said, 'If a superior man dwelt among them, what rudeness will there be?'
(James Legge's translation)

第八篇

臨江之麋

唐　柳宗元

作者 　見詩選《江雪》 p. 099

篇旨

藉小麋至死不悟的寓言，作者提醒世人處世當悟

外力庇護之不可永恃，要生存必須認清時勢及自立自強的道理。文筆簡潔生動，堪稱古文範例。

By way of a fable about a dim-witted elk, the author reminds people of the truth that one must never rely on the protection of outsiders, and that one must have a clear view of one's own situation, relying on one's own ability and will to survive in a competitive world. Written in a language that is lively and energetic, it can be considered a model essay in the ancient style.

臨江之人畋，得麋麑，畜之。入門，群犬垂涎，揚尾皆來，其人怒，怛之。自是日抱就犬，習示之，使勿動，稍使與之戲。積久，犬皆如人意。麋麑稍大，忘己之麋也，以為犬良我友，抵觸偃仆，益狎。犬畏主人，與之俯仰甚善，然時啖其舌。

三年，麋出門，見外犬在道甚眾，走欲與為戲。外犬見而喜且怒，共殺食之，狼藉道上。麋至死不悟。

Zhùyīn:

Línjiāng zhī rén tián, dé mí ní, xù zhī. Rù mén, jún quǎn chuí xián, yáng wěi jiē lái, qí rén nù, dá zhī. Zì shì rì bào jiù quǎn, xí shì zhī, shǐ wù dòng, shāo shǐ yǔ zhī xì. Jī jiǔ, quǎn jiē rú rén yì. Mí ní shāo dà, wàng jǐ zhī mí yě, yǐ wéi quǎn liáng wǒ yǒu, dǐ chù yǎn pū, yì xiá. Quǎn wèi zhǔ rén, yǔ zhī fǔ yǎng shèn shàn, rán shí dàn qí shé.

Sān nián, mí chū mén, jiàn wài quǎn zài dào shèn zhòng, zǒu yù yǔ wéi xì. Wài quǎn jiàn ér xǐ qiě nù, gòng shā shí zhī, láng jí dào shàng. Mí zhì sǐ bú wù.

注 解

1. **臨江** Lín jiāng 【名詞】唐代縣名，在今江西省清江縣 name of a district in present-day Qīngjiāng district of Jiāngxī province

2. **麋** mí 【名詞】獸名，與鹿同類但稍大 the name of an animal; an elk; a large deer that lives in northern Europe and Asia; in America, it is also called a moose

3. **畋** tián 【動詞】打獵 to go hunting

4. 麛麑 mí ní 【名詞語】小麛 a young elk; a baby elk

5. 畜 xù 【動詞】畜養；飼 (sì) 養 to raise [as with domestic animals]

6. 群 qún 【量詞】用於成群的人或東西 a group; a herd; a flock

7. 犬 quǎn 【名詞】狗 dogs

8. 垂 chuí 【動詞】落下；流下；滴下 to flow down; to drip

9. 涎 xián 【名詞】口水 saliva; mouth water

   垂涎 chuí xián 【動詞語】流口水 to slaver; to drool

10. 揚 yáng 【動詞】舉 (jǔ) 起 to raise
    豎起 to set upright; to erect

11. 尾 wěi 【名詞】尾巴 tail

12. 怒 nù 【形容詞】生氣 angry; furious

13. 怛 dá 【動詞】使…害怕；嚇唬 to frighten; to scare; to intimidate

14. 日 rì 【副詞】日日；天天；每天 day by day; every day

15. 抱 bào 【動詞】用手臂圍持；抱著 to hold in the arms

16. 就 jiù 【動詞】到…那兒去；靠近 to move toward

17. 習 xí 【副詞】習常地；常常 customarily; habitually; frequently

18. 示 shì 【動詞】給…看 to show; to point out to

19. 勿 wù 【副詞】不要；別 do not

20. 稍 shāo 【副詞】逐漸地；一點一點地 gradually; little by little

221

21. 戲 xì 【動詞】遊戲 to play

22. 積 jī 【動詞】積累 to accumulate

23. 久 jiǔ 【時間詞】時間長；長久 of a certain duration of time

積久 jī jiǔ 【動詞語】積累的時間長了 to accumulate over the course of time

24. 如 rú 【動詞】依照；順從 to follow; to be obedient to

如人意 rú rén yì 【動詞語】順從主人的意思 to be obedient to the owner's wish

25. 大 dà 【動詞】長大 to grow up; to be brought up

26. 以為 yǐ wéi 【動詞】認為；覺得 to think that; to feel that

　　　"以為"基本上是個意動動詞；它後面的小句所說的不是一件事實，而只是存在心裡的一種主觀的想法。"以為"可以合用，也可以分用。本句是合用的例子。

"Yǐ wéi" is basically a **putative verb**; what is said after it is not a fact, but a subjective idea held by the syntactic subject. This verb can be conjoined as "Yǐwéi..." or separated as "yǐ...wéi ...". Here it is conjoined.

27. 良 liáng 【副詞】的確 indeed

28. 抵 dǐ 【動詞】擠 to push against sb.

29. 觸 chù 【動詞】〔用角〕頂撞 to bump against sb. [with horn]

30. 偃 yǎn 【動詞】仰面倒下去；臉朝上地倒下去 to fall on one's back

31. 仆 pū 【動詞】臉朝下地倒下去 to fall forward; to prostrate

32. 益 yì 【副詞】更加 more; even more

33. 狎 xiá 【形容詞】親近而隨便 to be very intimate with sb.; to take liberties with sb.

益狎　【形容詞】更加親近而隨便 to take even more liberties with sb.
yì xiá

34. 畏 wèi　【動詞】畏懼；怕 to fear

35. 俯 fǔ　【動詞】低頭；面向下 to lower (or hang) one's head; to face down

36. 仰 yǎng　【動詞】抬頭；臉向上 to raise one's head; to face up

37. 啖 dàn　【動詞】吃 to eat ──→ 舔 (tiǎn) to lick

啖其舌　【動詞語】舔牠的舌頭；顯出一副饞 (chán) 相 to lick with the
dàn qí shé　　　　　　tongue; to reveal a lickerish expression

38. 道 dào　【名詞】路 a road; a street

39. 眾 zhòng　【形容詞】多 numerous

40. 走 zǒu　【動詞】跑 to run

41. 喜 xǐ　【形容詞】高興 glad; happy

42. 共 gòng　【副詞】共同；一起 together; jointly

43. 狼藉　【形容詞】縱橫散亂；亂七八糟，到處都是
láng jí　　　　in total disorder; scattered about in a mess

44. 至 zhì　【動詞】到 till; until

45. 悟 wù　【動詞】醒悟；了解；明白 to realize; to awaken

※ 至死不悟【成語】一直到死也還不明白
zhì sì bú wù　　　　did not come to realize [the truth, reason etc.] till death;
　　　　　　　　　to hold on to one's wrong belief till death

第九篇

賣油翁

宋　　歐陽修

作者　　見詞選《生查子》 P. 130

篇旨

通過射箭與瀝油說明"業精於勤"的道理。任何技藝只要不斷練習，就能得心應手，達到妙境。

Through the examples of archery and trickling oil, the author illustrates the points that excellence in work is only possible with diligence, and that hard and incessant practice in the sine qua non of achieving great facility.

　　陳康肅公堯咨善射，當世無雙；公亦以此自矜。嘗射於家圃，有賣油翁釋擔而立，睨之久而不去；見其發矢，十中八九，但微頷之。康肅問曰："汝亦知射乎？吾射不亦精乎？"翁曰："無他，但手熟爾。"康肅忿然曰："汝安敢輕吾射？"翁曰："以我酌油知之。"乃取一葫蘆置於地，以錢覆其口，徐以杓酌油瀝之，自錢孔入，而錢不濕。因曰："我亦無他，惟手熟爾。"康肅笑而遣之。

Zhùyīn:

　　　Chén Kāngsù gōng Yáozī shàn shè, dāng shì wú shuāng; gōng yì yǐ cǐ zì jīn. Cháng shè yú jiā pǔ, yǒu mài yóu wēng shì dàn ér lì, nì zhī jiǔ ér bú qù; jiàn qí fā shǐ, shí zhòng bā jiǔ, dàn wēi hàn zhī. Kāngsù wèn yuē: "Rǔ yì zhī shè hū? Wú shè bú yì jīng hū?" Wēng yuē: "Wú tuō, dàn shǒu shú ěr." Kāngsù fèn rán yuē: "Rǔ ān gǎn qīng wú shè?" Wēng yuē: "Yǐ wǒ zhuó yóu zhī zhī." Nǎi qǔ yì hú lú zhì yú dì, yǐ qián fù qí kǒu, xú yǐ sháo zhuó yóu lì zhī, zì qián kǒng rù, ér qián bù shī. Yīn yuē: "Wǒ yì wú tuō, wéi shǒu shú ěr." Kāngsù xiào ér qiǎn zhī.

注 解

1. 賣 mài 　【動詞】以貨物換錢 to sell

2. 油 yóu 　【名詞】食油；炒菜用的油 cooking oil

3. 翁 wēng 　【名詞】老頭兒 an old man

   賣油翁【名詞語】賣油的老頭兒 an old man who sells the cooking oil
   mài yóu wēng

4. 陳堯咨【名詞】人名，姓陳，名堯咨，字嘉謨 (Jiāmó)，康肅
   Chén Yáozī 　　　　(Kāngsù)是他的諡號。他是宋真宗時的進士，
   工隸書，善射，官至大學士。古代人寫文章
   提到已去世的大官時，常稱他的諡號來表示
   尊敬 name of an official during the reign of Emperor Zhēn of Sòng (r. 998-1122 A.D.). Surnamed Chén, and named Yáozī, Kāngsù was his posthumous honorific title. He was a presented scholar, good at calligraphy in the official script style. He was also a skilled archer, and served as a Grand Secretary. It was common to use the posthumous title to refer to a deceased person in order to show respect.

5. 公 gōng 　【名詞】對男子的尊稱 a respectful salutation to man

6. 善 shàn 　【形容詞】善於；精於；很會 to be good at; to be an expert in

7. 射 shè 　【動詞】射箭 to shoot with bow and arrow
   　　　　　【名詞】射藝；射箭的技巧 archery

8. 當 dāng 　【介詞】在某個時候或某個地方 at; indicating time, place, or range

9. 世 shì 　【名詞】時代 epoch; era; times

225

當世　　【名詞語】在他那個時代 during his time; in his days
dāng shì

10. 雙 shuāng【名詞】匹配(pèi)的人；敵手 an equal; a match; a rival

無雙　　【動詞語】沒有能跟他比的人
wú shuāng　　　　　　 unparalleled; unrivaled; matchless

11. 以 yǐ　　【介詞】拿；憑藉(píng jiè) using; taking; rely on; depend on

12. 此 cǐ　　【指示代詞】這個，本文中指"善射" this

13. 矜 jīn　　【動詞】矜誇(kuā)；誇耀 to brag; to boast

自矜　　【動詞語】自我矜誇；自己誇耀自己
zì jīn　　　　　　 singing one's own praise

14. 嘗 cháng【副詞】曾(céng)經 denoting a certain past experience or a certain
　　　　　　　　 state that existed at some time in the past

15. 圃 pǔ　　【名詞】菜園，種植蔬(shū)菜瓜果的園子 a vegetable garden;
　　　　　　　　 ground used for growing vegetables, flowers, or fruits

16. 釋 shì　　【動詞】放下 to lay down

17. 擔 dàn　　【名詞】擔子；挑(tiāo)在肩(jiān)上的東西 a carrying pole and
　　　　　　　　 the loads on it

18. 立 lì　　【動詞】站 to stand

19. 睨 nì　　【動詞】斜視；斜(xié)著眼看；從眼角看
　　　　　　　　 to look askance; looking sideways; to look at sb. disdainfully
　　　　　　　　 out of the corner of one's eyes

20. 久 jiǔ　　【副詞】時間長；長久；很久 for a long time

21. 發 fā　　【動詞】發射；射 to shoot

22. 矢 shǐ　　【名詞】箭 arrows

23. 中 zhòng【動詞】射中目標 to hit the target

24. 微 wēi 【副詞】微微 slightly

25. 頷 hàn 【動詞】點頭 to nod one's head; to nod

26. 汝 rǔ 【代詞】你 you (used in addressing an inferior)

27. 不亦…乎 【固定句型】不也…嗎？ Isn't it ...?
bú yì ... hū 以反問表肯定 use a rhetorical question for an affirmative sense

28. 精 jīng 【形容詞】精妙 exquisite; superb

29. 無他 【動詞語】沒有別的緣故 for no other reason than
wú tuō

30. 但 dàn 【副詞】僅僅；只不過 merely; only

31. 熟 shú 【形容詞】熟練 skilled; proficient

32. 爾 ěr 【助詞】用於句末，同"耳"；而已；罷了
used at the end of a sentence, meaning: only; merely; that is all

33. 忿然 【副詞】忿怒地 angrily; indignantly
fèn rán

34. 安 ān 【副詞】何；怎麼 how

35. 敢 gǎn 【助動詞】敢；膽敢 dare; to be brave enough to...

36. 輕 qīng 【動詞】輕視；看不起 to despise; to underestimate

37. 酌 zhuó 【動詞】倒 (dào)進 to pour into

酌油 【動詞語】倒油；把油倒進… to pour the oil
zhuó yóu

38. 乃 nǎi 【副詞】就 then

39. 取 qǔ 【動詞】拿 to take

40. 葫蘆 【名詞】葫蘆的果實；中間細，像兩個球連在一起，
   hú lú 古人常挖出它的瓤 (ráng)，用為貯 (zhù)酒之器
   a bottle gourd; a calabash

41. 置 zhì 【動詞】擱 (gē)；放 to place; to put

42. 錢 qián 【名詞】銅錢 a copper coin with a square hole in the center

43. 覆 fù 【動詞】蓋住 to cover

44. 其口 【名詞】它之口；此處指葫蘆之口；葫蘆嘴 the mouth of
   qí kǒu the bottle gourd

45. 徐 xú 【副詞】徐緩 (huǎn)地；緩緩地 slowly; gently

46. 杓 sháo 【名詞】杓兒 a spoon; a ladle

47. 瀝 lì 【動詞】滴下；液 (yè)體一滴一滴地落下 to drip; to trickle

   瀝之 【名詞】使之／油向下滴
   lì zhī to drip/trickle the oil

48. 孔 kǒng 【名詞】洞 a hole

   錢孔 【名詞語】銅錢中央 (yāng)的方洞
   qián kóng the rectangular hole in the center of a coin

49. 濕 shī 【動詞】沾 (zhān)濕 to moisten; to make wet

50. 因 yīn 【副詞】於是；就 thereupon

51. 亦 yì 【副詞】也 also; too

52. 惟 wéi 【副詞】只是 only; merely

53. 遣 qiǎn 【動詞】打發；讓某人離開 to send sb. away; to dismiss

第十篇

愛蓮說

宋　周敦頤

作者　周敦頤(1017-1073 A.D.)字茂叔，宋道州（今湖南省道縣）人；世稱濂溪先生。爲宋代理學大師，著有《太極圖說》、《通書》等。時人稱讚他"胸懷灑落，如光風霽月"。

Zhōu Dūnyí (1017-1073 A.D.), courtesy name Màoshú, was a native of Dàozhōu, present-day Dào district in Húnán province. He was commonly referred to as Master of Liánxī. He was one of the leaders of the Neo-Confucian intellectual movement during the Northern Sòng dynasty. His works include *Explanation of the Diagram of the Great Ultimate, Penetrating the Book of Changes,* and other philosophical writings. His contemporaries praised him as "casual and elegant in mental outlook, like a cheerful breeze on a sunny day, or a clear moon after rain."

篇旨　作者認爲花之有蓮正如人之有君子，兩者都具備挺直、清美、通達、莊重的特質，故值得讚美與愛賞。文字清雅有力，"出淤泥而不染，濯清漣而不妖，香遠益清，亭亭淨植"更是描繪蓮花的千古名句。

The author thinks that in the world of flowers the lotus is like the gentlemen in the human society; both possessing the attributes of erectness, elegance, openness, and sobriety; and as such, both deserving high praised and appreciation. The writing style is lucid and powerful, as exemplified by the lines "growing out of silt yet spotless; bathing in crystal clear water without being seductive; its sweet scent can be smelled far away, and it stands clean and erect," a description of lotus that has remained unsurpassed throughout the ages.

水陸草木之花，可愛者甚蕃；晉陶淵明獨愛菊。自李唐來，世人甚愛牡丹。予獨愛蓮之出淤泥而不染，濯清漣而不妖；中通外直，不蔓不枝；香遠益清，亭亭淨植，可遠觀而不可褻玩焉。

予謂：菊，花之隱逸者也；牡丹，花之富貴者也；蓮，花之君子者也。噫！菊之愛，陶後鮮有聞；蓮之愛，同予者何人？牡丹之愛，宜乎眾矣。

Zhùyīn:

Shuǐ lù cǎo mù zhī huā, kě ài zhě shèn fán; Jìn Táo Yuānmíng dú ài jú, zì Lǐ Táng lái, shì rén shèn ài mǔdān. Yú dú ài lián zhī chū yū ní ér bù rǎn, zhuó qīng lián ér bù yāo; zhōng tōng wài zhí, bú màn bù zhī; xiāng yuǎn yì qīng, tíng tíng jìng zhí, kě yuǎn guān ér bù kě xiè wán yān.

Yú wèi: "Jú, huā zhī yǐn yì zhě yě; mǔdān, huā zhī fù guì zhě yě; lián, huā zhī jūn zǐ zhě yě. Yì! Jú zhī ài, Táo hòu xiǎn yǒu wén; lián zhī ài, tóng yú zhě hé rén? Mǔdān zhī ài, yí hū zhòng yǐ."

注 解

1. 蓮 lián　　【名詞】蓮花；荷花 lotus

2. 陸 lù　　　【名詞】陸地 land

3. 蕃 fán　　　【形容詞】眾多 plentiful; numerous

4. 晉 Jìn　　　【名詞】朝代名。晉朝 (265-419 A.D)　the Jìn danasty

5. 陶淵明 【名詞】晉朝末年著名的隱逸詩人
   Táo Yuānmíng　　　　Táo Qián (365-427 A.D.), a famous poet who lived in seclusion

6. 獨 dú　　【副詞】單獨；只 only; merely

7. 菊 jú　　【名詞】菊花 chrysanthemums

8. 唐 Táng　【名詞】朝代名。唐朝 (618-907 A.D)　the Táng dynasty

李唐　【名詞語】唐朝由李淵建立，故稱李唐
Lǐ Táng　　　　　　　the Táng dynasty founded by the Lǐ clan

9. 自⋯來【介詞語】自⋯以來；從⋯到現在 since ...
zì ... lái

10. 牡丹　【名詞】花名 peony
mǔ dān

11. 淤泥　【名詞】水中沈澱 (chén diàn) 的泥沙；水底的污泥
yū ní　　　　　　　sediment at the bottom of a river, pond, etc.; silt

12. 染 rǎn　【動詞】染污；弄髒 to be contaminated

13. 濯 zhuó　【動詞】洗 to wash

14. 漣 lián　【名詞】水面因風吹而形成的波紋；漣漪；微波
　　　　　　　　　a small wave on the surface of water; ripples

清漣　【名詞語】清澈的水波 clear, rippling water [in a pond]
qīng lián

15. 妖 yāo　【形容詞】妖媚 (mèi) seductive; bewitching

16. 中 zhōng【名詞】裡面 the inside

17. 通 tōng　【形容詞】没有阻礙，可以通過；（比喻）通達
　　　　　　　　　to go, move, or flow unobstructed; hollow (literally)
　　　　　　　　　to understand clearly (figuratively)

18. 外 wài　【名詞】外面 the outside

19. 直 zhí　【形容詞】不彎曲；（比喻）正直
　　　　　　　　　straight (literally); upright (figuratively)

20. 蔓 màn;　【名詞】攀援植物的細長捲鬚 a thin curling stem that grows from
　　wàn　　　　　a climbing plant; creeping tendrils
　　　　　【動詞】生蔓 to grow tendrils

21. 枝 zhī　【名詞】樹枝；植物主幹旁生的莖條 branches; a part of tree
　　　　　　　　　that grows out from the main stem

231

【動詞】生枝 to have branches

不蔓不枝【動詞語】不生蔓不生枝 do not grow tendrils or branches
bú màn bù zhī

22. 香 xiāng 【形容詞】芳香 fragrant; aromatic

【名詞】香味 fragrance; aroma

23. 益 yì 【副詞】更 even more

24. 亭亭 【副詞】直直的 erect; upright
tíng tíng

25. 淨 jìng 【形容詞】乾淨；清潔 clean

26. 植 zhí 【動詞】立 to stand

27. 褻 xiè 【動詞】親近；親狎 to profane

褻玩 【動詞語】親狎地玩弄；親近但不莊重地玩弄
xiè wán to behave towards sb./sth.with disrespect because of over-intimacy

28. 予 yú 【代名詞】我 I

29. 謂 wèi 【動詞】說 to say; to remark

30. 隱逸 【形容詞】隱居避世 to be secluded
yǐn yì

花之隱逸者【名詞語】隱逸的花（形容詞後置）
huā zhī yǐn yì zhě a secluded flower (modifier postposition)
Cf. prose 1, n. 57, p. 163

31. 富貴 【形容詞】富裕高貴 to be wealthy and high ranked;
fù guì rich and honored

花之富貴者【名詞語】富貴的花（形容詞後置）
huā zhī fù guì zhě a rich and honored flower (modifier postposition)
Cf. prose 1, n. 57, p. 163

32. 君子　【形容詞】才德出眾的人 a man of great virtue; a true gentleman
jūn zǐ

花之君子者【名詞語】〔似〕君子的花（形容詞後置）
huā zhī jūn zǐ zhě　　　　　a gentleman-like flower (modifier postposition)
Cf. prose 1, n. 57, p. 163

33. 噫 yī　【嘆詞】咳，表示悲痛和嘆息 alas! to show being sad or sorry

34. 之 zhī　【助詞】"之"字的作用是把賓語提到動詞之前
the particle "zhī" functions as a marker for object inversion

菊之愛【特殊結構】愛菊　to love chrysanthemum
jú zhī ài

35. 鮮 xiǎn　【形容詞】少 few; little; rare

36. 有 yǒu　【助詞】動詞詞頭 here it functions as a verbal prefix

37. 聞 wén　【動詞】聽說 to hear; to be heard

有聞　【動詞】聽說 to hear; to be heard
yǒu wén

38. 宜 yí　【形容詞】適宜；應該 to be fitting; to be proper

39. 眾 zhòng【形容詞】多 to be numerous

第十一篇

前赤壁賦

宋　蘇軾

作者　見詩選《飲湖上初晴後雨》P.111

篇旨

藉主客問答，探索生存的意義以及在瞬息萬變而
又未嘗變的自然中，人當如何掌握暫短的生命妥
善自處。由迷茫而徹悟，由悲慨而超曠，作者通
過莊子自然主義的思想，對人生採取樂觀、豁達
的態度。達人智語，較之蘭亭集序之一味悲慨任
何美好情境都稍縱即逝，在精神境界上又進一層
。作者運用清風、明月、江水、詩、酒、樂等意
象，反覆迴環描述泛舟赤壁的一夜清遊。融敍事
、繪景、抒情、說理於一文，既富情趣，又含哲
思。至於文字之跌宕朗暢，意境之清奇超曠，千
百年來的文學愛好者無不稱美讚賞，堪稱散文中
的傑作。

Through dialogues between himself and a friend, the author probes into the
meaning of life and how one should handle one's own fleeting life in the
ever-changing yet never-changing world. Beginning in doubt and moving to
enlightenment, shifting from pessimism to transcendence, the author finally
adopts the view of the naturalist philosopher Zhuāngzǐ, to be optimistic and
broad-minded. This remarkable essay shows the wisdom of a man of great
understanding, and it is, in spirit, one step further than Wáng Xīzhī's lament
about the transience of any thing that is good or beautiful. The author ably
manipulates the images of a light breeze, a bright moon, river water, poems,
wine, and music, alternating the images to depict a night sail pass the Red-
cliff. It blends narrative, descriptive, lyric, and expository elements into a
single piece of writing that is full of interest and that elucidates a philosophical
theory. As for its artistic achievement, the work is free and easy, with a
flowing rhythm to its writing atyle, while novel and wonderful in its
conception. Readers have marvelled at it for nearly a thousant years, and it is
indeed a masterpiece, standing head and shoulders above other examples of
rhyme prose.

　　壬戌之秋，七月既望，蘇子與客泛舟，遊於赤壁之
下。清風徐來，水波不興。舉酒屬客，誦明月之詩，歌
窈窕之章。少焉，月出於東山之上，徘徊於牛斗之間。

白露橫江，水光接天。縱一葦之所如，凌萬頃之茫然。
浩浩乎如馮虛御風，而不知其所止；飄飄乎如遺世獨立
，羽化而登仙。

Zhùyīn:

Rénxū zhī qiū, qī yuè jì wàng, Sūzǐ yǔ kè fàn zhōu, yóu yú Chìbì zhī xià. Qīng fēng
xú lái, shuǐ bō bù xīng. Jǔ jiǔ zhǔ kè, sòng Míngyuè zhī shī, gē Yǎotiǎo zhī zhāng. Shǎo
yān, yuè chū yú dōng shān zhī shàng, pái huái yú niú dǒu zhī jiān. Bó lù héng jiāng, shuǐ
guāng jiē tiān. Zòng yì wěi zhī suǒ rú, líng wàn qǐng zhī máng rán. Hào hào hū rú píng xū
yù fēng, ér bù zhī qí suǒ zhǐ; piāo piāo hū rú yí shì dú lì, yǔ huà ér dēng xiān.

注 解

1. **赤壁**
   Chì bì

   【名詞】地名，又名赤鼻磯 jī，在湖北省黃州（今黃岡縣）城外。 a place name; the Red Cliff, also named Chìbíjī, is situated in Huángzhōu, just outside the city of present-day Huánggāng district in Húběi province

2. **賦 fù**

   【名詞】文體名；是一種有韻的散文
   name of a literary genre; a Rhyme Prose

3. **赤壁賦**
   Chìbì Fù

   【名詞】文章名；蘇軾因反對王安石的新法，被貶到黃州，他曾到黃州城外的赤壁（赤鼻磯）去遊覽過兩次，寫了兩篇遊赤壁的文章，本文是前一篇，故稱前赤壁賦。 title of an article;
   When Sū Shì was demoted to Huángzhōu because he objected Wáng Ānshí's reform policy, he visited the Red Cliff twice and wrote a rhyme prose for each occasion. This is the first one.
   文中談到了赤壁之戰 (208 A.D.)，其實赤壁之戰發生在湖北省嘉魚縣東北的赤壁，不是在黃州城外的赤鼻磯，蘇軾在遊覽的時候聯想到赤壁之戰以及當時的英雄人物，於是姑且把赤鼻磯當作赤壁寫了這篇文章。

   In this article Sū Shì referred to the Battle of Chìbì (208 A.D.); in fact that battle took place at another Chìbì -- to the northeast of present-day Jiāyú district in Húběi province, not this one also known as Chìbíjī. While on a boat outing Sū Shì recalled the historical event, and all the heroic figures involved, so he simply imagined that this was the actual location of the famous battle, and wrote this article.

4. 壬戌　【名詞】宋神宗趙頊(xù)元豐五年，當公元 1082 年，時蘇
rén xū　　　　　軾四十七歲　the year of Rén Xù (1082), when Sū Shì was
　　　　　　　　47 years old

5. 既 jì　【副詞】已經　already

6. 望 wàng　【名詞】月圓；也就是陰曆每月的十五日
　　　　　　　　full moon; the fifteenth day in a lunar month

　既望　【名詞】望後一日；陰曆每月的十六日
jì wàng　　　　　the day after the fifteenth; the sixteenth

7. 泛舟　【動詞語】划船　to row a boat
fàn zhōu

8. 清風　【名詞語】清涼的風　a clear breeze
qīng fēng

9. 徐來　【動詞語】緩慢地吹來　to blow gently
xú lái

10. 水波　【名詞語】水的波紋　waves; ripples
shuǐ bō

11. 興 xīng　【動詞】起　to rise

　水波不興【敘述句】江水平靜，沒有波紋
shuǐbō bùxīng　　　　the river was calm, without any ripples

12. 屬 zhǔ　【動詞】注入；斟 (zhēn) 酒　to pour the wine

　屬客　【動詞語】斟酒給客人　to serve wine to guests
zhǔ kè

13. 誦 sòng　【動詞】朗誦；大聲讀　to recite; to read aloud

14. 明月之詩【名詞】指《詩經・陳風・月出》篇。
míng yuè zhī shī　　　　It refers to the poem "Yuèchū" in the Book of Odes

236

15. 歌 gē 　【動詞】唱 to sing

16. 窈窕之章【名詞】《詩經・陳風・月出》第一章云：
　　 yǎotiǎo zhī zhāng　　The first stanza of "Yuè Chū" in *the Book of Odes* says:
　　　　　　　　　　"月出皎兮，佼人僚兮，舒窈糾兮，
　　　　　　　　　　勞心悄兮。"
　　　　　　　　　　A moon rising white
　　　　　　　　　　is the beauty of my loved one.
　　　　　　　　　　Ah, the tenderness, the grace,
　　　　　　　　　　Heart's pain consumes me!　(Arthur Waley's translation)
　　　　　　　　　　"窈窕"與"窈糾"聲音相近。
　　　　　　　　　　The sounds of "yǎo tiǎo" and "yǎo Jiǎo" are very close to
　　　　　　　　　　each other.

17. 少焉 　【副詞】少時；過了一會兒 after a while
　　 shǎo yān

18. 東山 　【名詞語】東邊兒的山 the mountain in the east
　　 dōng shān

19. 徘徊 　【動詞】徐行 to move slowly
　　 pái huái　　　　──→緩緩地上升 to rise slowly

20. 牛斗之間【名詞語】牽牛星和北斗星之間 between stars of the
　　 Niú Dǒu zhī jiān　　　　　　　　　Herdboy and the Big Dipper

21. 白露 　【名詞】白茫茫的水氣 vapor; mist
　　 bó lù
　　 bái lù

22. 橫 héng 　【動詞】橫越 to cross

　　 橫江 　【動詞語】橫穿過長江 to cross the river
　　 héng jiāng　　──→佈滿在長江上 to spread over the river
　　　　　　　　　　──→在長江上瀰漫著
　　　　　　　　　　　　to permeate above the river

23. 縱 zòng 　【動詞】放縱；放任 to let go; to give...a free rein

24. 葦 wěi 　【名詞】蘆 (lu) 葦；長在水邊兒的草 reeds
　　　　　　　　此處"葦"代表小船 here it stands for a boat

一葦　【名詞語】像一片葦葉似的小船兒
yì wěi　　　　　　　　a small reed-like boat

25. 如 rú　【動詞】往 to go; to move on

縱一葦之所如【動詞語】縱一葦之〔其〕所如。“之”是
zòng yìwěi zhī suǒrú　　　　動詞“到…去”的意思。
　　　　　　　　　　　　Let the boat go where it will go

〔蘇子與客〕　縱　一葦　之〔其〕所如
[s].　　　　　v　o/s　v　[mod]　o

這是兼語結構使動式，其中“一葦”是兼語，同時作動詞“縱”的
賓語和動詞“之”的主語。

This is a **causative pivotal construction**, in which the noun phrase "yì wěi" is called a **pivotal element** which functions both as the object of the first verb "zòng" and as the subject of the second verb "zhī".

26. 凌 líng　【動詞】乘駕 to ride [over the waves]

27. 頃 qǐng　【名詞】一百畝 a hundred mǔ, about 15.13 acres;
　　　　　　　　　　　　a [Chinese] hectare

28. 茫然　【形容詞】廣大 vast
máng rán　　　　　此處指長江的廣大的水面
　　　　　　　　　Here it refers to the vast surface of the Yángzǐ River

凌萬頃之茫然【動詞語】乘駕在萬頃廣大的水面上
líng wàn qǐng zhī máng rán　　　──→泛舟在無邊無際的水面上
　　　　　　　　　　　　　　　　──→在無邊無際的水面上泛舟
　　　　　　　　　　　　　　　to row/float over the boundless waves

29. 浩浩乎【形容詞】廣大啊 [said of water] vast; expansive; extensive
hào hào hū

30. 馮 píng　【動詞】同“憑”，憑藉；依靠 to depend upon; to rely on;
　　　　　　　　　　　　to ride on

31. 虛 xū　【名詞】空虛 the void; a large empty space

238

32. 御風　【動詞語】駕風；駕著風〔飛行〕 to ride on winds
    yù fēng

　　　　〔江水〕　　浩浩乎　　〔舟之浮於水上〕　如　　馮虛御風，
　　　　[s]　　　　pa　　　　[s]　　　　　　　l.v.　v o v o
　　　　　　　　　　　　　　　　　　　　　　　　　　　　　　　p
　　　　　　　　　　　　　　　好像是…一樣

　　　　　　　　　　　　　　　　　　　　舟之
　　　　　　　　　　　而　　不知　其所止
　　　　　　　　　　conj　adv　v　o

33. 飄飄乎【形容詞】〔在空中〕飄動啊
    piāo piāo hū　　　　──→輕輕地飛揚啊 floating [in the air]

34. 遺 yí　　【動詞】遺棄；扔下 to abandon

    遺世　　【動詞語】遺棄世界 to desert the world
    yí shì　　　　　　──→離開人世 to desert the human world

35. 羽化　【動詞語】古人稱"成仙"為"羽化"；變成仙人
    yǔ huà　　　　　　Ancient people used the term "yǔ huà" (changed into a
    　　　　　　　　　winged creature) to express the idea of "metamorphosed
    　　　　　　　　　into an immortal"

36. 登 dēng　【動詞】升登 to ascend

37. 仙 xiān　【名詞】仙境 fairyland

    登仙　　【動詞語】登上仙境 to ascend to the fairyland
    dēng xiān

    羽化登仙【動詞語】變成仙人，登上仙境 to become an immortal and
    yǔ huà dēng xiān　　　　　　　ascend to the fairyland

　　　　〔人之處於舟中〕　飄飄乎　　〔人之感覺〕　如　　遺世獨立，
　　　　[s]　　　　　　　pa　　　　[s]　　　　l.v.　v o v o
　　　　　　　　　　　　　　　　　　　　　　　　　　　　p
　　　　　　　　　　　　好像是…一樣

　　　　　　　　　　羽化　　而　　登仙
　　　　　　　　　　o-v　　conj　v o
　　　　　　　　　　　　　　p

於是飲酒樂甚，扣舷而歌之。歌曰：" 桂櫂兮蘭槳，擊空明兮泝流光；渺渺兮予懷，望美人兮天一方。" 客有吹洞簫者，倚歌而和之。其聲嗚嗚然，如怨如慕，如泣如訴；餘音嫋嫋，不絕如縷，舞幽壑之潛蛟，泣孤舟之嫠婦。

Yúshì yǐn jiǔ lè shèn, kòu xián ér gē zhī. Gē yuē: " Guì zhào xī lán jiǎng, jī kōng míng xī sù liú guāng; miǎo miǎo xī yú huái, wàng měi rén xī tiān yì fāng." Kè yǒu chuī dòng xiāo zhě, yǐ gē ér hè zhī. Qí shēng wū wū rán, rú yuàn rú mù, rú qì rú sù; yú yīn niǎo niǎo, bù jué rú lǚ, wǔ yōu huò zhī qián jiāo, qì gū zhōu zhī lí fù.

38. 扣 kòu 【動詞】敲 (qiāo) to tap

39. 舷 xián 【名詞】船的邊緣 bulwarks of a ship

扣舷而歌之：敲著船邊唱歌 to sing while tapping the bulwarks of a ship
kòu xián ér gē zhī

40. 桂 guì 【名詞】桂樹 cassia

41. 櫂 zhào 【名詞】划船時撥水的用具，長的叫櫂，短的叫槳 oars

桂櫂 【名詞】用桂樹的木頭做的櫂
guì zhào oars made of cassia wood

42. 蘭 lán 【名詞】木蘭樹 deciduous magnolia

蘭槳 【名詞】用木蘭樹的木頭做的槳
lán jiǎng oars made of magnolia wood

43. 擊 jī; jí 【動詞】敲打 to hit sth. many times
此處應解釋做 " 撥動 " to row

44. 空明 【名詞】月光下的清波 the clear waves under the moonlight
kōng míng

45. 泝 sù 【動詞】同 " 溯 " ；逆流而上，逆著水流的方向向上

划　to go against the stream (current)

46. 流光　【名詞】流動閃爍的光──→隨著水波流動閃爍的月光
liú guāng　　　　　the glittering moon light reflected on the waves

洬流光【動詞語】逆著隨著水波浮動的月光向上划
sù liú guāng　　　to row against the current that reflects the glittering moonlight

47. 渺渺兮【形容詞】渺遠啊；遙遠啊　distant
miǎo miǎo xī

48. 懷 huái　　【動詞】懷念　to think of; to long for

渺渺兮　　余懷．　　　　　倒裝句 (a transposed sentence - for emphasis)
　pa　　　s　v
　　　　　　　　s

49. 美人　　【名詞】美麗的人；思慕的人（傳統的解釋認為借指
měi rén　　　　　君主）　the beloved person one is thinking of; traditionally
this is interpreted as a euphemism for "the ruler"

50. 天一方【名詞】天的一方；天的另一邊 the other end of the sky
tiān yì fāng

51. 洞簫　　【名詞】用竹子做的單管直吹的樂器　a kind of bamboo flute;
dòng xiāo　　　　a bamboo flageolet; a bamboo flute blown at one end

　　[prep] o
〔於〕客　有 吹洞簫者　　存在句 (an existential sentence)
　s　　　　v　　o

在客人裡有個吹洞簫的　　　Among the guests there is one who plays flageolet
＝有 吹洞簫之客　　　　There is a guest who plays flageolet
　v　　o

52. 倚歌　　【動詞語】隨著歌　to go along with the song
yǐ gē

53. 和 hè　　【動詞】以聲相應；跟著唱腔伴奏　to match; to harmonize; to
play or sing music that combines with the main tune to make a
pleasing sound

和之　【動詞語】應和它（歌）；伴和它（歌）
hè zhī　　　——→隨著歌吹出簫聲來　to harmonize the song

54. 嗚嗚然【形容詞】低沈的；嗚嗚的
wūwū rán　　　　　low pitched; sounds like 'wūwū'

55. 怨 yuàn　【動詞】埋怨；責怪　to complain; to grumble

如怨　【形容詞】如同怨；好像怨
rú yuàn　　　　　　as if complaining; as if grumbling

56. 慕 mù　【動詞】思慕；想念　to long; to miss

57. 泣 qì　【動詞】無聲地哭；啜(chuò)泣　to weep; to sob

58. 訴 sù　【動詞】陳訴；訴說　to relate; to explain

59. 餘音　【名詞】未消失完的聲音　the wavering resonance
yú yīn

60. 嫋嫋　【形容詞】悠揚婉轉
niǎo niǎo　　　　　[said of sound] lingering in the air

61. 絕 jué　【動詞】斷絕　to cease; to break up; to snap off

62. 縷 lǔ　【名詞】線　thread; yarn

不絕如縷【動詞語】不斷絕，好像一條很細的線
bù jué rú lǔ　　　　　like a thread of sound [which did not snap off]

63. 壑 huò　【名詞】山谷　a gully

幽壑　【名詞語】深谷　a deep gully
yōu huò

64. 潛 qián　【形容詞】潛伏的　concealed; hidden

65. 蛟 jiāo　【名詞】蛟龍　a flood dragon

潛蛟　【名詞語】潛伏的蛟龍　a hidden flood dragon
qiáo jiāo

66. 孤舟　【名詞語】孤單的小船　a lone boat
gū zhōu

67. 嫠婦　【名詞】寡婦　a widow
lí fù

舞幽壑之潛蛟【動詞語】使幽壑之潛蛟跳舞 to make the flood-
wǔ yōu huò zhī qián jiāo　　　　　dragon in a deep gully dance

泣孤舟之嫠婦【動詞語】使孤舟之嫠婦低聲地哭 to cause the
qì gū zhōu zhī lí fù　　　　　widow in a lone boat sobbing

〔簫聲〕　舞 幽壑之潛蛟, 泣 孤舟之嫠婦。　使動句變式 atypical
[s]　　　v　o　　　v　o　　causative construction

舞、泣，此處都是動詞的使動用法

When the verb that would usually follow the pivotal element in a typical causative sentence is transposed in front of the pivotal element, it functions as a **causative verb**, and there is no need to add another verb to express the causative meaning. Cf. prose 2, n. 51, p. 172

〔簫聲〕　使 幽壑之潛蛟 舞，使 孤舟之嫠婦 泣。　使動句常式 typocal
[s]　　v　o/s　　　v　v　o/s　　　v　causative construction

　　蘇子愀然，正襟危坐，而問客曰：“何為其然也？”客曰：“‘月明星稀，烏鵲南飛’，此非曹孟德之詩乎？西望夏口，東望武昌，山川相繆，鬱乎蒼蒼，此非孟德之困於周郎者乎？方其破荊州，下江陵，順流而東也，舳艫千里，旌旗蔽空，釃酒臨江，橫槊賦詩，固一世之雄也，而今安在哉！況吾與子漁樵於江渚之上，侶魚蝦而友麋鹿，駕一葉之扁舟，舉匏樽以相屬。寄蜉蝣於天地，渺滄海之一粟。哀吾生之須臾，羨長江之無窮。挾飛仙以遨遊，抱明月而長終。知不可乎驟得，託遺響於悲風。”

　　Sūzǐ qiǎo rán, zhèng jīn wéi zuò, ér wèn kè yuē: "Hé wèi qí rán yě?" Kè yuē: "'yuè

243

míng xīng xī, wū què nán fēi', cǐ fēi Cáo Mèngdé zhī shī hū? Xī wàng Xiàkǒu, dōng wàng , shān chuān xiāng liáo, yù hū cāng cāng, cǐ fēi Mèngdé zhī kùn yú Zhōuláng zhě hū? Fāng qí pò Jīngzhōu, xià Jiānglíng, shùn liú ér dōng yě, zhú lú qiān lǐ, jīng qí bì kōng, sī jiǔ lín jiāng, héng shuò fù shī, gù yí shì zhī xióng yě, ér jīn ān zài zāi! Kuàng wú yǔ zǐ yú qiáo yú jiāng zhǔ zhī shàng, lǚ yú xiā ér yǒu mí lù, jià yí yè zhī piān zhōu, jǔ páo zūn yǐ xiāng zhǔ. Jì fú yóu yú tiān dì, miǎo cāng hǎi zhī yí sù. Āi wú shēng zhī xū yú, xiàn chángjiāng zhī wú qióng. Xiá fēi xiān yǐ áo yóu, bào míng yuè ér cháng zhōng. Zhī bù kě hū zòu dé, tuō yí xiǎng yú bēi fēng."

68. 愀然　【副詞】難過地〔改變了臉色〕 sadly [showing a sudden change
    qiǎo rán　　　　　　　　　　　 of facial expression]

69. 襟 jīn　【名詞】衣襟　the lapel of a garment or robe

    正襟　【動詞語】使襟正；拉正衣襟
    zhèng jīn　　　　　　to straighten one's lapel of garment

70. 危坐　【動詞語】直坐；端正地坐　to sit upright
    wéi zuò

    正襟危坐【動詞語】拉正衣襟，端正地坐〔表示出一種嚴肅的
    zhèng jīn wéi zuò　　　　　態度〕to straighten one's lapel and sit upright

71. 何為　【介詞語】為何；為什麼　for what reason? why
    hé wèi　　　　　　疑問代詞用作賓語時，放在介詞前
    　　　　　　　　　When an interrogative pronoun is used as an object, it should precede
    　　　　　　　　　the preposition that governs it.

72. 然 rán　【繫詞】如此　to be like this

    　　　　　　s　　　　p
    　　　　　簫聲〔之〕　如此
    　　何為　　　其　　　然　也？　　　倒裝句 (a transposed sentence)
    　　　p　　　　s　　　part　　　　 creating an emphatic effect

73. 烏 wū　【名詞】烏鴉　a crow

74. 曹孟德【名詞】人名，曹操，字孟德，東漢末的權臣，善用兵
    Cáo Mèngdé　　　　，詩也作得很好。"月明星稀，烏鵲南飛。"

是他的詩《短歌行》裡的句子

Cáo Cāo, the powerful prime minister at the end of the Eastern Hàn dynasty (25-220 A.D.), who was an able general and also a good poet; the previous line is quoted from his famous poem "A Short Song"

此 非　曹孟德之詩　乎？　反問表肯定 (rhetorical for affirmative)
s l.v.　　pn　　part　　Cf. prose 9, n. 27, p.227

此 乃　曹孟德之詩　也。
s l.v.　　pn　　part

75. 夏口　【名詞】地名，今湖北漢口
Xiàkǒu　　　　name of a place, present-day Hànkǒu in Húběi province

76. 武昌　【名詞】地名，今湖北武昌
Wǔchāng　　　name of a place, present-day Wǔchāng in Húběi province

77. 川 chuān【名詞】河流 a river

78. 繆 liáo　【動詞】同"繚"，繚繞 to wind around; to encircle

山川相繆【敍述句】山河互相繚繞
shān chuān xiāng liáo　　mountains and rivers wind around each other
山環水繞
mountains encircle and rivers meander
山繞著水，水繞著山
The mountains are girdled by the meandering rivers and the rivers are surrounded by the winding mountains

79. 鬱 yù　【形容詞】草木茂盛(mào shèng)　luxuriant; lush

80. 蒼蒼　【形容詞】青翠 verdant
cāngcāng

鬱乎蒼蒼【形容詞語】草木茂盛啊〔非常〕青翠(cuì)
yù hū cāng cāng　　—→ 草木又茂盛又青翠
the grass and foliage are luxuriant and verdant

81. 困 kùn　【動詞】圍困；包圍　to besiege; to be besieged

82. 於 yú　【介詞】在被動句中介紹主動者；可看作被動記號
a preposition that introduces the agent in a passive sentence, it can be regarded as a passive marker

83. 郎 láng 【名詞】青少年男子 a young man

周郎 【名詞】姓周的青年，此處指周瑜 (yú)
Zhōu láng
東漢建安十三年 (208 A.D.) 曹操的軍隊佔領荊州、江陵，順著長江向東走，孫權派周瑜與劉備合力抵抗曹操，十一月，在赤壁打了一次仗，周瑜用火攻之計燒毀了曹操的戰船，曹軍大敗
the young man Zhōu, here it refers to Zhōu Yú
In the year 208 A.D., after his troops conquered Jīngzhōu and Jiānglíng, Cáo Cāo led a fleet sailing eastward along the Yángzǐ River to attack Sūn Quán at Wú. Sūn appointed Zhōu Yú as the commander, to form an alliance with Liú Bèi and fight against Cáo Cāo. In the eleventh lunar month, Zhōu set Cáo Cāo's entire fleet on fire with a clever scheme, and Cáo Cāo was badly defeated.

之處
此 非 曹孟德之困於周郎者 乎？ 反問表肯定 (rhetorical for affirmative)
s l.v. pn part

此 乃 曹孟德之困於周郎者 也。
s l.v. pn part

孟德 困 於周郎 被動句 (a passdive sentence)
s p(v prep o) "於"：被 (preposition and a passive marker)

孟德之 困 於周郎 "之"字化句子爲主謂短語
s 之 p(v prep o) "之" turns a sentence into a clausal phrase

84. 荊州 【名詞】地名，在今湖北
Jīngzhōu　　　　　　name of a place, Jīng Zhōu in present-day Húběi province

破荊州【動詞語】打破荊州
pò Jīngzhōu　　　　　to break in (to conquer) Jīng Zhōu

85. 江陵 【名詞】地名，在今湖北省
Jiānglíng　　　　　　name of a place, Jiāng Líng in present-day Húběi province

下江陵【動詞語】攻下江陵
xià Jiānglíng　　　　to break in and take over Jiānglíng

86. 舳艫 【名詞】船尾叫舳，船頭叫艫；泛指船
zhú lú　　　　　　　stems and sterns; here it means "boats"

舳艫千里 【敘述句】 船尾船頭相連接，有一千里那麼長
zhú lú qiāng lǐ　　　　　　　the sterns and stems stretching to a thousand lǐ

87. 旌旗　【名詞】 軍隊的旗子　banners and flags
jīng qí

88. 蔽 bì　【動詞】 遮蔽；擋住　to cover; to block

蔽空　【動詞語】 擋住天空　to block the sky
bì kōng

89. 釃酒　【動詞語】 斟酒；倒酒　to pour wine
sī jiǔ

90. 臨 lín　【動詞】 面對　to face

91. 槊 shuò　【名詞】 長矛　a long spear; a lance

橫槊　【動詞語】 橫拿著槊　to hold a lance horizontally
héng shuò

92. 賦詩　【動詞語】 作詩　to compose poems
fù shī

93. 雄 xióng　【名詞】 英雄　a hero

一世之雄 【名詞語】 一代的英雄　the hero of a generation
yí shì zhī xióng

94. 而今　【時間詞】 現在　now
ér jīn

95. 安在哉 【動詞語】 在何處呢？在哪裡呢？　Where is [he]?
ān zài zāi　　　　　　　疑問詞用作賓語時，應倒置在動詞前
　　　　　　　　　　When a question word is used as an object, it should precede the verb that governs it.

96. 漁 yú　【動詞】 打魚；捕魚　to fish

97. 樵 qiáo　【動詞】 打柴　to gather firewood; to collect firewood

98. 渚 zhǔ 　【名詞】小洲；水裡的小塊陸地　an islet

99. 侶 lǚ 　【名詞】伴侶　a companion

　　　　　【名詞意動】以…為伴侶；跟…作伴
　　　　　　　　　　to regard/take ... as companions

100. 蝦 xiā 　【名詞】水生有殼動物，可食；蝦　a small shellfish; a shrimp

　　侶魚蝦【動詞語】以魚蝦為伴侶；把魚蝦當作伴侶
　　lǚ yú xiā 　　　　　　　to take fish and shrimps as companions

101. 麋 mí 　【名詞】一種形體比較大的鹿，生活在歐、亞，及北美
　　　　　　　　a large deer that lives in Northern Europe, Asia, and North
　　　　　　　　America; an elk; a moose

102. 鹿 lù 　【名詞】一種動物，尾短，腿細長，毛黃褐色，有白
　　　　　　斑，性情溫順，雄的有樹枝狀的角
　　　　　　a good natured animal with long legs and short tail, the males
　　　　　　grow bony antlers like branches; a deer

　　友麋鹿【動詞語】以麋鹿為友
　　yǒu mí lù 　　　　　　　to take elks and deers as friends

　　吾與子 漁樵 於 江渚之上，
　　　s 　v v　prep　o

　　侶 魚蝦 而 友 麋鹿。　　"侶" "友" 為名詞之意動用法
　　v 　o 　conj v 　o 　　"侶" "友" are nouns used as putative verbs

　　　　　意動結構 (N1以N2為N3;) 中的N2是兼語。若把N3移放到
　　　　　兼語N2之前，它就有了意動的作用。

　　　　　In a **putative construction** (N1 yǐ N2 wéi N3), N2 is the **pivotal element**.
　　　　　If N3 is transposed in front of the **pivotal element** N2, it then assumes a
　　　　　putative function.　　　　　Cf. prose 8, n. 26, p. 222

　　以 　魚蝦 為 侶，以 麋鹿 為 友。
　　v 　o/s 　v 　o 　v 　o/s 　v 　o

103. 扁舟 　【名詞】小船　a small boat
　　piān zhōu

104. 匏 páo 　【名詞】葫蘆 (húlú)　gourds

105. 樽 zūn 　【名詞】盛酒器　a wine vessel; a drinking vessel

248

匏樽　【動詞語】用葫蘆做的盛酒器　a wine vessel made of gourd
páo zūn

106. 相屬　【動詞】相注；互相斟酒；你給我斟酒，我給你斟酒
xiāng zhǔ　　　　　　to pour (serve) wine for each other

107. 寄 jì　【動詞】寄居；暫時住在…　to sojourn

108. 蜉蝣　【名詞】小蟲，活在水邊，生命極短，朝生而暮死（只
fú yóu　　　　　　能活幾小時）　a very small insect that lives near water
and only lives for a very short time; mayflies

寄蜉蝣於天地【動詞語】〔如〕蜉蝣寄於天地；寄居於天地如
jì fú yóu yú tiān dì　　　　　蜉蝣（比喻人生存於世間的短暫）
to sojourn between heaven and earth as a mayfly
(to liken to the transience of human life)

109. 渺 miǎo　【形容詞】渺小　tiny

110. 滄海　【名詞語】大海；青綠色的大海　the vast blue sea
cāng hǎi

111. 一粟　【名詞】一粒 (lì) 小米　a grain of millet
yí sù

渺滄海之一粟【形容詞】渺〔如〕滄海之一粟；渺小得像大
miǎo cāng hǎi zhī yí sù　　　　海裡的一粒小米（比喻人極渺小）
tiny as a millet in a vast sea; (to liken to the
insignificance of human being)

112. 須臾　【時間詞】片刻　an instant
xū yú　　　　　　　　短暫　short; transient; fleeting

113. 羨 xiàn　【動詞】羨慕　to envy

114. 窮 qióng　【形容詞】窮盡　exhausted; ended

無窮　【形容詞】無盡；沒有窮盡　inexhaustible; endless; boundless
wú qióng

〔予〕哀 吾生之須臾， 羨 長江之無窮。
[s] v o v o

"之"字的作用是把句子"吾生須臾""長江無窮"化成主謂短語，作動詞"哀""羨"的賓語。

The particle "zhī" here serves to transform the sentences "wú shēng xū yú" and "chángjiāng wú qióng" into **clausal phrases** to function as the objects of the verb "āi".

115. 挾 xiá, xié 【動詞】依傍(bàng)；伴隨　to accompany

116. 飛仙　【名詞語】會飛的仙人　flying immortals
fēi xiān

117. 遨遊　【動詞】漫遊；逍遙自在地遊玩 to roam about freely
áo yóu

118. 長終　【形容詞】長久；永久 to last long; everlasting
cháng zhōng

119. 驟得　【動詞語】突然地得到 to gain suddenly and easily
zòu dé

120. 託 tuō　【動詞】寄託　to consign ... to; to commit... to; to place ... in

121. 遺響　【名詞】餘音；還未完全消失的簫聲
yí xiǎng　　　　　the lingering sound of the flute

122. 悲風　【名詞】悲涼的秋風 the sad autumnal wind
bēi fēng

託遺響於悲風：意思是藉簫聲傳達出自己悲哀、遺憾的心
tuō yí xiǎng yú bēi fēng　情，把它寄託在淒涼的秋風中
to consign the lingering sound [along with my regretful feeling] to the sad autumnal wind

蘇子曰："客亦知夫水與月乎？逝者如斯，而未嘗往也；盈虛者如彼，而卒莫消長也。蓋將自其變者而觀之，則天地曾不能以一瞬；自其不變者而觀之，則物與我皆無盡也。而又何羨乎？且夫天地之間，物各有主，

250

苟非吾之所有，雖一毫而莫取。惟江上之清風，與山間之明月，耳得之而為聲，目遇之而成色；取之無禁，用之不竭。是造物者之無盡藏也，而吾與子之所共適。”

Sūzì yuē: "Kè yì zhī fú shuǐ yǔ yuè hū? Shì zhě rú sī, ér wèi cháng wǎng yě; yíng xū zhě rú bǐ, ér zú mò xiāo zhǎng yě. Gài jiāng zì qí biàn zhě ér guān zhī, zé tiān dì céng bù néng yǐ yí shùn; zì qí bú biàn zhě guān zhī, zé wù yǔ wǒ jiē wú jìn yě. Er yoù hé xiàn hū?, Qiě fú tiān dì zhī jiān, wù gè yǒu zhǔ, gǒu fēi wú zhī suǒ yǒu, suī yì háo ér mò qǔ. Wéi jiāng shàng zhī qīng fēng, yǔ shān jiān zhī míng yuè, ér dé zhī ér wéi shēng, mù yù zhī ér chéng sè; qǔ zhī wú jìn, yòng zhī bù jié. Shì zào wù zhě zhī wú jìn zàng yě, ér wú yǔ zǐ zhī suǒ gòng shì."

123. 夫 fú 　【指示代詞】彼；那個　that; those

124. 逝 shì 　【動詞】過去　to pass; to depart

125. 斯 sī 　【指示代詞】此；這個，指水　this; here referring to water

126. 未嘗 　【副詞】未曾　to have not ...; to have never ...
　　 wèi cháng

127. 盈 yíng 　【形容詞】滿　to be full; to wax

128. 虛 xū 　【形容詞】空；缺 (quē) 　to be empty; to wane

129. 彼 bǐ 　【指示代詞】彼；那個，指月　that; here referring to the moon

130. 卒 zú 　【副詞】終於；到底　to the end; eventually

131. 莫 mò 　【副詞】用在動詞、形容詞前，表示否定　not; didn't; hasn't

132. 消 xiāo 　【動詞】減少　to decrease; to dissipate

133. 長 zhǎng 　【動詞】增長　to grow; to increase

卒莫消長【動詞語】到底沒有消失或增長
zú mò xiāo zhǎng 　　　　 eventually it neither decreased nor increased

134. 蓋 gài 【副詞】大概地說 generally speaking

135. 將 jiāng 【連詞】連接分句，表示假設，可譯成 "如果"
a conjunction used at the beginning of a subordinate clause to express a supposition, it can be rendered as "if"

136. 自 zì 【介詞】從 from

137. 變 biàn 【動詞】改變 to change

138. 曾 zēng 【副詞】表示事實出人意外，語氣帶誇張，可譯作 "竟然" 或 "簡直" somewhat to one's surprise ...; simply

139. 以 yǐ 【動詞】通 "已"，止 interchangeable with "yǐ", meaning "to stop"

140. 瞬 shùn 【動詞】眨 (zhǎ) 眼 to wink

一瞬 【動詞語】一眨眼 to wink once
yí shùn
【名詞語】一眨眼〔那麼短的時間〕an instant; a wink

曾不能以一瞬【動詞語】簡直不能停止一眨眼〔那麼短的
zēng bù néng yǐ yí shùn   時間〕（極言天地間一切事物變化的迅速）
cannot stay static for an instant
(stressing the fleeting nature of all things in the world)

141. 物 wù 【名詞】萬物 things; all things under the sun

142. 盡 jìn 【形容詞】窮盡 exhausted; ended

143. 何羨乎【動詞語】羨什麼呢？ what to envy?
hé xiàn hū   疑問代詞用作賓語時，放在動詞前
When an interrogative pronoun is used as an object, it should precede the verb that governs it.

144. 且夫 【連詞】況且；而且，承接上文，表示更進一層的語氣
qiě fū   moreover; besides, following the previous text, meaning to take a step further

145. 各 gè 【代詞】各自 each

146. 有主 【動詞語】有主人 to have a master; to have an owner
    yǒu zhǔ

147. 苟 gǒu 【副詞】如果 if

148. 所有 【名詞語】有的東西 things owned
    suǒ yǒu

149. 一毫 【名詞語】一根毫毛；比喻極小或極少 a tiny hair; very
    yì háo   small or very little [in size or quantity]

150. 取 qǔ 【動詞】拿 to take

　　　且夫 〔於〕 天地之間 物各有主，
　　　conj [prep]   o   s adv v o

　　　　　〔物〕 苟 非 吾之所有,
　　　　　[s] conj l.v. pn

　　　　　　　　〔物〕 〔僅爲〕 〔吾〕
　　　　〔則〕 雖 一毫 而 莫取,
　　　　[conj] [s] conj [l.v.] p conj [s] adv v

　　　苟…則…：假若…那麼…
　　　雖…而…：雖然…可是…

151. 惟 wéi 【副詞】表示限於某個範圍，用在主語或謂語的前面，
        可譯為"只有""只"等 an adverb indicating
        the limit of a scope, used before the subject or predicate, can be
        rendered into modern Chinese as "zhǐ yǒu" or "zhǐ".

152. 禁 jìn 【動詞】禁止 to prohibit; to prevent ... from...

153. 竭 jié 【形容詞】竭盡；窮盡 to be exhausted; to be used up

154. 造物者 【名詞語】創造萬物的 N the Creator; Mother Nature
    zào wù zhě

155. 藏 zàng 【名詞】寶藏 treasury

　　無盡藏【名詞語】沒有窮盡的寶藏；永遠不會用完的寶藏
    wú jìn zàng   an inexhaustible treasury

253

156. 適 shì 【動詞】悅；喜愛；欣賞 to like; to enjoy; to appreciate

所適 【名詞語】喜愛的對象 Cf. poem 12, n. 10, p. 49
suǒ shì   ——→欣賞的對象
        what we enjoyed and appreciated

所共適【名詞語】所共同喜愛／欣賞
suǒ gòng shì   共同喜愛的對象
      ——→共同欣賞的對象
      what we enjoyed and appreciated in common

惟 江上之清風與 山間之明月。
adv   o (extra.posed)

       清風 〔清風〕   明月 〔明月〕
耳 得 之 而   為聲，且 遇 之 而   成色
s   v   o conj [s]   v o   s   v   o conj [s]   v o

〔吾與子〕 清風、明月   〔人〕   〔清風、明月〕
   取 之 無 禁，用 之.   不竭,
  [s] v   o   v [o/s] v   v   o   [s]   adv pa

清風明月
是   〔乃〕造物者之無盡藏也，
s   [l.v.]   pn   part

而 〔清風明月〕〔為〕吾與子之所共適。
adv   [s]   [l.v.]   pn

客喜而笑，洗盞更酌。肴核既盡，杯盤狼藉。相與枕藉乎舟中，不知東方之既白。

  Kè xǐ ér xiào, xǐ zhǎn gèng zhuó. Yáo hé jì jìn, bēi pán láng jí. Xiāng yǔ zhèn jiè hū zhōu zhōng, bù zhī dōng fāng zhī jì bái.

157. 喜 xǐ 【形容詞】快樂；高興 happy; glad

158. 盞 zhǎn 【名詞】酒杯 wine cups

159. 更 gèng 【副詞】再；又 once again

160. 肴 yáo 【名詞】魚肉之類的葷 (hūn)菜
      cooked food, especially meat and fish

161. 核 hé 　【名詞】果核 pit
　　　　　　　　此處指水果 here it means "fruit"

162. 既盡　【形容詞】已經窮盡；已經〔被〕吃光
　　jì jìn　　　　　　　　to have been exhausted; to have been eaten up

163. 杯盤　【名詞】酒杯菜盤 wine cups/glasses and plates
　　bēi pán

164. 狼藉　【形容詞】縱橫交錯
　　láng jí　　　　　　亂七八糟很不整齊地攤著
　　　　　　　　　　　in total disorder or disarray

※ 杯盤狼藉【成語】酒杯菜盤亂七八糟地攤著
　　bēi pán láng jí　　　　Empty glasses and plates are scattered all over -- the feast
　　　　　　　　　　　　is over.

165. 枕藉　【動詞】枕著靠著
　　zhèn jiè　　　　　to lie on as on a pillow or to lean against; to lie in complete
　　　　　　　　　　disarray

　　相與枕藉【動詞語】互相枕著靠著
　　xiāng yǔ zhèn jiè　　　　resting on or leaning against one another

166. 既白　【動詞語】已經發白
　　jì bái　　　　　　〔天〕已經亮了 it has dawned; it's been daybreak already

第十二篇

寒花葬志

明　歸有光

作者　歸有光 (1506 -1571 A.D.) 字熙甫，號震川，江蘇崑山
　　　人。三十五歲中舉，六十歲時始中進士，任知縣

，其間講學二十餘年，從學的人很多，世稱"震
川先生。"長於散文，著有《震川文集》四十卷
傳世。

Guī Yǒuguāng (1506-1571 A.D.), courtesy name Xīfǔ and style name
Zhènchuān, was a native of Kūnshān in Jiāngsū province. He passed the
provincial examination at the age of 35, but did not succeed in the last stage
of civil service exam until he was 60. In the intervening years, he lectured for
over two decades in Jiādìng in Jiāngsu, attracting many followers from near
and far. He was honored as "Master Zhènchuān" by his contemporaries. He
excelled in writing prose and left to posterity his *Collection of Literary Works
by Zhènchuān* in 40 rolls.

篇旨

作者為妻子的婢女寒花寫葬志，追憶她幼年的嬌
憨伶俐，悲傷往日共處的歡樂不可復得。簡潔平
淡中含有真摯的情感，十足呈現歸文的特色。

The author writes this burial note for Hánhuā, a young servant of his wife,
remembering the lovely and nimble girl in her younger days, and then
lamenting the fact that the happy times they once had together were now gone
forever. Concise and plain, it nevertheless is suffused with sincere and rueful
feelings, demonstrating the unmistakable characteristics of Guī's writing style.

　　婢，魏孺人媵也。嘉靖丁酉五月四日死，葬虛丘。
事我而不卒，命也夫！

　　婢初媵時，年十歲，垂雙鬟，曳深綠布裳。一日，
天寒，爇火煮荸薺熟，婢削之盈甌；予自外入，取食之
；婢持去，不與。魏孺人笑之。孺人每令婢倚几旁飯，
即飯，目眶冉冉動。孺人又指予以為笑。

　　回思是時，奄忽便已十年。吁！可悲也已！

Zhùyīn:

　　Bì, Wèi Rúrén yìng yě. Jiājìng dīng yǒu wǔ yuè sì rì sǐ, zàng Xūqiū. Shì wǒ ér bù
zú, mìng yě fū!

　　Bì chū yìng shí, nián shí suì, chuí shuāng huán, yì shēn lù bù shēng. Yí rì, tiān hán, rè huǒ zhǔ bí qí shú, bì xiāo zhī yíng ōu; yú zì wài rù, qǔ shí zhī; bì chí qù, bù yǔ. Wèi Rúrén xiào zhī. Rúrén měi lìng bì yǐ jī páng fàn, jí fàn, mù kuàng rǎn rǎn dòng. Rúrén yòu zhǐ yǔ yǐ wéi xiào.

　　Huí sī shì shí, yān hū biàn yǐ shí nián. Xū! Kě bēi yě yǐ!

注 解

1. 寒花　　【名詞】文中婢女之名
   Hán huā　　　　　　　name of the deceased handmaid who was being buried

2. 葬志　　【名詞語】下葬時為死者寫的墓志
   zàng zhì　　　　　　a note or text to be inscribed on a stele; an epitaph

3. 婢 bì　　【名詞】婢女；使女　a handmaid; a maid servant

4. 孺人　　【名詞】明清兩代七品以下職官之妻子封 “孺人”
   rú rén　　　　　　during the Míng and Qīng dynasties, a title granted to wives
   　　　　　　　　of officials in the Seventh Grade or below

   魏孺人　【名詞語】作者之妻；姓魏，原籍蘇州，後遷居崑山
   Wèi rú rén　　　　Madam Wèi, the wife of Guī Yǒuguāng, originally from
   　　　　　　　　Sūzhōu, and later moved to Kūnshān, both in present-day
   　　　　　　　　Jiāngsū province

5. 媵 yìng　　【名詞】陪嫁的婢女
   　　　　　　a maid who accompanies a bride to her new home

6. 嘉靖　　【名詞】明世宗朱厚熜 (zǒng) 的年號 (1522-1566 A D.)
   Jiā jìng　　　　reign title of Emperor Shì of Míng (1522-1566 A.D.)

7. 丁酉　　【名詞】嘉靖十六年 (1537) 為丁酉
   Dīng yǒu　　　the year of Dīng Yǒu, i.e., 1537 A.D.

8. 虛丘　　【名詞語】地名　a place name; the Void Hill, where the maid was
   Xū qiū　　　　　　being buried

9. 事 shì　　【動詞】事奉　to serve; to wait upon

10. 卒 zú　　【動詞】終；到底　to complete; to reach the end

257

11. 命 mìng 【名詞】命運 fate

12. 垂 chuí 【動詞】掛著 to hang down

13. 鬟 huán 【名詞】 環形的髮髻 [the hair dressed in] a coiled knot

　　垂雙鬟【動詞語】低梳著一對環形的髮髻
　　chuí shuāng huán　　　　the hair dressed low in a pair of coiled knots

14. 曳 yì 【動詞】拖著 to trail

15. 布裳 【名詞語】布裙 a skirt made of cotton cloth
　　bù shāng

16. 爇 ruò; rè【動詞】燃燒 to burn

　　爇火 【動詞語】燒火 to make a fire
　　rè huǒ

17. 煮 zhǔ 【動詞】把食物放在開水鍋裡燒 to boil; to cook sth. in a pan of boiling water

18. 荸薺 【名詞】水栗 water chestnuts
　　bí .qí

19. 削 xiāo 【動詞】削去外皮 to peel; to pare the skin

20. 盈 yíng 【動詞】裝滿 to fill up

21. 甌 ōu 【名詞】小瓦盆 a small earthen bowl

22. 持 chí 【動詞】拿 to take

　　持去 【動詞語】拿走 to take away
　　chí qù

23. 與 yǔ 【動詞】給 to give

24. 倚 yǐ 【動詞】靠 to lean against

25. 几 jī 【名詞】小桌 an end table

26. 飯 fàn 【動詞】吃飯 to eat; to have meals

27. 眶 kuàng 【名詞】眼眶 the socket of the eye; here: eyes

28. 冉冉 rǎn rǎn 【副詞】慢慢地；徐徐地 slowly; gradually; imperceptibly

29. 動 dòng 【動詞】移動；轉動 to move; to roll

30. 笑 xiào 【名詞】可笑的事 something that is funny

以為笑 yǐ wéi xiào 【動詞語】以〔之〕為笑；把〔它〕當作可笑的事；以為是可笑的事 to regard [it] as something funny

31. 奄忽 yǎn hū 【副詞】忽然 suddenly; abruptly; rapidly

32. 已 yǐ 【副詞】已經 already

33. 吁 xū 【嘆詞】唉 to sigh

34. 可悲 kě bēi 【形容詞】使人難過、悲傷 sad; lamentable

35. 也已 yě yǐ 【助詞】句末助詞，表示強調，可譯成"啊" an emphatic final particle that can be rendered as "indeed!"

第十三篇

湖心亭看雪

明　張岱

作者　張岱 (1597-1689 A.D.) 字宗子，號陶菴，山陰（今浙江

259

紹興）人，僑寓杭州，好遊山水。他的文章，筆致清越，描寫生動，造句新奇，是晚明散文創作成就最高的作家。著有《陶菴夢憶》等。

Zhāng Dài (1597-1689 A.D.), courtesy name Zōngzǐ, style name Táoān, was a native of Shānyīn, present-day Shàoxīng in Zhèjiāng province, and later settled in Hángzhōu. He was fond of travelling to scenic places. His writing style is lucid, vivid, and freshly descriptive. He ranks among the most accomplished essayists at the end of the Míng dynasty. His works include *Táoān Mèngyì*, and other collections.

篇旨

作者描寫夜晚冒寒遊賞西湖雪景之潔與靜。文字簡雅，意境清奇，雅士懷抱，展露無遺。

The author describes a boating adventure on West Lake in a cold and snowy night. The panoromic vista exudes an aura of overwhelming cleanliness and serenity, a unique artistic conception revealing the refined instinct of a rather sophisticated scholar.

崇禎五年十二月，余住西湖。大雪三日，湖中人鳥聲俱絕。

是日，更定矣，余拏一小舟，擁毳衣爐火，獨往湖心亭看雪。霧凇沆碭，天與雲與山與水，上下一白，湖上影子，惟長堤一痕、湖心亭一點、與余舟一芥、舟中人兩三粒而已！到亭上，有兩人鋪氈對坐，一童子燒酒爐正沸。見余大喜曰："湖中焉得更有此人！"拉余同飲。余強飲三大白而別。問其姓氏，是金陵人，客此。及下船，舟子喃喃曰："莫說相公癡，更有癡似相公者。"

Zhuyīn:

Chóngzhēn wǔ nián shí èr yuè, yú zhù Xīhú. Dà xuě sān rì, hú zhōng rén niǎo shēng jù jué.

260

Shì rì, gēng dìng yǐ, yú nāo yì xiǎo zhōu, yǒng cuì yī lú huǒ, dú wǎng Húxīntíng kàn xuě. Wù sōng háng dàng, tiān yǔ yún yǔ shān yǔ shuǐ, shàng xià yì bái, hú shàng yǐng zǐ, wéi Chángtí yì hén, Húxīntíng yì diǎn, yǔ yú zhōu yí jiè, zhōu zhōng rén liǎng sān lì ér yǐ! Dào tíng shàng, yǒu liǎng rén pū zhān duì zuò, yì tóng zǐ shāo jiǔ lú zhèng fèi. Jiàn yú dà xǐ yuē :Hú zhōng yān dé gèng yǒu cǐ rén!" Lā yú tóng yǐn. Yú qiǎng yǐn sān dà bái ér bié. Wèn qí xìng shì, shì Jīnlíng rén, kè cǐ. Jí xià chuán, zhōu zǐ nán nán yuē: "Mò shuō xiànggōng chī, gèng yǒu chī sì xiànggōng zhě."

注 解

1. **湖心亭** 【名詞語】湖水中間的亭子
   Húxīn Tíng　　　　　　a pavilion built in the middle of a lake

2. **崇禎** 【名詞】明朝最後一位皇帝宗朱由檢的年號(r.1628-1644
   Chóng zhēn　　　　A.D.)，崇禎五年是 1632 年
   reign tile of the last Emperor of Míng (r. 1628-1644 A.D.)
   The fifth year of Chóngzhēn was 1632 A.D.

3. **西湖** 【名詞語】湖名，在浙江杭州城外
   Xí hú　　　　the West Lake, outside the city of Hángzhōu in Zhèjiāng
   province

4. **俱** jù 【副詞】都 both; all; altogether

5. **絕** jué 【動詞】斷絕；停止 to break up; to cease [coming and going]

6. **更** gēng 【名詞】古時將一夜分為五更：自晚七時至次晨五時，
   每兩小時為一更
   in ancient times, the night was divided into five periods with
   each covering two hours, from 7:00 p.m. to 5:00 a.m.; the
   watch of the night

   更定 【敘述句】起更；更聲已起，表示入夜
   gēng dìng　　　　the night watch has begun

7. **拏舟** 【動詞語】撐船；駕船 to ride [on] a boat
   ná zhōu

8. **擁** yǒng 【動詞】圍裹 to be wrapped in

261

9. 毳衣　【名詞語】皮衣　a fur coat
cuì yī

10. 爐火　【名詞語】生火的爐子　a stove fire
lú huǒ

11. 霧淞　【名詞語】如霜的寒霧　rime fog; freezing fog
wù sóng

12. 沆碭　【形容詞】白茫茫地瀰漫著
háng dàng　　　　　　showing a vast expanse of whiteness

13. 一　yì　【副詞】全　completely; universally

14. 影子　【名詞】輪廓(lún kuò)；模糊的形象　an outline; a vague image
yǐng.zǐ

15. 長堤　【名詞】很長的堤，指蘇堤　either of two dikes in the West Lake,
cháng tí/dī　　　　　　built by the Sòng dynasty poet Sū Shì

16. 痕　hén　【名詞】痕跡　a trace; a stroke

17. 點　diǎn　【名詞】點　a dot

18. 芥　jiè　【名詞】芥子，比喻極小的東西
　　　　　　　　　mustard seed, to liken to a tiny thing

19. 粒　lì　【名詞】顆粒　a grain

20. 氈　zhān　【名詞】氈毯；厚毯子　a felt rug

鋪氈　【動詞語】舖開毯子
pū zhān　　　　　　to spread out a thick blanket/rug

21. 對坐　【動詞語】面對面坐
duì zuò　　　　　　to sit face to face

22. 童子　【動詞】僮僕　a young servant; a house boy
tóng zǐ

23. 燒　shāo　【動詞】點火；燃燒　to start a fire; to burn

24. 沸　fèi　【形容詞】燒開　boiling

25. 焉　yān　【疑問詞】怎麼　how

26. 更　gèng　【副詞】另外　in addition

27. 拉　lā　【動詞】拉　to drag

28. 強飲　【動詞語】勉強地喝
　　qiǎng yǐn　　　　　　　to drink compulsively, i.e., beyond one's capacity

29. 大白　【名詞語】大酒杯　a large wine cup
　　dà bái

30. 姓氏　【名詞】姓名　name
　　xìng shì

31. 金陵　【名詞】地名，即今南京　place name; present-day Nánjīng
　　Jīnlíng

32. 客　kè　【動詞】旅居　to sojourn; to stay at a place temporarily

33. 及　jí　【介詞】到⋯〔時〕　by the time ...

34. 舟子　【名詞語】船夫；撐(chēng)船的人　a boatman
　　zhōu zǐ

35. 喃喃　【動詞】嘟囔(dū náng)；低聲說　to mumble
　　nán nán

36. 莫　mò　【副詞】不要　do not; not to

37. 相公　【名詞】舊時對讀書人的敬稱，後多指秀才
　　xiàng gōng　　[in ancient time] an address for a scholar, later it was mainly
　　　　　　　　　used to address someone who passed the first stage of civil
　　　　　　　　　service examination

38. 癡　chī　【形容詞】癡迷　to be infatuated

39. 似　sì　【準繫詞】像　to be like
　　　　　　　　　用於比較時，表示程度更深
　　　　　　　　　N1 Adj. 似 N2 = N1 is more Adj. than N2

When used to introduce the second part of a comparison, it functions like the conjunction "[more]...than" in English.

癡似相公者【名詞語】比相公更癡的人　one who is more infatuated
chī sì xiànggōng zhě　　　　　　　　than this scholar

第十四篇

板橋題畫

清　鄭燮

作者　鄭燮 (1693 -1765 A.D.) 字克柔，號板橋，揚州興化
（今江蘇省）人。乾隆元年 (1736 A.D.) 進士，曾任山
東范縣及濰縣的知縣，有惠政，能愛民。因觸犯
上官，辭官歸隱，以賣書畫終老揚州。所畫蘭竹
，秀勁精妙，爲世所寶。著有《板橋集》。

Zhèng Xiè (1693 -1765 A.D.), courtesy name Kèróu and style name Bǎnqiáo,
was a native of Xīnghuà at Yángzhōu, in present-day Jiāngsū province. In
1736 he became a presented scholar and then served as magistrate in Fànxiàn
and Wéixiàn, both in Shāndōng province, where he gained a reputation for
governing the people with benevolent affection. Later, after offending his
superior and being forced to resign from office, he made a living by selling
his paintings and calligraphy. His paintings of orchids and bamboos have
been treasured by art collectors ever since for their vitality and grace. His
prose is preserved in *Collections of Bǎnqiáo*.

篇旨

作者通過石濤與八大的畫藝，討論畫作儘管題材
專博不同，風格簡繁殊異，然各臻其妙，無優劣
之分。至於別號之多寡也每與畫風相應，皆爲畫
家性情趣味之自然流露。其個人在藝術上的追求

則務專尚簡，捨石濤而隨八大。簡雅有力，文如
其畫。

The author uses the paintings of Shí Tāo and Bādà Shānrén as examples,
describing their difference in both subject matters and painting styles. One
covers a broad range of subjects and utilizes a variety of painting skills, and
the other concentrates on just a few themes and paints in a simple and direct
style. Similarly, one can assume many different pen-names or only one. The
author considers these choices to be the natural outcome of distinctive
personalities and tastes of the different artists, and regards both as worthy,
each in its own way, with neither one superior to the other. As for the author
himself, he seems more akin to Bādà Shānrén than to Shí Tāo. Laconic,
elegant, and very powerful, this article of his shows the same qualities that can
be seen in his paintings.

石濤善畫，善有萬種，蘭竹其餘事也。板橋專畫蘭
竹，五十餘年，不畫他物。彼務博，我務專，安見專之
不如博乎？石濤畫法，千變萬化，離奇蒼古而又能細秀
妥帖，比之八大山人殆有過之無不及者。然八大名滿天
下，石濤名不出吾揚州，何哉？八大純用減筆而石濤微
茸耳。且八大無二名，人易記識。石濤宏濟，又曰清湘
道人，又曰苦瓜和尚，又曰大滌子，又曰瞎尊者，別號
太多，翻成攪亂。八大只是八大，板橋亦只是板橋，吾
不能從石公矣。

Zhùyīn:

 Shǐ Tào shàn huà, shàn yǒu wàn zhǒng, lán zhú qí yú shì yě. Bǎnqiáo zhuān huà
zhú, wǔ shí yú nián, bú huà tō wù. Bǐ wù bó, wǒ wù zhuān, ān jiàn zhuān zhī bù rú bó hū?
Shǐ Tào huà fǎ, qiān biàn wàn huà, lí qí cāng gǔ ér yòu néng xì xiù tuǒ tiē, bǐ zhī Bā Dà
Shānrén dài yǒu guò zhī wú bù jí zhě. Rán Bā Dà míng mǎn tiānxià, Shǐ Tào míng bù chū
wú Yángzhōu, hé zài? Bā Dà chún yòng jiǎn bǐ ér Shǐ Tào wēi róng ěr. Qiě Bā Dà wú èr
míng, rén yì jì zhì. Shǐ Tào Hóng Jì, yòu yuē Qīng Xiāng Dàorén, yòu yuē Kǔguā Héshàng,
yòu yuē Dàdízǐ, yòu yuē Xiā Zūnzhě, bié hào tài duō, fān chéng jiǎo luàn. Bā Dà zhǐ shì Bā
Dà, Bǎnqiáo yì zhǐ shì Bǎnqiáo, wú bù néng cóng Shí Gōng yǐ.

注 解

1. **板橋** 【名詞】鄭燮的號 courtesy name of Zhèng Xiè
   Bǎnqiáo

2. **題** tí 【動詞】書寫 to write

3. **畫** huà 【動詞】畫 a painting

   題畫 【名詞】在畫面上題寫詩文 to write on a painting
   tí huà

4. **石濤** 【名詞】清僧，名道濟，又名弘濟，字石濤，號清湘老
   Shí Tāo 人，又號大滌子、苦瓜和尚、瞎尊者，明靖江
   王之後，與八大山人同時；精分隸，善畫山水
   蘭竹；筆意縱恣，江以南稱第一。著有《苦瓜
   和尚畫語錄》

   A monk in the Qīng dynasty, named Dàojì and also Hóngjì,
   courtesy name Shítāo, style name Qīngxiāng Láorén, also Dàdízǐ,
   Kǔguā Héshàng, Xiā Zūnzhě, he was a descendant of the Prince
   of Jìngjiāng of the Míng dynasty, and lived at the same time with
   Bādà Shānrén, also a scion of the Míng royal family. He excelled
   in the Lì style of calligraphy and was good at painting landscape,
   orchid, and bamboo. His brush strokes are free and expressive,
   and considered to be the best in the Jiāngnán region. He wrote a
   book entitled *Kǔguā Héshàng Huàyǔlù*.

   ◆ **號** hào   a style name

5. **善** shàn 【形容詞】善於；很會 good at; professed in

6. **蘭竹** 【名詞】蘭花跟竹子 orchid and bamboo
   lán zhú

7. **餘事** 【名詞語】正業之外的事；無須投入主要精力的事
   yú shì   extra tasks; matters of secondary importance

8. **專** zhuān 【副詞】專門；只是 specially; exclusively

9. **他物** 【名詞語】別的東西 other things
   tuō wù

266

10. 彼 bǐ 【代名詞】他，指石濤 he, referring to Shí Tāo

11. 務 wù 【動詞】致力；把力量都放在… to devote oneself to ...

12. 博 bó 【形容詞】廣博 broad; in a great variety

　　務博　【動詞語】把力量都放在〔求〕廣博上；
　　wù bó　　　　　把力量都放在〔畫〕各種題材的畫上
　　　　　　　　　to devote oneself to painting a variety of themes

13. 專 zhuān 【形容詞】專一；專精 specialized; concentrated

　　務專　【動詞語】把力量都放在〔求〕專精上；
　　wù zhuān　　　　把力量都放在〔畫〕一種題材的畫上
　　　　　　　　　to devote oneself to painting a specific theme

14. 安見　【動詞語】怎見得；不見得；不一定
　　ān jiàn　　　　How do you know that...; not necessarily...

15. 專之不如博【繫詞語】專不如博 A is not as good as B
　　zhuān zhī bù rú bó　　　to be specialized is not as good as to be broad

　　之 zhī　【助詞】放在主語和謂語之間，把句子化成主謂短語，
　　　　　　　用作動詞見的賓語 When the particle "zhī" is inserted
　　　　　　　between the subject and the predicate, it change the sentence
　　　　　　　into a clausal phrase, to serve as the object of the verb "jiàn"

16. 千變萬化【動詞語】複雜多變
　　qiān biàn wàn huà　　　　intricate, colorful, and ever changing

17. 離奇　【形容詞】十分奇特；不同平常；怪誕
　　lí qí　　　　　odd; fantastic; strange and imaginative

18. 蒼古　【形容詞】蒼勁（筆力雄健）古樸
　　cāng gǔ　　　　vigorous and ancient-looking

19. 細秀　【形容詞】精致秀麗 delicate and exquisite
　　xì xiù

20. 妥帖　【形容詞】穩當；合適 properly arranged; fitting
　　tuǒ tiē

21. 比之　　【動詞語】比之〔於〕；拿他跟…比　to compare him [with]
　　bǐ zhī

22. 八大山人【名詞語】姓朱名耷(Dá)，本為明宗室，居南昌。
　　Bā dà shān rén 　　明亡後入泰新山為僧，字雪箇，號箇山
　　　　　　　　　　　，又號八大山人，佯狂嗜酒，工書，善
　　　　　　　　　　　畫花鳥、山水、竹木，筆致縱恣，清超
　　　　　　　　　　　絕俗

Zhū Dá, a member of the Míng royal clan, lived in Nánchāng of Jiāngxī province. After the fall of Míng, he went to the Tàixīn mountain to become a Buddhist monk. He had a courtesy name Xuěgè, and styles Gèshān and Bādà Shānrén. He faked insanity and drank a lot; he was good with calligraphy, and painted in flowers, birds, landscapes, bamboos and trees, in free style of superior quality.

23. 殆 dài　　【副詞】恐怕；大概　probably; almost

24. 過之　　【動詞語】超過他　to surpass him; to be better than he is
　　guò zhī

25. 不及　　【動詞語】趕不上；比不上　not so adj. as ...; inferior to ...
　　bù jí

26. 然 rán　　【連詞】然而；但是　but

27. 滿 mǎn　　【動詞】盈滿；布滿；遍布　to spread all over

　　名滿天下【敘述句】名聲遍布於天下；在天下到處都有名
　　míng mǎn tiān xià　　　　to be world-famous; to enjoy world-wide fame

28. 出 chū　　【動詞】超出　to go beyond

29. 揚州　　【名詞語】地名，在今江蘇省　Yángzhōu, in present-day
　　Yáng zhōu 　　　　　　Jiāngsū province

30. 純 chún　　【副詞】純粹(cuì)　purely; exclusively

31. 減筆　　【名詞語】減省的筆畫；很少的筆畫；以寥寥數筆畫
　　jiǎn bǐ 　　　　一幅畫　a few strokes; sketchy strokes

32. 微 wēi 【副詞】稍微 slightly

33. 茸 róng 【形容詞】茸密；茂密 luxuriant; detailed in a complicated way

34. 記識 【動詞語】識同"誌"；記誌；記住 to remember
jì zhì

35. 弘濟 【名詞】石濤的別名
Hóngjì an alias of Shí Tāo

36. 曰 yuē 【動詞】叫作 to be called

37. 清湘道人【名詞語】從清澈的湘水來的道人；石濤別號之一
Qīngxiāng Dàorén Monk from the Clear Xiāng River; one of Shí Tāo's styles

38. 苦瓜和尚【名詞語】像苦瓜似的和尚；石濤別號之一
Kǔguā Héshàng Monk Bitter Gourd; one of Shí Tāo styles

39. 大滌子【名詞語】徹底清洗的人；石濤別號之一
Dàdí zǐ Master Thorough Cleansing; one of Shí Tāo's styles

40. 瞎尊者【名詞語】瞎眼的尊者；石濤別號之一
Xià Zūnzhě The Blind Reverend; one of Shí Tāo's styles

◆ 尊者 zūnzhě an honorific term for a monk; a reverend

41. 別號 【名詞】在名，字以外另取的化名
bié hào a style; a pen name in addition to given name and courtesy name

42. 翻 fān 【副詞】反而 on the contrary

43. 攪亂 【形容詞】混亂 confused
jiǎo luàn

44. 從 cóng 【動詞】跟從；跟隨 to follow; to take after

45. 石公 【名詞語】石老先生，指石濤
Shí gōng Mater Shí, meaning Shí Tāo

269

第十五篇

答謝中書書

梁　　陶弘景

作者　陶弘景 (452 - 536 A.D.)，字通明，秣陵（今江蘇江寧縣）人。齊、梁時代著名的隱士。

Táo Hóngjǐng (452-536 A.D.), courtesy name Tōngmíng, was a native of Mòlíng, present-day Jiāngníng district in Jiāngsū province. He was a famous recluse during the Qí and Liáng dynasties.

篇旨

全篇以四字對句描寫雲山清流，四時竹木，晨夕魚鳥，種種自然美景，靜中寓動，生意盎然。文筆清綺，音調和諧，是典型的早期駢文小品。

This article describes the marvellous landscape through four syllablic lines. These incorporate the use of artistic parallelism to describe the clouds, the mountains, and the rivers; to show the daily and seasonal changes that occur in the bamboos and trees, the fish and the birds, etc., in such a natural and charming manner and with such great vitality. Its style lucid and elegant, its language euphonious, this is a fine example of parallel prose in its formative years.

山川之美，古來共談。高峰入雲，清流見底。
兩岸石壁，五色交輝。青林翠竹，四時俱備。
曉霧將歇，禽鳥亂鳴。夕日欲頹，沈鱗競躍。
實是欲界之仙都。自康樂以來，未復有能與其
奇者。

Zhùyīn:

Shān chuān zhī měi, gǔ lái gòng tán. Gāo fēng rù yún, qīng liú xiàn dǐ.
Liǎng àn shí bì, wǔ sè jiāo huī. Qīng lín cuì zhú, sì shí jù bèi.

Xiǎo wù jiāng xiē, qín niǎo luàn míng. Xī rì yù tuí, chén lín jìng yuè.
Shí shì yù jiè zhī xiān dū. Zǐ Kāng Lè yǐ lái, wèi fù yǒu néng yù qí qí zhě.

注 解

1. 答 dá 　　【動詞】回答　to answer

2. 謝中書【名詞】指謝徵（或作微），字元度，陽夏（今河南太
   Xiè Zhōngshū　　康縣）人，曾作中書鴻臚，所以稱謝中書
   Xiē Zhēng (or Wēi), once served as Master of Ceremony in the
   Imperial Secretariate in Qí Dynasty (479-502)

   ◆ 中書省　　　　　Imperial Secretariate
   　 zhōngshūshěng
   ◆ 鴻臚 hónglú　　　herald; master of ceremony

3. 書 shū 　　【名詞】書信；信　a letter

4. 山川 　　【名詞】山河　mountains and rivers; landscape
   shān chuān

5. 美 měi 　　【名詞】美　beauty; being beautiful

6. 古來 　　【時間詞】自古以來；從古代到現在　since antiquity
   gǔ lái

7. 共談 　　【動詞語】共同談論；古人今人都談論
   gòng tán　　　　　to be talked of by all people, past and present

8. 高 gāo 　　【形容詞】高　high; tall

9. 峰 fēng 　　【名詞】高峻的山頂　peaks; the pointed top of a mountain

10. 入雲 　　【動詞語】插入雲中　to stick into the clouds
    rù yún

11. 清 qīng 　　【形容詞】清澈　crystal-clear; limpid

12. 流 liú 　　【名詞】河流　river water

271

清流　【名詞語】清澈的河流　clear river water
qīng liú

13. 見　xiàn　【動詞】呈現　to reveal; to show

14. 底　dǐ　【名詞】河底　the bottom; the river bed

見底　【動詞語】呈現河底　to reveal the river bed
xiàn dǐ

15. 兩　liǎng　【數詞】兩邊的　two; both

16. 岸　àn　【名詞】河岸　banks

兩岸　【名詞語】兩邊河岸上　on both banks
liǎng àn

17. 石　shí　【形容詞】岩石的；石頭的　stony; rocky

18. 壁　bì　【名詞】峭壁；陡峭的山石　cliffs

◆ 陡峭 dǒuqiào　　precipitous

石壁　【名詞語】石質的峭壁　rocky cliffs
shí bì

19. 五色　【名詞】青、黃、赤、白、黑五色　five colors
wǔ sè

20. 輝　huī　【動詞】輝映；光彩照耀；反映　to shine; to reflect

交輝　【動詞語】互相輝映　to shine on (or reflect on) each other
jiāo huī

五色交輝　【敘述句】五種光彩互相輝映
wǔ sè jiāo huī　　various colors shine on each other

21. 青　qīng　【形容詞】綠色的　green

22. 林　lín　【名詞】樹林　woods; forests

青林　【名詞語】綠色的樹林　green forests
qīng lín

23. 翠 cuì　【形容詞】翠綠色　emerald green

24. 竹 zhú　【名詞】竹子　bamboos

翠竹　【名詞語】翠綠色的竹子　emerald green bamboos
cuì zhú

25. 四時　【名詞語】四季；春夏秋冬　four seasons; year round
sì shí

26. 俱備　【動詞語】完全具備；全都有　to have; to be provided
jù bèi

27. 曉 xiǎo　【形容詞】天明；早晨　daybreak; early morning

28. 霧 wù　【名詞】霧氣　fog; vapor

29. 將 jiāng　【副詞】將要　to be about to

30. 歇 xiē　【動詞】盡；消失　to die out; to disappear

曉霧將歇【敘述句】早晨的霧將要散盡
xiǎo wù jiāng xiē　　　　the morning vapor is about to disperse completely

31. 禽 qín　【名詞】飛禽　birds

32. 鳥 niǎo　【名詞】鳥　birds

33. 亂 luàn　【副詞】雜亂地　disorderly

34. 鳴 míng【動詞】叫　to chirp

亂鳴　【動詞語】雜亂地叫；混雜著叫
luàn míng　　　　to chirp disorderly; to chirp wildly or noisily

35. 夕日　【名詞語】夕陽；傍晚的太陽
xì rì　　　　the setting sun

273

36. 欲 yù　【副詞】將要 to be about to

37. 頹 tuí　【動詞】墜；落 to fall; to set

38. 沉 chén　【形容詞】沉在水中的 immersed

39. 鱗 lín　【名詞】鱗片 fish scales
　　　　　　　　此處指魚 here it stands for "fish"

沈鱗　【名詞語】沒入水中的魚 fish in the water
chén lín

40. 競躍　【動詞語】比賽跳躍 to jump up competitively;
jìng yuè　　　　　　　　　to jump up one after another

41. 實 shí　【副詞】確實 surely; indeed

42. 欲界　【名詞語】指人世 this world; the human world
yù jiè　　　　佛家把死生往來的世界分為三界：一、欲
　　　　　　界，有淫欲和食欲；二、色界，在欲界之
　　　　　　上，此界已無淫食二欲，但還有形色的愛
　　　　　　好，有物質的障礙；三、無色界，在色界
　　　　　　之上，此界中已無一切物質

　　　　Buddhists classify the world into three realms: 1, the realm
　　　　of desire where sex asd food are dominant; 2, the realm of
　　　　form, where sex and food no long exist, but there is still
　　　　form and matter to care for; 3, the realm of formlessness,
　　　　where material aspects disappear.

43. 仙都　【名詞語】仙人居住的地方；仙境 fairyland; wonderland;
xiān dū　　　　　　　paradise; where immortals live

欲界之仙都【名詞語】人間之仙境 a fairyland in the human world
yù jiè zhī xiān dū

44. 康樂　【名詞】指山水詩的始祖謝靈運 (Xiè Língyùn 385 - 433)，
Kānglè　　　他在劉宋時曾經被封為康樂公 Duke of Kānglè,
　　　　　　referring to Xiè Língyùn (385-433 A.D.), the earliest and
　　　　　　greatest landscape poet.

274

◆ 劉宋 *Liú Sòng*　　The Southern Dynasties Sòng (420-479)
　　　　　　　　　　founded by Liú Yù

45. 自 … 以來 【時間詞】從 … 到現在　ever since ...
　　zì ... yǐ lái

46. 未　wèi　【副詞】還沒有　to have not yet

47. 復　fù　【副詞】再　again; once more

48. 與　yù　【動詞】稱讚；讚揚　to praise; to commend; to speak highly of
　　　　　　　　這裡意為 "欣賞"
　　　　　　　　here: to appreciate

49. 奇　qí　【名詞】佳妙；美妙；美好　exquisite beauty; wonder

　　與其奇【動詞語】欣賞它（山水）的奇妙　to appreciate its wonder
　　yù qí qí

275

駢 文 簡 介
A Brief Introduction to Parallel Prose

漢語的特性是單音節及有聲調，駢文即是由此特性發展出來的一種文體。駢文的特點有三：

Parallel prose is a natural outcome of the Chinese language which is mono-syllabic and tonal by nature. Parallel prose has three distinctive features:

（一）語句方面的特點：駢偶和四六。

Syntactic characteristics: Parallel lines with tetra-syllables and hexa-syllables.

一、 駢偶是用平行的兩句話，兩兩相對。最應注意的是詞語互相配對，原則上總是名詞對名詞，動詞對動詞，形容詞對形容詞，副詞對副詞，連詞，介詞也與連詞，介詞相對。

Parallelism means using pairs of antithetical lines throughout the text. The two lines in a pair must be syntactically identical, with corresponding words belonging to the same grammatical category and function, whether they are nouns, verbs, adjectives, adverbs, conjunctions, or prepositions.

例如：

高峰入雲，
adj n v n

清流見底。　　　　　陶弘景《答謝中書書》
adj n v n

窮者欲達其言，
adj pron aux v pron n

勞者須歌其事。　　　庾信《哀江南賦》
adj pron aux v pron n

駢文中偶然夾雜著一些散句，這種散句的作用是引起下文或結束上文。

There are occasionally loose (non-parallel) words used between parallel elements to facilitate a transition or a conclusion.

二、 四六：是用四字句和六字句，因此駢文又叫四六文。四六文的基本結構有五種：

Parallel prose is mainly comprised tetra- and hexa-syllablic lines, so it is also called essays in tetra- and hexa-syllabic lines. The basic sentence patterns of parallel prose include the following:

1. 四四　　　tetra/tetra

例如 ：

　　　高峰入雲，

　　　清流見底。　　　　陶弘景《答謝中書書》

2. 六六　　　hexa/hexa

例如 ：

　　　窮者欲達其言，

　　　勞者須歌其事。　　庾信《哀江南賦》

3. 四四四四　　　tetra, tetra/tetra, tetra

例如 ：

　　　兩岸石壁，五色交輝。
　　　adj n　n　n　　num n adv v

　　　青林翠竹，四時具備。
　　　adj n　n　n　　num n adv v

　　　　　　　　陶弘景《答謝中書書》

4. 四六四六　　　tetra, hexa/tetra, hexa

例如 ：

　　　老當益壯，寧知白首之心。
　　　adj aux adv adj　adv v adj n part n

　　　窮且益堅，不墜青雲之志。
　　　adj adv adv adj　adv v adj n part n

　　　　　　　　王勃《滕王閣序》

5. 六四六四　　　hexa, tetra/hexa, tetra

例如 ：

　　　屈賈誼於長沙，非無聖主。
　　　v　n　prep n　adv v adj n
　　　　person　place

277

竄梁鴻於海曲，豈乏明時？
v　　n　prep　n　　adv　v　adj　n
　person　　place

王勃《滕王閣序》

（二）語音方面的特點，即平仄相對。

The phonetic characteristics lie in the contrast and alternation of words in the level tone and in the deflected tone

平仄是跟四六對仗（對偶）有關的。平是平聲（即國語中的第一、二聲），仄是上聲（即國語中的第三聲）、去聲（即國語中的第四聲）、入聲（已轉變成國語中的第一、二、三四聲）。在對仗時應該以平對仄，以仄對平，特別是每句中的第二、四、六字，必須嚴守這項規律。這種注重平仄相對的規則，開始於於齊、梁（479-557 A.D.），完成於唐代（618-907 A.D.）

The tonal variation is related to the parallelism. Words in the level tone -- the first and second tones in Mandarin Chinese--have a pitch that is even and long, while words in the deflected tones--the third and fourth tones plus the entering tone that used to have a stop ending lost in Mandarin Chinese--have pitches that are relatively short with changing contours. Between a couplet of antithetical lines the level tone words in one line should be matched with the deflected tone words in its corresponding line, especially for words in the 2nd, 4th, and 6th position. This is the distinctive feature of parallel prose that began during the Qí and Liáng dynasties (479-557 A.D.) and reached its maturity in Táng dynasty (618-907 A.D.)

例如：

老當益壯，寧知白首之心。
｜－｜｜　　－－｜｜－－

窮且益堅，不墜青雲之志。王勃《滕王閣序》
－｜｜－　　｜｜－－－｜

（三）用詞方面的特點，即用典和藻飾。

The characteristics in diction: allusions and ornateness.

一、用典：又叫"用事"，就是引述古人之言證實自己的論點，或引述古事映發情懷。目的在以最濃縮精簡的方式來加強並豐富文章的內涵，使文章精煉、典雅、委婉、含蓄，耐人尋味。

Allusions, also called "yòngshì"; thit is a literary device of quoting written references or citing past events to support one's arguments, or to illustrate a special sentiment or emotion. The purpose is to enrich or strengthen the meaning of one's writing in the most economic and effective way, to make the writing more concise, elegant, suave, implicit, and to afford much food for thought.

例如：

屈賈誼於長沙，非無聖主。

竄梁鴻於海隅，豈乏明時？　　王勃《滕王閣序》

In this couplet the author cites the stories of Jiǎ Yì who was very talented but did not fulfill his political aspiration, even though Emperor Wén of Hàn was an enlightened ruler, and also of the hermit Liáng Hóng, who lived in obscurity during the reign of Emperor Zhāng of Eastern Hàn, considered a peaceful and well-governed period in Chinese history. The point here is to stress that success and failure are predestined.

二、　藻飾：極力追求文詞華美。
Ornateness: To strive for an ornate diction.

例如：

雹碎春紅，霜凋夏綠。
n　v　n　n　　n　v　n　n

劉令嫻《祭夫涂敬業文》

大體說來，對偶和四六能使文章產生整齊的美感，用典容易引起聯想並使文章變得典雅，協調平仄能增強聲音的和諧悅耳。它的缺點是若過分追求形式的整練，典故的艱深，文詞的華美，會使文章顯得板滯、晦澀、和內容貧乏。

In general, the parallel form can create an esthetic sense of neatness, while the use of allusions can bring to minds covert references and thus enrich the meaning, while the alternation and contrast of tonal patterns can increase aural delight. The weakness of parallel prose, however, is its excessive pursuit of formal beauty, which makes its style unvarying, abstruse, and deficient in content.

注 解

1. 駢文　【名詞】古代的一種文體，文中用對偶的句子，與散
   pián wén　　　　　　文不同　a stylized antithetic form of writing prevalent in the 6th and 7th centuries; parallel prose

2. 駢 pián 　【形容詞】兩馬並駕　two horses harnessed to a carriage

3. 偶 ǒu 　【形容詞】兩人並立　two persons standing side by side

　駢偶 　【形容詞】兩兩相對　two things in a pair
　pián ǒu

4. 夾雜 　【形容詞】攙 (chān) 雜；混雜　mixed up
　jiā zá

5. 窮者 　【名詞語】不得志的人　one who does not have his ambition
　qióng zhě 　　　　　　　　　fulfilled

6. 達 dá 　【動詞】表達；表露　to express

7. 勞者 　【名詞語】勞動的人　laborers
　láo zhě

8. 歌 gē 　【動詞】唱　to sing

9. 庾信 　【名詞】人名，性庾名信字子山，曾事梁朝及西魏、北
　Yǔ Xìn 　　　　　　周，是六朝著名作家之一

　　　　　personal name. Surnamed Yǔ, named Xìn, and courtesy name
　　　　　Zǐshān (513-581 A.D.), he served in Liáng dynasty in the
　　　　　south, and Western Wèi-Northern Zhōu in the north. He was
　　　　　one of the best known writers in the Six Dynasties period.

10. 哀江南賦【名詞】篇名庾信作　title of a Rhyme Prose, "Lament for the
　Aī Jiāngnán Fù 　　　　　Southland," written by Yǔ Xìn

11. 益 yì 　【副詞】更　more; even more

12. 壯 zhuàng【形容詞】強壯；雄壯　strong; with lofty aspirations

13. 寧 níng 　【副詞】豈；怎　how; why

14. 移 yí 　【動詞】改變　to change [to]

15. 白首之心【名詞語】年老的心境；衰頹 (shuāi tuí)的心境
　bái shǒu zhī xīn 　　　　　mood of an old man; discouraged and despondent mood

16. 墜 zhuì 【動詞】墜落；掉下 to fall down

降低 to lower

17. 青雲之志【名詞語】攀登雲間的志向；高遠的志向
qīng yún zhī zhì　　　　　　　a soaring aspiration; high and noble ambition

18. 王勃 【名詞】人名，姓王名勃字子安，長於詩文，為"初唐
Wáng Bó 四傑"之一。其餘三人為楊炯、盧照鄰、及
駱賓王。

personal name. Surnamed Wáng, named Bó, and courtesy name Zǐān (649-676 A.D.), he was a talented writer in both prose and poetry, and was best known as one of the "Four Excellent Writers in the Early Táng period." The other three were Yáng Jiǒng (634-688 A.D.), Lú Zhàolín (635-684 A.D.), and Luò Bīnwáng (640-684 A.D.).

19. 滕王閣序【名詞】篇名，王勃作 Title of an article, "Preface to the Poem
Téngwáng Gé Xù 　　　　on the Téngwáng Pavilion," written by Wáng Bó

20. 屈 qū 【動詞】屈抑；壓抑 to crush; to repress; to suppress

21. 賈誼 【名詞】西漢著名的年輕有才幹的政治家
Jiǎ Yì 　　　　name of a famous young, talented statesman of Hàn dynasty

22. 長沙 【名詞】地名，在今湖南省
Chángshā 　　　　name of a place in present-day Húnán province

23. 聖主 【名詞語】聖明的君主，指漢文帝
shèng zhǔ 　　　　a sagacious ruler, referring to Emperor Wén of Hàn

24. 竄 cuàn 【動詞】逃竄 to flee; to run away
使⋯逃竄 to make sb. flee

25. 梁鴻 【名詞】東漢的賢士
Liáng Hóng 　　　　name of a respected scholar in the Eastern Hàn dynasty

26. 海曲 【名詞語】海邊的隱僻的地方
hǎi qū 　　　　a secluded area near the sea shore

27. 明時 【名詞語】政治清明的時代，指東漢章帝時
míng shí 　　　　time of good government, referring to the reign of Emperor Zhāng during the Esaetern Hàn

281

28. 典故　【名詞】詩文等作品中引用的古代故事和有來歷出處的
diǎn gù　　　　　詞語 allusions from history, literature, or classics

29. 委婉　【形容詞】曲折；婉轉 suave and moving; round about
wěi wǎn

30. 含蓄　【形容詞】〔語言、詩文等〕意未盡露，耐人尋味 with
hán xù　　　　　concealed or implied deep meanings; implicit

31. 典雅　【形容詞】〔文章、言辭〕有典籍上的根據，高雅而不
diǎn yǎ　　　　　淺俗 refined; elegant (writing)

32. 精鍊　【形容詞】〔遣詞造句〕精美凝鍊 concise; succinct
jīng liàn

33. 藻飾　【動詞】用華美的文辭來修飾文章 to embellish; to make
zǎo shì　　　(writing) more beautiful by embellishing/adorning it

　　　　【名詞】華美的文辭 embellishment in writing

34. 雹 báo　【名詞】雹子 hail

35. 碎 suì　【動詞】打碎 to smash

36. 春紅　【名詞語】春天的紅花，指徐敬業
chūn hóng　　　　red flowers in Spring, standing for her young husband

37. 霜 shuāng【名詞】霜 frost

38. 凋 diāo　【動詞】使…凋謝 to cause to wither and fall

39. 夏綠　【名詞語】夏天的綠葉，指徐敬業
xià lù　　　　　green leaves in Summer, standing for her young husband

40. 聯想　【動詞語】因關聯而想到 to associate; to connect in mind
liáng xiǎng

41. 協調　【動詞語】使…和諧 to harmonize
xié tiáo

42. 和諧　【形容詞】悅耳 harmonious; pleasing to the ear
hé xié

43. 整練　【形容詞】整齊簡練　neat and concise
    zhěng liàn

44. 艱深　【形容詞】艱難深奧　difficult and abstruse
    jiān shēn

45. 華美　【形容詞】華麗　beautiful; gorgeous; splendid; magnificent
    huá měi

46. 板滯　【形容詞】僵硬；呆板　stiff; dull; monotonous; unvarying
    bǎn zhì

47. 晦澀　【形容詞】隱晦；不易懂　obscure; hard to understand
    huì sè

48. 內容　【名詞】內涵的意思　contents; substance; meaning
    nèi róng

49. 貧乏　【形容詞】欠缺、不足　deficient; wanting
    pín fá

詩韻韻目表

上平	上	去	ending	入	ending
1 東	1 董	1 送	-ung; -iung	1 屋	-uk; -iuk
2 冬	2 腫	2 宋	-ong; -iong	2 沃	-ok; -iok
3 江	3 講	3 絳	-ɔng	3 覺	-ɔk
4 支	4 紙	4 寘	-i; -ui		
5 微	5 尾	5 未	-əi; -iəi		
6 魚	6 語	6 御	-io		
7 虞	7 麌	7 遇	-u; -iu		
8 齊	8 薺	8 霽	-iei; -uei		
9 佳	9 蟹	9/10 泰 卦	-ai; -uai		
10 灰	10 賄	11 隊	-ɔi; -uɔi		
11 真	11 軫	12 震	-in; -iun	4 質	-it; -iut
12 文	12 吻	13 問	-iuan	5 物	-iuat
13 元	13 阮	14 願	- ɑn; -u ɑn; -i ɑn	6 月	- ɑt; -u ɑt; -i ɑt
14 寒	14 旱	15 翰	-ɑn; -uɑn	7 曷	-ɑt; -uɑt
15 刪	15 潸	16 諫	-an; -uan	8 黠	-at; -uat

下平	上	去	ending	入	ending
1 先	16 銑	17 霰	-iɛn; -iuɛn	9 屑	-iɛt; -iuɛt
2 蕭	17 篠	18 嘯	-iɛu		
3 肴	18 巧	19 效	-au		
4 豪	19 皓	20 號	-ɑu		
5 歌	20 哿	21 箇	-a; -uɑ; -iuɑ		
6 麻	21 馬	22 禡	-a; -ia; -ua		
7 陽	22 養	23 漾	-ang; -uang; -iang	10 藥	-ak; -uak;-iak; -iuak
8 庚	23 梗	24 敬	-ɐng; -uɐng; -iɐng;	11 陌	-ɐk; -uɐk; -iɐk; -iuɐk
9 青	24 迥	25 徑	-ieng; iueng	12 錫	-iek; -iuek
10 蒸			-əng; -uəng; -iəng	13 職	-ək; -uɐk; -iɐk; -iuɐk
11 尤	25 有	26 宥	-əu; -iəu		
12 侵	26 寢	27 沁	-im	14 緝	-ip
13 覃	27 感	28 勘	-ɑm	15 合	-ɑp
14 鹽	28 琰	29 豔	-iɛm	16 葉	-iɛp
15 咸	29 檻	30 陷	-am	17 洽	-ap

Rhyme Books

Ancient people wrote poems according to their own speech sounds. While they were transliterating some Buddhist texts into Chinese, scholars in the 4th century A.D. for the first time took notice of the tonality in Chinese, and they began to compile rhyme books. The 601 A.D. *Qiè Yùn* by Lù Fǎyán represented the joint efforts of eight leading scholars and incorporated into it regional differences and historical changes of Chinese phonology, classifying Chinese characters-syllables into 193 rhymes of four tones. Later, in 706 A.D. this work was expanded by Sūn Miǎn to 195 rhymes in his book, *Táng Yùn*, and further expended to 206 rhymes by Chén Péngnián and Qiū Yōng in thier book, *Guǎng Yùn*, published in 1008 A.D. These were the standard reference books for versification over a period of four hundred years. Later, at the end of the Sòng dynasty, Liú Yuān, a man from Píngshuǐ, simplified *Guǎng Yùn* and reclassified the characters into 106 rhymes because he found that poets throughout the ages did not make the minute distinctions that *Guǎng Yùn* had specified. His book was known as the *PíngShuǐ Rhyme Book*, or simply the *Poetic Rhyme (Shī Yùn)*, and it has prevailed ever since. As later poets would invariably consult *Poetic Rhyme* in their versification, and since poems composed prior to its publication were taken into consideration in the writing of *Poetic Rhyme*, this work can be said to suit almost all the poems and lyrics contained in this volume, except for the first two selections taken from the *Book of Odes*.

The sound values given in the table represent the most up-to-date scholarship in the field of Chinese phonology. However, as the Chinese language has never been alphabetical, the reconstructed sound value is at best a close approximation.

The *Poetic Rhyme* or *Shī Yùn* is readily available in Chinese book stores. One can even get a pocket size edition, smaller than a cellphone, in Beijing.

The *Book of Odes* of 6th century B.C. was put together at a time when Chinese people were not yet aware of the tonal distinctions. Only twenty-nine rhyme groups were known to be distinguishable. These rhyme groups and sound values of the rhyming words are also given at the end of poems one and two.